CE

TYPES OF SOCIAL STRUCTURE IN EASTERN INDONESIA

KONINKLIJK INSTITUUT
VOOR TAAL-, LAND- EN VOLKENKUNDE
TRANSLATION SERIES 11

F. A. E. VAN WOUDEN

TYPES OF SOCIAL STRUCTURE IN EASTERN INDONESIA

ENGLISH TRANSLATION
BY RODNEY NEEDHAM

PREFACE BY
G. W. LOCHER

THE HAGUE - MARTINUS NIJHOFF - 1968

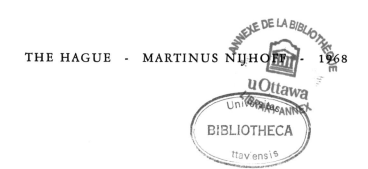

This book is published under a grant from the
Netherlands Ministry of Education and Sciences.
Original title:
"SOCIALE STRUCTUURTYPEN IN DE GROOTE OOST"
Published by J. Ginsberg, Leiden, 1935

PREFACE

BY

G. W. LOCHER

Some years ago, in a discussion of the modern concept of structure, Lévi-Strauss contended that the extraordinarily widespread employment of the term "structure" since 1930 reflected a rediscovery of the concept and the term rather than the continuation of a prior usage. This assertion may be correct in general, but it does not apply to the Netherlands, at least not so far as the *concept* of structure is concerned. The transmission of the concept in that country can in fact be quite easily traced.

It began in 1917 with the publication by van Ossenbruggen of a study of the Javanese notion of *montjå-pat*,[1] a paper which was influenced to a high degree by the famous monograph by Durkheim and Mauss, "De quelques formes primitives de classification", which had been published at the beginning of the century.[2] An even clearer structural approach is to be found in the extensive Leiden thesis of W. H. Rassers, *De Pandji-Roman*.[3] This dissertation itself refers with particular emphasis to van Ossenbruggen's paper and to the monograph by Durkheim and Mauss, as well as to various other publications by them. The studies later made by Rassers were also of such a kind that when a collection of them was published in English in 1959, under the title *Pañji, The Culture Hero*,[4] they were aptly subtitled "A Structural Study of Religion in Java".

The concept of structure in the Netherlands had in the meantime been passed on from Rassers to J. P. B. de Josselin de Jong. It was

---

[1] F. D. E. van Ossenbruggen: „De Oorsprong van het Javaansche Begrip Montjå-Pat", *Verslagen en Mededeelingen der Koninklijke Akademie van Wetenschappen*, Afdeeling Letterkunde, 5e reeks, 3e deel, 1918, pp. 6-45.

[2] E. Durkheim and M. Mauss, „De quelques formes primitives de classification: contribution à l'étude des représentations collectives", *Année sociologique*, vol. VI (1901-2), Paris, 1903, pp. 1-72.

[3] Antwerpen, 1922.

[4] Koninklijk Instituut voor Taal-, Land- en Volkenkunde Translation Series 3, The Hague, 1959.

chiefly due to the influence of Rassers that in the early twenties de Josselin de Jong took up again the study of Durkheim and Mauss. Topics such as myth and kinship systems, which were prominent in the work of Rassers, were also matters with which he proceeded to concern himself, more than had previously been done and with a different method of approach. In doing so, de Josselin de Jong quite soon arrived at novel insights in the field of kinship structures, particularly with regard to the relation between matrilineal and patrilineal modes of grouping. When in 1952 he presented his exposition and critical assessment of Lévi-Strauss's theory of kinship structures,[5] in a laudatory review of the latter's book,[6] it was not only at Leiden that it became evident that there had developed in the Netherlands a structuralist trend in cultural anthropology which had its own characteristics. But this development had already been under way for some thirty years.

In the late twenties, when van Wouden and I together attended the lectures delivered by de Josselin de Jong, the latter was already giving a detailed course on kinship structures in which he used not only the concept of structure but the word as well. These lectures by de Josselin de Jong, who had been a supernumerary professor under the Leiden University Fund since 1922, were not part of the prescribed programme of study. We attended them simply because we wanted to do so, van Wouden as a student under the programme for intending civil servants in the Netherlands East Indies, and I at that time as a history student. We were also both members of the anthropological debating society, W.D.O., which was founded in that period by a number of enthusiastic students, from different fields of study, who not only attended de Josselin de Jong's courses but also considered themselves more or less as his followers.

After taking his master's degree, van Wouden did not in the event go to the Netherlands East Indies as an administrative officer. Because of the world economic crisis, and the attendant restriction on the despatch of new personnel to the Indies, he was released from various obligations in this respect and was able to turn to research on social organisation and kinship structures in Indonesia. This resulted in his dissertation, in 1935, on types of social structure in eastern Indonesia, which now appears in an English translation.

---

[5] *Lévi-Strauss's Theory on Kinship and Marriage* (Mededelingen van het Rijksmuseum voor Volkenkunde, Leiden, No. 10), Leiden, 1952.
[6] Claude Lévi-Strauss, *Les Structures élémentaires de la parenté*, Paris, 1949.

It is exceptionally gratifying that this translation has been produced, thanks principally to Needham's assistance. Van Wouden's thesis is indeed of no less importance in the development of structural anthropology in the Netherlands than is Held's Leiden thesis on the Mahābhārata, which appeared in English in the same year,[7] and which has become better known through the extended attention paid to it by Lévi-Strauss in *Les Structures élémentaires de la parenté*. In a letter which Lévi-Strauss wrote to de Josselin de Jong in 1953, with reference to the latter's monograph *Lévi-Strauss's Theory on Kinship and Marriage*, in which special reference was made to van Wouden,[8] he remarked that he regarded his ignorance of van Wouden's work as one of the greatest omissions in his knowledge of the literature on the subject of his book.

In a thesis, what is due to the supervisor and what to the pupil is frequently hard to make out, particularly when the student has for years attended the lectures given by his supervisor. A comparison with Held's thesis of the same year, 1935, and especially with the inaugural lecture on the Malay Archipelago as an ethnological field of study,[9] delivered then by J. P. B. de Josselin de Jong (as a regular professor), shows that van Wouden was working along the same lines and with the same background as his supervisor and the latter's other pupils of the same period. The prominent place given to van Wouden's thesis by de Josselin de Jong in his lecture is certainly not fortuitous. However much difficulty de Josselin de Jong may have had, also, in helping van Wouden to produce a readable book out of the drafts which he handed in, he was throughout persuaded (to my knowledge) that the content of van Wouden's thesis made a contribution which in various respects was exceptional and very original.

In this connexion, moreover, the condition of contemporary studies on kinship structures and socio-political organisation should not of course be overlooked. Certainly it should be kept in mind that van Wouden had to base his study, as he himself stresses in his introduction, on a defective ethnographic literature on the region in question. This did not prevent de Josselin de Jong from still making special reference to van Wouden's work many years later, as appears from his 1952 monograph on Lévi-Strauss's book, and also from Needham's report (in his translator's note below) of the recommendation which he

---

[7] G. J. Held, *The Mahābhārata: an ethnological study*, Amsterdam, 1935.

[8] pp. 55, 57.

[9] *De Maleische Archipel als Ethnologisch Studieveld*, Leiden, 1935.

received from de Josselin de Jong in 1950 that he should work through this book.

Needham's appreciation of van Wouden's book, "for all its acknowledged defects", is similarly an important indication of its significance, since he himself has not only carried out field research in part of the region dealt with by van Wouden but also has a very good understanding of structural anthropology. My own experience with van Wouden's book during my research in the Atoni area of Timor (1940-41) is a parallel confirmation of the great importance of the work, notwithstanding the fact that the data on Timor which van Wouden cites turned out to be not only defective but in some respects mistaken as well. The evidence which I accumulated (lost during the war) clearly indicated, in my view, the correctness of some of the fundamental insights and interpretations advanced by van Wouden. My friend and colleague H. G. Schulte Nordholt can attest that this was my opinion when we came across each other on Timor and argued about van Wouden's book in a debate which was not occasioned simply by the circumstance that he had studied at Utrecht and I at Leiden. In 1966, in his thesis on the political system of Timor,[10] he wrote (in connexion with a comment by C. E. Cunningham to the effect that he had studied at Leiden): "The first acquaintance with Leiden was the reading of van Wouden's thesis when I was already on Timor. At that time I had not yet perceived the importance of his brilliant theory, and the way in which he had drawn up a scheme of Timorese social structure, merely from very scanty and not entirely trustworthy evidences, provoked a resistance in me, because it seemed to me that it did not accord with the factual situation in the Atoni area. The fact that a detailed and faithful description of a political community, made by an administrator who had not been educated at Leiden, should nevertheless call 'Leiden' to mind, is testimony to the importance of the 'Leiden school' " (p. 3).

This all brings us to the question of how van Wouden was able to arrive at what is in many respects a correct interpretation when the evidence on the different areas with which he was concerned was so insufficient and in parts even mistaken. The answer to this lies in what J. P. B. de Josselin de Jong had to say in his 1935 lecture on the importance of ethnological fields of study. He was not only convinced of the great importance in general of continual interchange between

---

[10] *Het Politieke Systeem van de Atoni van Timor*, Driebergen, 1966.

theory-building and empirical work in the field, but he ascribed in this connexion a special place to the idea of fields of study. The reason is that one is then dealing with culture areas which are sufficiently homogeneous and distinctive to form separate fields of investigation, and at the same time display enough local variation to permit a profitable internal comparison to be carried out.

By means of the study of such areas it is possible to arrive at well-defined structural types, namely structural models. By reference to these the evidence from a given part of such a field of study can provide an indication that one is dealing with the same type of structure as in other parts of the area in question. This can be done even though the information from the former place, taken by itself — i.e. when an attempt is made to study such a limited region in isolation from the wider field of study to which it belongs — may be inadequate to such an understanding. It was this technique which allowed van Wouden to make interpretations of kinship and political systems which were largely correct, considering the time of publication of his thesis, despite the fact that the ethnographical material did not in itself provide sufficient evidence. Naturally, in adopting this method a distinction has to be maintained between the interpretation of data by means of structural models, on the one hand, and a factual description of societies on the other. That such an interpretation can provide a stimulus to the description of a given empirical reality, as Schulte Nordholt reports of his own case, has to do with the nature of the essential interchange, mentioned above, between theorising and field research.

An important aspect of analysis by means of models, as exemplified in van Wouden's argument, is that diverse possibilities can be implicit in the model, not all of which will necessarily be realised in empirical phenomena; that is, they may be present but remain in a latent state. Thus P. E. de Josselin de Jong emphasised a few years ago how van Wouden had demonstrated that a diagram of asymmetric connubium among a given number of unilineal groups, defined by one rule of descent, contains simultaneously a model of an asymmetric connubium among the same number of unilineal groups with the other rule of descent, and that this same diagram can also serve as a model for a system of asymmetric connubium in a society organised by double-unilineal descent.[11] The extent to which such possibilities may be

---

[11] "Circulerend Connubium en het dubbel-unilineale Principe", *Bijdragen tot de Taal-, Land- en Volkenkunde*, vol. 120 (Anthropologica VI), 1964, pp. 181-194 (see p. 183).

realised in the form of distinct social groupings in empirical societies is of course a question for closer research in the field. At present, however, we suspect that the realisation of such possibilities in a society with unilineal groups can have occurred in manifest forms to only a slight degree.

The great advance in understanding effected in the thirties was primarily the idea that accentuated matrilineal grouping, similarly marked patrilineal grouping, and double-unilineal grouping could belong to one and the same structure. For an area such as the Lesser Sunda Islands, in which all three forms of organisation occurred, this structural insight provided an entirely different perspective from that afforded by starting from three sharply distinguished main types of unilineal kinship systems, studied exclusively in a functionalist way or else placed in a diffusionist or evolutionary historical sequence, as for the most part had previously been done.

University of Leiden, March 1968.

TRANSLATOR'S NOTE

The translation of Dr. F. A. E. van Wouden's work has presented a special interest which it may be useful to indicate. To do so should underline the value of the book itself, and may also permit a more confident reception of this English version.

When I first went to Leiden as a graduate student in 1950, in order to work under the late Professor Dr. J. P. B. de Josselin de Jong, the first product of the Leiden school which was recommended to me, as an Oxford social anthropologist, was *Sociale Structuurtypen in de Groote Oost*. Not only did it much impress me at the time, but in later years, in the course of work on prescriptive alliance (a subject to which Dutch anthropologists have made such fundamental and indispensable contributions), Van Wouden's pioneering theoretical study proved to be of increased and continuing relevance. Today, it strikes me the more forcibly as a work which, for all its acknowledged defects, well deserves to be far better known, and I am very pleased to help make it so.

There are three topics in particular on which it seems to me to have an outstanding claim to attention, and which justify its republication. I trust I shall not encroach upon the preface by Professor Dr. G. W. Locher if I mention them very briefly. The first is the study of connubium, in the sense of "fixed affinal alliances" perpetuated by means of cross-cousin marriage, in symmetric and asymmetric forms. A point of basic theoretical importance, especially in comparison with certain views propounded much later by others, is that cross-cousin marriage is argued to be, not just a preferential mode of union among close relatives, but the logical expression of a systematic communication of women *(huwelijksverkeer)* among social groups. Whereas the symmetric form of connubium had long been recognised, the concentration here on the asymmetric form, with its "closed chain" of alliances and relativity of differential affinal status, is genuinely exploratory. A more particular theoretical advance concerns patrilateral cross-cousin marriage. Fortune had previously pointed out (in a paper which Van Wouden does not cite) that this form of marriage, regularly practised, would lead to a constant alternation in the direction in which women were transferred between lines.[1] But it was Van Wouden who went on to discern, for the first time in the literature, and forestalling Lévi-Strauss by fourteen years, that this practice would make a systematic ordering of affinal alliances impossible and would lead to "total confusion".[2]

It is not Van Wouden's prime intention, however, to explain a particular type of marriage; the marriage regulations are simply a starting point for arriving at an insight into the "totality" of the cultures under study. This line of analysis introduces the second topic, namely the comprehensive kind of classification which is associated with positive marriage rules, such that "cosmos and human society are organised in the same way". The classification is analysed in terms of ideological "oppositions", with prominent reference to the symbolism of numbers. By such an approach to this type of society it becomes possible, Van Wouden maintains, to demonstrate "the essential unity of social organisation, myth, and ritual".

Thirdly, as a defining aspect of these integral social and symbolic forms, there is the topic of dual sovereignty, or complementary governance, as exercised through the essential conjunction of secular power and mystical authority.

Now it is true that the way in which Van Wouden actually conducts his investigation into these cardinal matters is open to scholarly criticism, and that his conclusions are by no means indisputable. It is plain also that such concerns, and certain of the theoretical positions adopted, reflect dominant anthropological interests at the University of Leiden, and specifically the teaching of Professor J. P. B. de Josselin de Jong.[3] But the combined analysis of this variety of fundamental topics, in an

---

[1] R. F. Fortune, "A Note on Some Forms of Kinship Structure", *Oceania*, vol. IV, no. 1, September 1933, pp. 1-9 (see pp. 3-4).

[2] Cf. Claude Lévi-Strauss, *Les Structures élémentaires de la parenté* (Paris: Presses Universitaires de France, 1949), chs. XXVI, XXVII; see also second edition, revised and corrected (Paris & The Hague: Mouton, 1967), pp. xix-xx. (Lévi-Strauss makes no reference in the first edition to Fortune's crucial paper or to Van Wouden's work; in the second edition, see the note on the latter at p. 360 n. 9).

[3] J. P. B. de Josselin de Jong, *De Maleische Archipel als Ethnologisch Studieveld* (Leiden, 1935); cf. G. J. Held, *The Mahābhārata: An Ethnological Study* (Amsterdam, 1935); F. D. E. van Ossenbruggen, "Het Oeconomisch-Magisch Element in Tobasche Verwantschapsverhoudingen", *Mededeelingen der Koninklijke Akademie van Wetenschappen*, Afdeeling Letterkunde, deel 80, serie B, no. 3, pp. 63-125 (Amsterdam, 1935).

extensive comparative study, nevertheless gives Van Wouden's work a remarkable and lasting importance.

Perhaps I may also be permitted to mention a further persuasion to undertake the translation of this book, viz., my own professional interest in the social anthropology of eastern Indonesia. I have made an ethnographical reconnaissance there (Sumba, 1954-55), and other anthropologists who have worked with me at Oxford have since carried out highly effective investigations, in a continuing series of linked expeditions to the area, into matters raised by Van Wouden. These circumstances are no guarantee of the translation, and cannot be claimed to have contributed decisively to it, but they testify to a practical involvement which may add a degree of authority.

No general editing has been attempted, but a number of changes from the original publication have been made in the interest of accuracy and convenience. Van Wouden's own list of corrigenda (1935, p. [190]) has of course been acted upon, and a further dozen or so misprints have also been taken into account. A few expository corrections have been tacitly incorporated; the only one worth specifying is the reading "schoondochter" for "schoonmoeder" (1935, p. 21; cf. below, p. 20). The bibliographical references have been standardised in a modern form, and the bibliography itself has been checked and supplied with full particulars. The references cited have not been examined except in cases of doubt or as aids to a more exact interpretation of the points at issue. The index has been considerably augmented, especially in analytical respects.

The translation is fairly direct, and preserves a formal correspondence with the original in its division into paragraphs and sentences, but it is not meant otherwise to be minutely literal. Van Wouden's Dutch is not the most pellucid, and my chief care has therefore been, not to convey faithfully all the qualities of the author's prose, but to achieve a simple and accurate rendering of the argument. The temptation to employ technical expressions which have become current in more recent analyses of prescriptive alliance has been scrupulously resisted, and particularly in the theoretical chapters (III and VI), which have been kept deliberately close to the terms of the text. A term of another kind which may give pause to some readers is *negorij*, denoting a territorial political unit. The dictionary equivalent in English is given as "nagaree", but this is so unhelpful that the Dutch word, with its ethnographical connotations, has been retained. Van Wouden quotes some passages from Schadee and from Tauern in German, and these have been translated directly from that language. The names of places, groups, and individuals have been left in the forms adopted by Van Wouden, with the following Dutch and German consonants: *dj* = English *j*; *tj* = English *ch*; *j* = English *y*. The vowel *e* has generally the phonetic value of the French *é*. Van Wouden has substituted *u* for the Dutch *oe*, but with this qualification the proper names thus remain readily identifiable with their originals as reported in the ethnographical literature or as located on maps of the area.

I am most grateful to the following persons for their help. Mrs. J. T. Ros kindly added certain bibliographical particulars which were not discoverable in Oxford, and rectified an omission in the text (1935, p. 49). Mr. J. J. Fox, from the vantage of his own recent researches on the island of Roti, was so good as to make a first critical reading of the translation. I take great pleasure in acknowledging the advice and corrections of my former class-mate at Leiden, Mrs. E. Postel, who with admirable efficiency collated the entire translation against the Dutch; I am obliged to her, not only for her conscientious detection of certain oversights and mistakes, and for other suggestions for improvement, but chiefly for the added sense of security with which this rendering of Van Wouden's intricate exposition and analysis can now be presented to a wider public.[4]

It is pleasant to be associated in this undertaking with Professor Dr. G. W. Locher, formerly my learned mentor at Leiden. Finally, I am indebted to the Editorial Committee of the Koninklijk Instituut voor Taal-, Land- en Volkenkunde for the compliment of inviting me to make this translation, and I wish to register my warm appreciation of this new opportunity for amical collaboration with my colleagues in the Netherlands.

R. N.

University of Oxford, October 1967.

---

[4] By a gratifying chance, it turns out that Dr. Louis Berthe has independently prepared a translation of Van Wouden into French. This additional version, which incidentally confirms the value of the work, may be expected to permit a fuller consideration of the argument, and should also furnish an interesting gauge of the adequacy of the present English translation. It is to be published, under the title *Les Structures sociales de l'Indonésie orientale*, by François Maspero, Paris.

CONTENTS

INTRODUCTION

The area covered by this investigation extends over the whole of the south-east of Indonesia: it stretches from the Timor Archipelago in the west to the Southeastern Islands in the east, and is bordered to the north by the islands of Seran and Buru. The choice of this area, which takes in such far-separated territories, has not been determined by geographical or other more or less arbitrary factors, but is based upon various points of similarity from an ethnographical point of view. The different societies of these islands are practically all characterised by the possession of clan systems, still fairly intact, coupled with an explicit preference for cross-cousin marriage in its restricted form. In this respect they are strongly distinguished from the societies of Celebes and Halmahera, the two other large culture areas of eastern Indonesia, in which in general there is no question of clan systems but where more bilateral modes of reckoning kinship seem to predominate. The latter observation applies chiefly to Celebes; on Halmahera the memory of a former clan system seems still not entirely to have disappeared. However this may be — and the defectiveness of the data is an element which should not be overlooked — the above points of difference are well enough established to justify a separate treatment of the area in question.

The spatial limits of this study are thus quite simply established, but the demarcation of cultural boundaries between the peoples and groups inhabiting these islands presents more difficulty. The essential unity of each culture makes it rather unfeasible to make an exact separation and delimitation of the extent and elements of each of its components. To try to do so would result in gross errors and inaccuracies which would give a very problematical character to the results obtained. Although we shall be dealing primarily with the social factors of these cultures, as is declared by the title of the work, it should be kept constantly in mind that these social phenomena are firmly rooted in the totality of the culture. We intend, therefore, not to detach the social component arbitrarily from the culture, and to consider it in isolation, but to proceed in a precisely converse fashion.

Starting from particular social elements, we shall attempt to determine the place of such elements in the culture, and then examine what their task is in relation to other elements. As starting point for such attempts we have taken exclusive cross-cousin marriage, which, as we have observed, occupies throughout the area a position of eminent importance. This general cultural factor provides us with the firm basis which is essential amid the multiplicity of cultural influences. We hope to be able to show that this marriage custom is the pivot on which turns the activity of the social groups, the clans. The scheme of social categories thus found serves as the model for an all-embracing classification. Cosmos and human society are organised in the same way, and through this there emerges the essential interconnexion and similarity of the human and the cosmic. According to our conceptions these are totally different things, but here they form a higher unity, the sacred forces of which are reflected in myth and ritual. Myth is a sacred narrative, set in the very distant past, about the nature of things. On the distinction between the present and the mythical past rests the differentiation of the sacred and the profane. But the continuity of the profane present is interrupted by ritual, sacred ceremonies, by which the mythical events of prehistory are repeated over and over again for the living generation. The preservation and continuation of everything is ensured by the interaction of human and cosmic powers in the ritual. This rhythmic character of time, the interconnexion of human and cosmic forces, and the comprehensive classifications based on social criteria are at once consequences and causes of the essential unity of culture, in which myth, rite, and social structure are the three great components. The distinction, also, between social and religious will be seen to be extremely closely connected with social phenomena. As we shall see, it is connected with the opposition between maternal and paternal principles of grouping. By bearing constantly in mind all these associations, and the underlying interconnexion of the various cultural elements, we shall be able to concentrate especially on social phenomena without falling into a sterile one-sidedness. As a last qualification, we should add that the discussion will centre almost exclusively on the internal organisation of the tribe. We hope to examine the inter-tribal relations in this area, interesting as they are, in another place.

The greatest difficulty which one encounters in the study of cultural phenomena in these parts is the serious inadequacy of the ethnographical material. Scientific writings by anthropologically trained investigators are at present entirely lacking, and one relies for the most part on more or less incidental reports by government officials and missionaries. The few works which are the fruit of special expeditions (e.g., Tauern's *Patasiwa und Patalima*), or major publications brought out at the instance of the government (Van Suchtelen's monograph on Endeh, and Sachse's on Seran, in the *Mededeelingen van het Encyclopaedisch Bureau*), do not differ essentially from the run of the material published in learned periodicals (particularly the *Bijdragen tot de Taal-, Land- en Volkenkunde van Nederlandsch-Indië* and the *Tijdschrift* and *Verhandelingen* of the Bataviaasch Genootschap van Kunsten en Wetenschappen) and are of no more than middling value. The chief defects in this sort of ethnographical literature are lack of precision and confusion of terminology. The lack of precision marks particularly those writings which are the result of an impulse to tell of interesting and exotic situations with which, through accidental circumstances, the author has become acquainted; this defect is less evident in those reports which owe their origin to some superior or external initiative. Usually the experience of the situations described is expressed in general observations, without any attempt at a more detailed description of the social groups (village, the inhabitants of a house, lineage, clan, district, etc.) with which the communication is concerned. A detailed and trustworthy description of the nature, extent, and composition of such groups is absolutely necessary if any judgement of the meaning and import of the communication is to be arrived at. Very often one would readily exchange generalities of the kind mentioned above for examples taken from concrete data: the composition of a certain village, its relationship to other villages, the number and names of such villages, etc. — in short, exact descriptions of the actual social units in place of generalities. The fairly bulky work by Geurtjens on the Kei Islands provides a striking example of this kind of fault. The complicated relationships and affinal alliances of the various clans are discussed in completely general terms, without a solitary instance in which these links are demonstrated in concreto. For no single district or village do we learn anything whatever about the number, names, and relationships of the component villages or clans. This imprecision is clearly not the result of ignorance, but comes from the desire, pushed to extremes, to be interesting, and one of the consequences of which, naturally, is a certain fear of the aridity of particular enumerations. If an author has set himself no other aim than to be interesting, then it is hard to reproach him for this; but usually there are other factors which it is perfectly legimimate to criticise. In publications which are written with more serious ends in view the vagueness in question is for the most part not so prominent, though the essential difference is often not particularly great. A happy exception to this rule is presented by, for example, Grijzen's monograph on central Timor (1934), which, although it is far from being entirely satisfactory, is very advantageously marked off from other publications of the kind by its large quantity of concrete data. Drabbe's papers on Tanimbar differ also from other ethnographies intended to cover the whole culture, not so much in the above respect as in the detailed descriptions of certain elements of the culture. The numerous writings of Kruyt are not entirely free from the defects under discussion. His grasshopper-method of ethnographic research makes him dependent on the statements of resident Europeans, and on fleeting contacts with natives, who rightly or wrongly are recognised as authorities. This method brings him into touch merely with the surface of the cultures which he discusses, and it gives his works the character of compilations which can be used only with caution and in which contradictions and improbabilities are repeatedly encountered.

Terminological uncertainty more often than not makes a correct assessment of the material extraordinarily difficult. Terms such as family, extended family, and lineage are frequently used for the most disparate groups, without any indication of what precisely they are meant to denote. Even without having to learn an extensive vocabulary of technical terms, the difficulty occasioned by this terminological confusion can to a large extent be obviated by sticking so far as possible to the indigenous terminology. By indigenous terminology we mean really indigenous linguistic usages, and not the words and designations which have acquired authoritative currency in the course of contact between Europeans and the local peoples. The unlimited use of such terms (e.g., *fettor, soa, negorij, tuan tanah*, and so on) as a rule only makes the confusion worse.

In the light of these defects in the ethnographical literature, and the fact that it is difficult to get at (being dispersed throughout a number of periodicals, many of which are little known), it has seemed useful to precede the analysis with a summary of the available material. In this part so far as possible all of the ethnographical literature is arranged and sifted and composed into a critical whole — or so we hope. Since we are not dealing with a well-described area, the literature on which has become generally known, such an introductory description seems to us to be indispensable. In the four succeeding chapters we shall then make a more theoretical examination of the facts set out in the survey.

Given the above-mentioned terminological uncertainty in most of the descriptive sources, it seems helpful to provide a short list of the terms to be employed here and the meanings attached to them:

FAMILY: a term which causes the greater part of the confusion. We shall use it in the very restricted sense of closest relatives: brothers, sisters, parents. Whenever there is occasion to do so, we shall make our particular meaning clearer.

LINEAGE: a unilateral (unilineal) descent group comprising only traceable relatives.

CLAN: an exogamous, unilateral, traditional descent group. Exogamous in that marriage within the clan is excluded; unilateral in that kinship is reckoned either patrilineally or matrilineally; traditional in that the clan also includes numerous relative whose genealogical connexions cannot be traced.

GENS: the same as clan. It has been proposed that the term gens be employed for a patrilineal descent group, and the term clan for a matrilineal descent group.

PHRATRY: an exogamous unilateral half of a tribe; it may or may not include a number of clans.

MOIETY: the term moiety is used for an exogamous half of a tribe without internal division into clans, as distinguished from phratry, which in this case is used to denote each grouping of clans when the tribe contains more than two such groups. As will be seen below, we use the term moiety in one instance with a very special meaning, namely as denoting, not an exogamous half of a tribe with clans of the same rule of descent, but halves composed of clans with opposite rules of descent.

TRIBE: the highest unit into which the descent groups (lineages, clans, phratries) are joined. Within this unit the clans etc. can exercise a completely social function in their fundamental relationships, particularly in affinal relations. Although there may sometimes exist higher units (such as *federations*), the tribe is an independent unit; no clan need go outside it in order to provide for its social needs. Often a number of tribes form a unit, from an ethnographical point of view, in which case one has to do with a *people*. Naturally, a single tribe can likewise be considered as forming a people, on a smaller scale. It is completely incorrect that, as happens in fact, a descent group should be referred to as a tribe.

UNILATERAL: kinship is reckoned solely through the feminine line (*matrilineal, matrilateral*) or solely through the masculine line (*patrilineal, patrilateral*). Such lines can be referred to as *maternal* and *paternal* respectively.

BILATERAL: relationship is reckoned through the father and the masculine line, and also through the mother and the feminine line. In these respects the family is a bilateral group. A bilateral kin group usually includes only a few generations, since obviously the boundaries of such a group quickly become blurred. In most cases also unilateral tendencies make their appearance, either because of the operation of economic forces or as a result of customs of marital residence. In such circumstances it is best to speak of a *loose bilateral kin group*.

DOUBLE UNILATERAL: this term denotes the co-presence of both patrilineal and matrilineal clans within a single tribe. Any individual then belongs to the patrilineal clan of his father and also to the matrilineal clan of his mother.

EXOGAMOUS, ENDOGAMOUS: the former term denotes a prohibition on marriage within the group to which one belongs, the latter a prohibition on marriage outside it. The terms are opposed to each other only in a conceptual sense; it cannot be said that a particular group is either one or the other. A clan is by definition exogamous, and in this context it cannot be said that there is an opposition with endogamy. Similarly, we can hardly speak of the endogamy of a tribe; one of the essential characteristics of a tribe is that social life is carried on within its boundaries, though marriages outside the tribe can indeed occur. The term *endogamous classes* refers to class-groups, or rather caste-groups, of which endogamy is a foremost characteristic. The loose employment of the term endogamy to mean in-breeding, which is sometimes come across, is to be avoided.

CONNUBIUM: Fixed affinal relationships between two or more descent groups. Connubium is termed *symmetric* if two descent groups are linked by repeated marriages, i.e., if brother-and-sister exchange is permitted. Connubium is *asymmetric* if the affinal relationships are unilateral: in this case a descent group gives women to another but cannot receive women from that same group, so that brother-and-sister exchange is not permitted.

COUSINS: children of two brothers, of two sisters, or of brother and sister. The first and second kinds are called *parallel* cousins and the last *cross*-cousins. Marriage between parallel cousins is often not permitted, whereas marriage between cross-cousins is permitted. In the case of cross-cousin marriage there is a distinction to be made according to whether the man's choice is or is not restricted to the mother's brother's daughter. If a man is allowed to marry only a mother's brother's daughter, we are dealing with *exclusive cross-cousin marriage*: if he is also allowed to marry a father's sister's daughter it is *ordinary cross-cousin marriage*. In discussing such forms of marriage it is advisable never to rely on terms such as uncle, aunt, nephew, and niece, but invariably to define the relationship in question as precisely as possible.

CLASSIFICATORY SYSTEM OF KINSHIP TERMS: among many peoples the kinship terms diverge to a very important degree from our own. One of the most consequential differences is presented by the classificatory system, in which terms which for us apply to a strictly individual relationship are extended to an entire group: e.g., the term father is also used for father's brothers or for all male clan-mates of the same generation as the father. It is obvious that an ethnographer unfamiliar with these classificatory usages will very easily draw all sorts of mistaken conclusions. Classificatory systems are of the greatest importance for the understanding of social structure; they should therefore be recorded with the greatest possible precision and completeness.

We should also add a note on the literature that is to be cited and reproduced. As far as the more descriptive publications are concerned, we shall draw upon only those works which make a direct contribution to our exposition. We shall thus leave unmentioned various publications which may perhaps have helped indirectly towards the development of the argument, but which are of no direct use. This applies all the more strongly to the more theoretical literature. Only when there is special reason to do so is a general work on social anthropology cited. It has seemed to us that it would be rather unfeasible to list all the literature which has in any way contributed to our understanding, and it would in any case be difficult to draw a line between what deserved to be mentioned and what did not.

We have already indicated the extreme defectiveness of the material on which our investigation is largely based. In the following pages the reader will repeatedly find that we have had to refrain from definite conclusions and have had to resort to conjecture, precisely because of the incompleteness of the evidence. With the exception of Duyvendak's thorough study of the Kakehan society and its place in Seran culture, practically none of the older theoretical writings on this area have supplied the kind of material on which we ought to have been able to base our research. Our work should therefore be taken more as a preliminary orientation than as a definitive solution of the various problems with which it deals.

CHAPTER I

ASYMMETRIC CONNUBIUM

Among various peoples of eastern Indonesia we find a remarkable system of regulations governing non-reciprocal marriages; this system is clearly of the greatest significance for our investigation into the nature and the systematic character of the culture of these peoples. It completely determines the interrelations and activities of the social groups, and is reflected also in myth and ritual. By starting from this system we shall arrive at a clear understanding of the form and meaning of these culture-types, and we shall find it possible to demonstrate the essential unity of social organisation, myth, and ritual.

Let us take in the first place the *Tanimbar Islands,* where on the east coast of Jamdena, the largest and central island, the archaic relationships have been maintained the longest and in their purest form.[1] One's own descent group is called *mirwan'awai,* which literally means "men brothers". The description of it given by Drabbe indicates beyond question a patrilineal clan,[2] but he goes back considerably on his own words when he finally says that it is "practically" only trace-able kin ("so long as they are recognised as blood relatives") who are reckoned as members of the *mirwan'awai.* In other places, how-ever, he gives descriptions which can only refer to patrilineal clans. Moreover, the use of the word "practically" is not entirely clear, for to be "recognised as blood relatives" is not necessarily synonymous with being "traceable kin". However this may be, it may be taken as very probable that the original structure was that of a system of patri-lineal clans.[3]

The social organisation is characterised by a triple classification: *mirwan'awai,* one's own clan; *nduwe* (lord, master), the clan from which one takes wives; and *uranak* (sister's child), *tomwatte*-people, or *lollat*-row, the clan to which one gives one's daughters and which

---

[1] Drabbe, 1927, pp. 181 ff.
[2] See Introduction.
[3] Drabbe, 1925, p. 32; 1923, p. 552.

is regarded as inferior. The *mirwan'awai* is thus *nduwe* in relation to its *uranak*, and *uranak* in relation to its *nduwe*. Drabbe leaves open the possibility that such an affinal relationship, i.e., in only one direction, may be established with more than one clan. Indirectly related *nduwe*, finally, are termed by him the *nduwe* of one's *nduwe*.[4]

In the choice of a wife one has always to reckon with the wishes of one's *nduwe*. A recalcitrant party runs the risk of one day finding himself trapped in a house with a fire set underneath, or even of being poisoned or murdered, and the *nduwe* will break off all connexions with an *uranak* who does not fulfil his obligations towards them. Such considerations apart, it is possible to marry either a daughter of one's *nduwe* (*bate nduwe*) or an unrelated woman (*bat-waljete*).

It is a point of concern that one's *uranak* should not die out but should multiply, for it contributes very greatly to anyone's prestige that they should possess an extensive body of *uranak*; this brings power, influence, and riches. Exclusive cross-cousin marriage [5] is the designated means by which the *nduwe-uranak* relationship is maintained. It is customary that at all events one son — the eldest, or if the circumstances make it desirable the youngest — should contract such a marriage.[6] Two brothers may not marry two sisters; the first married would regard this as "a blow in the face" or even as "making use of his wife". An *nduwe*-wife is inescapably committed to a leviratic marriage. A man's mother's brother is his "real, true *nduwe*", and his sister's son is his "real, true *uranak*". He calls both kinds of female parallel cousins, his father's sister's daughters, and his sisters all by the same term; the mother's brother's daughters are addressed by a distinct term. Nothing more is known of the kinship nomenclature than that all members of one's own clan who are of the same generation are addressed as brothers and sisters.

Marriage with an *uranak*-woman is absolutely out of the question, "because in that case we should be swallowing our own blood". This relationship continues and infinitum, just as does the prohibition on marriage with the descendants of two brothers or two sisters.[7]

Marriage with a "strange woman" has the consequence that the *nduwe-uranak* relationship is created between two groups which were previously unrelated. It requires a protracted ritual, accompanied by

---

[4] Drabbe, 1923, pp. 547 ff.
[5] See Introduction.
[6] Geurtjens, 1921, p. 304.
[7] Drabbe, 1923, pp. 549 ff.

an expensive and complicated ceremonial exchange of gifts, and is not entered upon without grave reasons.[8]

A similar asymmetric connubium grouping is found in the *Kei Islands*, to the northeast of Tanimbar. The *fām* (a segment of a patrilineal clan, sub-clan)[9] which provides another with wives acquires a certain ascendancy of rank and authority over the latter. The maintenance of the long-established relationships and interconnexions established by the marriages of the *fām* ancestors is the primary aim of the existing marriage regulations. Each *fām* is committed by these regulations to seek wives for its sons among a limited number of other *fām* which are precisely determined. Reciprocal exchange of women between these *fām* is absolutely excluded. If a young man marries outside these narrowly demarcated boundaries, without the foreknowledge of the *fām* heads, the latter may in many cases later recognise the marriage, and the *wilin* (bridewealth) will in the event be paid, but usually the new relationship established by this marriage will not be long-lasting; the required payments will be completed as soon as possible, in order to be relieved of all obligations towards the *fām* of the wife.[10] Elsewhere we read: "No new alliances can come into being through any irregularly contracted marriage."[11]

The *fām* which are interconnected by marriage are termed *jan ur* and *mang ohoi*. *Mang ohoi* means villager, and denotes in particular the male inhabitants, since men are destined to remain in the village. By contrast, the women of the village, who at marriage are forced to leave, are called *marwutun* (strangers), whereas women whom marriage brings to settle in the village are accordingly called *mang ohoi*. *Jan ur* — from *janan uran*, children sisters — are the daughters who have been married out to other villages and their descendants. *Mang ohoi* are thus the wife-giving *fām*, and *jan ur* are the wife-takers. The *mang ohoi*/*jan ur* relationship is also called *jāb waein*. The *jan ur* are required to acknowledge the primacy of the *mang ohoi* by paying them respect and offering them gifts at such family occasions as births, marriages, and deaths.[12] It appears that the *jan ur*/*mang ohoi* relationship often exists between different *fām*, which probably means *fām* of two clans.

---

[8] Drabbe, 1923, pp. 556 ff.
[9] Geurtjens, 1921, pp. 376, 178.
[10] Geurtjens, 1921, p. 302.
[11] Geurtjens, 1921, p. 324.
[12] Geurtjens, 1921, p. 303.

Here too the unilateral affinal relationships are accompanied by cross-cousin marriage in its restricted form as the preferred marriage possibility. The eldest son is obliged to marry the eldest daughter of his mother's brother. Once the eldest brother has concluded such a marriage, his brothers may no longer marry "in this degree of consanguinity". All the children of one's parents' brothers and sisters are called brother and sister, and marriage with them, with the above exception, is forbidden. If no daughter is born to the mother's brother, he has to go to his *mang ohoi* for a wife for his sister's son. Geurtjens, however, reports one case in which a man who had no daughters contracted another marriage in the hope that this one would be luckier. His young nephew, who was already quite grown-up, had in the meantime to bear himself with patience.[13]

Less prominent members actually married the daughter of the father's elder brother, in order to evade the great expense entailed by a marriage with another *fām*. Among the lower classes, to whom the "high politics of marriage" of the aristocrats is foreign, marriages are contracted on mutual terms: daughters are exchanged.[14] Another report, which demonstrates also the disintegration of the clan system, seems to refer especially to the lower classes. We read in Geurtjens, namely, that marriage with a woman who is "not closer related by blood than the third degree" is simply punished with a fine.[15] The position of the more prominent *fām*, however, is extremely closely connected with their interrelationships by marriage, and such departures from tradition as we has just mentioned would greatly endanger this position. According to Geurtjens, "a family which cannot or will not any longer pay for its wives is disgraced throughout Kei." [16]

A relationship which bears a great similarity to that between *jan ur* and *mang ohoi* is that between *kōi* (or *mardu*) and *maduan*. In order to be able to meet the obligations of the ceremonial gift-exchange which accompanies a marriage, the head of the *fām* often calls on the aid of other heads. He who buys wives for a *fām* is the *maduan* (master, owner); all the members of the *fām* are known as his *kōi* or *mardu*, and they are his "inferiors". In all kinds of situations they have to render him service and homage, and they offer him gifts at family events such as births, marriages, and deaths. The children do not

---

[13] Geurtjens, 1921, p. 304.
[14] Geurtjens, 1921, p. 295.
[15] Geurtjens, 1921, p. 330.
[16] Geurtjens, 1921, p. 326.

belong to the father, but to the *maduan*, or, in general, to whomever paid the bridewealth for the mother. The *maduan* of a bridegroom is the person who is primarily responsible for the bridewealth. Often there is a *kōi/maduan* relationship between a "traditional slave" [17] and his master. The *maduan* can also, in his turn, be the *kōi* of a higher *maduan*.[18] A man may not remove to another place without the prior knowledge and agreement of his *maduan*.[19] It is plain from these reports that the *kōi/maduan* relationship obtains not only between groups but also between individuals. Thus we read further that the children owe various duties to the *maduan*; e.g., they have to work for him, and he can levy a distraint on part of their earnings.[20] A *maduan* can take back the wife of his *kōi* of inferior origin, if the *kōi* neglects his obligations towards him, but the *maduan* has no sexual rights in the woman.[21]

Our ethnographer Geurtjens also speaks, however, to a quite different effect about the *maduan*. He says: "The *maduan* is a long-suffering creditor ... If the debtor shows himself to be altogether too negligent, one simply takes one's daughter back ..." In spite of the use of the indeterminate "one" in the latter part of this quotation, there appears to be no other possible interpretation that that here the *maduan* represents the wife-giving group.[22] An indication to the same effect is seen in the statement that the "family relationships of *jan ur* and *mang ohoi*, or *kōi* and *maduan*" form a marriage bar founded upon the "affinal relationships of family groups" rather than of individuals.[23]

In central *Timor* we find a people calling themselves Emma Tétun (Tétun people) and speaking a language called Tétun. The name Bélu, by which they are usually designated, comes from their Dawan-speaking western neighbours, who call them Attoni Bélu. *Bélu* is a Tétun word meaning "friend".[24] This people is divided into a northern group and a southern group, which in addition to slight differences of language, are markedly divergent in social structure.

We are the better informed on the northern Tétun. Each member

---

[17] A "traditional slave" is, according to Geurtjens, someone whose slave status is purely traditional and who is otherwise scarcely distinguished from ordinary freemen.
[18] Geurtjens, 1921, pp. 294 ff.
[19] Geurtjens, 1921, p. 303.
[20] Geurtjens, 1921, p. 309.
[21] Geurtjens, 1921, p. 308.
[22] Geurtjens, 1921, p. 301.
[23] Geurtjens, 1921, p. 332.
[24] Grijzen, 1904, pp. 16 ff.

of the society stands in the closest and unbreakable relationships to a
triad of descent groups. These relationships, the influence of which
extends to the most important as well as the least things in life, are
based in the first instance on the marriage regulations. The first of the
three groups is that of *alin maun* (younger and older brother). Grijzen
describes it by listing so far as possible all traceable members of a
patrilineal kin group. The second group, the *fettoh sawa* (literally,
woman girdle) comprises the patrilineal kin groups into which the
women of the *alin maun* are married. To the third, the *umah manèh*
(literally, house man), belong the patrilineal groups from which men
of the *alin maun* have chosen their wives. The *alin maun* are more or
less obliged to take their wives from among their *umah manèh*. Anyone
who marries a woman from outside his *umah manèh* must inform the
latter. The *umah manèh* protest their offence and anger, and have
to be mollified with gifts. If the *umah manèh* consist of a number of
different descent groups, then each of them has to be given something,
and at least one brother or nephew has to take his wife from the
umah manèh. Poor people especially often marry within the *alin maun*,
since such a marriage entails no great expense or complicated ceremonies. The better-off usually marry a girl from their *umah manèh*,
since in that case no "money" has to be given in order to ward off
their anger, and because it is not thought desirable to increase by one
more the total of their *umah manèh*. In order to assure themselves of
regular affinal relationships, parents often betroth their sons while they
are still small to the little daughters of their *umah manèh*. From a
number of particulars it appears that whereas at present a descent
group has a number of *umah manèh* groups, it is certain that the
situation originally was that each descent group (apparently a patrilineal clan) had only one *umah manèh* group and one *fettoh sawa*. From
Grijzen's wording, also, when he discusses the compensation paid to
the *umah manèh* on the occasion of an irregular marriage, it can be
inferred that one of the *umah manèh* is the oldest and possesses first
interest in the matter. The *umah manèh* is the least respected and liked
of the three kin groups which make up a person's consanguineous and
affinal relatives, but also the most feared.[25]

At practically all family events the *umah manèh* concerned must be
present, and in some circumstances in fact all of them must be there.
The *umah manèh* are usually less well entertained than are the *alin*

---

[25] Grijzen, 1904, pp. 60 ff.

maun or the *fettoh sawa*, but in compensation they receive payment for the slightest thing they do or the least service they may perform. If the *umah manèh* are ignored they become angry and will pour out curses on the offenders, who will immediately fall sick or suffer other misfortunes. Often in the case of sickness the *mak'dōk* (shaman) comes to the conclusion that the cause is anger on the part of the *umah manèh*, and only by securing their favour through the making of gifts can the sufferer be cured.

Among prominent people the *alin maun* are called *husar datu*, the *fet'sawa* are called *nai o'an nai fettoh*, and the *umah manèh* are called *nai malun*.[26]

After a death, the *umah manèh* of the deceased must be informed. If this involves highly placed people, the communication is made very circumspectly and is accompanied by the presentation of gifts. The *umah manèh* burst out in a fury on hearing the news, and wrathfully reply that *buan* (evil magicians) have eaten the soul of the deceased, that the *buan* still remain in the surroundings, and that the *umah manèh* demand that they be seized so that the *umah manèh* can kill them — something which often happens.[27]

The author says nothing whatever about forms of preferential marriage, but even without such explicit report it is clear that we have to do here with a system which is entirely identical with that found on Tanimbar.

Steinmetz [28] informs us of the occurrence of unilateral affinal relationships in Insana, Beboki, and Mio Maffo (districts which lie further to the west and form part of the Dawan language area).[29] Upper-class people marry for the most part women from their *atoni amaf*, i.e., the descent group of the mother's brother, the clan from which ego's clan (*olif tata*) by long tradition takes its wives. Although it is not said in so many words, it is clear that the *fetto son* is the clan to which one gives wives, and that this group never coincides with the *atoni amaf*. Poor people mostly marry within the *olif tata*. An express confirmation of the unilateral marriage grouping is lacking for the remaining kingdoms or principalities in this part of Timor, but the part played by the triad of descent groups with which we have

---

[26] Grijzen, 1904, pp. 39, 55 ff.
[27] Grijzen, 1904, pp. 66 ff.
[28] In Kruyt, 1923*a*, p. 367.
[29] Grijzen, 1904, pp. 16 ff.

become familiar, and which according to Heijmering and Kruyt [30] features in all kinds of feasts and important occasions, points unmistakably in that direction. In western Timor, according to Kruyt, marriage between parallel cousins is forbidden in any circumstances. The marriage of cross-cousins is welcomed, but it is not demanded that the wife be a daughter of the mother's brother "as on Sumba". In Amarassi there is said to be a preference for brother-and-sister exchange, though the ruler of Mollo declared that it was forbidden. Marriage is forbidden with the sister's daughter, sister's son, and the sister of either parent-in-law. In Amarassi, however, it is reported that the mother-in-law's sister may be married. It may be that the report of ordinary cross-cousin marriage refers especially to the kingdoms on the south coast (Amanuban, Amanatun, and Amarassi).

Each of the various *nusak* (district, kingdom, tribe) [31] into which the population of *Rote* is divided comprises a number of *leo* (patrilineal clans), which in their turn are segmented into *nggi leo* (sub-clans). Although marriage within the *leo* continues to be regarded as incest, it nevertheless happens today that members of different *nggi leo*, but belonging to the same *leo*, do marry one another. [32]

A myth from the district of Ti relates how the two ancestors of this district agreed together, in connexion with a case of incest, that henceforth no one should marry in their own "tribe" (i.e., *leo*), but that the descendants of the one ancestor should always marry the descendants of the other. Each of the consequent phratries consists of eight clans. [33] We read elsewhere that affinal relations between two particular *leo* of one *nusak* are laid down by the ancestors, but that departures often occur at the present day. [34] That these connubial relationships were once more of the asymmetric type which we have already encountered is made very probable by the fact that exclusive cross-cousin marriage was also known on Rote. Van de Wetering describes cross-cousin marriage as the favoured type, [35] but he says nothing about unilaterality or bilaterality. The term for this form of marriage, namely *kabi toök* ("marriage with mother's brother"), would indicate the former. Another term is *sau tuti talike*, i.e., a marriage in which

---

30 Heijmering, 1844, pp. 247, 280, 303; Kruyt, 1923a, pp. 387, 352 ff.
31 Van de Wetering, 1925, p. 8.
32 Van de Wetering, 1925, pp. 8, 11.
33 Van de Wetering, 1925, p. 10.
34 Van de Wetering, 1925, p. 14.
35 Van de Wetering, 1925, pp. 3, 14; 1923b, p. 409.

the belts are tied together. Kruyt informs us that cross-cousin marriage of both types is practised.[36] Marriage with the brother's wife's brother, although permitted, is regarded by many as very undesirable. This can only mean that exclusive cross-cousin marriage must have obtained, since the impermissibility of brother-and-sister exchange is a direct consequence of the affinal relationships which are obviously entailed by unilateral cross-cousin marriage. That the system is already less strictly observed appears from the fact that marriage is permitted between sisters' children, though this report, which we likewise owe to Kruyt, appears generally not to be correct. As we have already observed elsewhere, the social standing of the persons involved will have a strong influence on the strictness with which the traditional marriage arrangements are observed.

We learn from the same author [37] that the wife's brother's wife, mother's brother's wife, and mother's sister's husband are not reckoned as "kin", whereas the father's brother's wife and father's sister's husband are. Kruyt does not explain what we are to understand by the term "kin". It probably refers to the representatives of the wife-giving and wife-taking groups.

The "lineages or tribes" into which the districts on *Savu* are divided are no longer exogamous.[38] Marriage is allowed both between brothers' children and between sisters' children. A preference is found for cross-cousin marriage, and brother-and-sister exchange is permitted.[39] Colenbrander reports, however, that marriages between cousins are forbidden, and that the preferred marriage is that between the daughter of a male cousin and the son of a female cousin.[40] What sorts of cousins the writer had in mind is unknown.

Obligatory cross-cousin marriage is reported in a number of sources on *Sumba* also. Wielenga speaks merely of cross-cousin marriage, without closer definition.[41] We may take it as fairly certain, however,

---

[36] Kruyt, 1921a, p. 271.
[37] Kruyt, 1921a, p. 270; Van de Wetering, 1923b, p. 404.
[38] Van de Wetering, 1926, pp. 488 ff., 494.
[39] Van de Wetering, 1926, p. 494.
[40] Colenbrander, 1916, p. 44.
[41] Wielenga, 1913, p. 223; cf. pp. 61, 73, 119, 143, 200, 257, 263, 266. The same author provides a text (1917, p. 93) which translates approximately as follows: "I pile up good upon good, basket upon basket". His accompanying note, to the effect that this refers to someone who has married off his sister and later gives his son to her daughter, thus twice over assuming responsibility for the bridewealth, cannot be entirely correct. Cf. Wielenga, 1913, p. 224, where the marrying out of the sister's sons is discussed.

that he refers to the restricted form, since practically all of the marriages which appear in the tales published in his article are exclusive cross-cousin marriages. The same author also reports in another place that ordinary cross-cousin marriage may accur as well.[42] Kruyt reports exclusive cross-cousin marriage, but at the same time he refers to certain departures from this form. In Wadjewa (western Sumba), also, ordinary cross-cousin marriage is said to be practised, and it is said to be permitted elsewhere if the brother has only sons and the sister only daughters, but in this case only after a purification rite. The general prohibition on marriage with the sister's husband's sister — i.e., the prohibition on brother-and-sister exchange — is a logical consequence of exclusive cross-cousin marriage. The relationship between a man and his sister's husband's sister is that of brother and sister.[43]

The *kabisu* (patrilineal clan) may be divided into two halves, and marriage is said to be permitted into the other half of one's own *kabisu*. But Kruyt hastens to contradict himself in the succeeding pages, where he says that if a girl wishes to marry a man from the other half she must first be made officially a member of another *kabisu* by means of a certain rite.[44] It is an open question whether we are perhaps faced with a merely apparent contradiction, such that marriage within the *kabisu* is in fact permitted in only one direction.

Some *kabisu*, according to Kruyt, are "related". By this he means that such *kabisu* stand in a relationship to each other of regular affinal alliance. The prevalence of exclusive cross-cousin marriage leads one to suppose that this relationship of connubium is asymmetric.[45]

On Sumba also the clan system is in the process of disintegration, as is shown by the rather undemanding character of the ways in which purification from incest can be effected. Marriage between sisters' children is absolutely forbidden in the districts of Kambera, Lewa, Lakoka, and Lamboja. Of these four districts, only Lamboja is situated in the western part of the island. In the western districts of Laura, Wadjewa, Wanokaka, and Anakala, and in the central districts of Bolobokat and Napu, marriage is permitted only with the daughter of an elder sister, and when the fathers belong to different *kabisu*.[46]

---

[42] Wielenga, 1917, p. 93.
[43] Kruyt, 1922a, p. 493.
[44] Kruyt, 1922a, pp. 497, 498.
[45] Kruyt, 1922a, p. 501.
[46] Kruyt, 1922a, p. 493.

It is well known that there used to be a patrilineal clan system in *Endeh* (middle Flores).[47] The clan is called *pu'u*, the clan head is *raki pu'u*, and the head of the patrilineage is termed *raki*. Today the clan system is in a state of full decline. The lineages are the main genealogical groups, and the marriage regulations take account only of traceable relatives. The prohibition on marriage between parallel cousins deserves special mention. This is accompanied by a preference for cross-cousin marriage in its restricted form. The prohibition on marriage with the father's sister's daughter is formulated as follows: "blood which has been taken out of the tribe must not be put back into it" (for "tribe" understand "clan"). Exclusive cross-cousin marriage is not obligatory, but it influences kinship relations to the extent that a woman calls the children of her father's sister's son, even though he may not in fact be married to her, by the term *ana* (children). There is a reciprocal taboo on pronouncing the names of the spouses of brother and sister.

If a lineage is threatened with extinction, a small son of a son-in-law is adopted (*nduëh*), or the son-in-law himself may be adopted, or else a stranger, for example a slave. The adopted individual is completely incorporated into the lineage, so that for instance the daughter of an adopted son-in-law may be married to her mother's sister's son.[48] This possibility is entirely in accord with a unilateral marriage system, the existence of which, on the grounds of the practice of exclusive cross-cousin marriage and what we have learned of this institution elsewhere, may be taken as certain. The daughter of a man who is thus adopted comes to belong to the same group as her mother's sister, and therefore marries a man from the same group as that to which the husbands of these relatives belong. In such a case, she and her mother's sister marry a son and his father. It is particularly remarkable that it is precisely this relationship that is specified, and not, for example, the marriage of a son of the adopted man with his mother's sister's daughter, which similarly would not conflict with clan-exogamy but which would, however, run counter to the unilateral marriage grouping.

The relationship terminology of the *Sikka*, who live further to the east, in the Maumere sub-division, clearly reflects exclusive cross-cousin marriage.[49] The following are some of the terms:

---

[47] Van Suchtelen, 1921, pp. 69, 88, 90, 102.
[48] Van Suchtelen, 1921, pp. 107, 115, 122.
[49] Calon, 1892a, pp. 190 ff.

ama	father, father's brother
ina	mother, mother's sister
tiu (or: *pulameng*)	mother's brother, father-in-law (m.s.)
naa	father's sister, mother-in-law (w.s.)
tuang	father-in-law (w.s.), daughter-in-law (m.s.)
pu	mother-in-law (m.s.), son-in-law, sister's children (m.s.)
wari	daughter-in-law (w.s.), younger sister (w.s.)

The following equivalences speak for themselves: father = father's brother; mother = mother's sister; mother's brother = father-in-law (m.s.); father's sister = mother-in-law (w.s.); son-in-law (m.s.) = sister's children (m.s.). It is noteworthy, too, that in the relationship between parents-in-law and children-in-law persons of the same sex address each other by different terms, whereas persons of opposite sex address each other by reciprocal terms. The former are closely related to each other by exclusive cross-cousin marriage, which of course has led to the terminological differentiation. Thus the relationship between son-in-law and father-in-law is identical with the important relationship between sister's son and mother's brother, and it is easily understandable that the terminology is not reciprocal. A man's mother-in-law, however, belongs to a group which in a unilateral system is entirely unrelated to his own. They address each other by a reciprocal term, the woman employing the same term as her husband. Under this system, father-in-law and daughter-in-law might even marry, for there is no real kinship between them, and they have a separate reciprocal term. For a woman, her daughter-in-law is identical with her brother's daughter: to address her as younger sister accords with the fact that both belong to the same patrilineal descent group.

laet	mother's brothers' daughter (m.s.)
wine	father's sister's daughter (m.s.), sister (m.s.)

The word *laet* means "to play, to joke, to tease"; there is thus apparently a joking relationship between these potential spouses.

In the *Solor Islands* exclusive cross-cousin marriage is, when possible, obligatory; otherwise, ordinary cross-cousin marriage is permitted.[50]

---

[50] Ten Kate, 1894, p. 242.

A third major culture area, which links up in many respects with that of Kei and Tanimbar, is formed by Seran, Buru, and a few smaller islands. Exclusive cross-cousin marriage, with its associated type of social structure, is known to us from this region also. The Manusela people, who inhabit the the interior of middle Seran, comprise four tribes (*ninia nia, amani*), each divided into a number of patrilineal clans (*uku, iba, ifa,* or *ifan*) and several hamlets (*lohoki*).[51] Tauern [52] and Schadee [53] mention exclusive cross-cousin marriage in the Manusela area, the former ascribing it to the tribes living to the east of the area as well. According to Schadee, this is the preferred type of marriage. Marriages between brothers' children, sisters' children, aunt and nephew, and uncle and niece are forbidden. Schadee reports that at the present day the exogamy of the clan has entirely lapsed, and that the *latu* (chief) of the Manusela *amani* (tribe, here in the narrower sense) does not scruple to encourage both kinds of parallel cousin marriage, precisely in order to create the possibility of marriage within one's own clan. The practice of exclusive cross-cousin marriage indicates the existence, or the former existence, of a unilateral marriage system. The following information from Willer [54] is interesting in this regard. After listing the five *ifan* of the Wai(ha)rama *amani*, viz. (1) Hapisoa, (2) Lihaya, (3) Manusawa, (4) Kopa, and (5) Ituhunia, he writes: "This division relates merely to kinship relations between one lineage and another, and especially with respect to marriage, since no one may marry in their own tribe". For both "lineage" and "tribe" we should read *ifan*. Should this report perhaps be taken to mean that the order in which the *ifan* are listed is that of a chain of affinal relationships? A widow may marry only in the *ifan* of her husband, and with one of his closest relatives.

In the several villages located on the south coast of the *Amahei* division (middle Seran) the original character of the society has been quite changed.[55] Van Schmid has provided certain information on marriage customs in this area. Here also exclusive cross-cousin marriage is practised, if not preferred. There is a joking relationship between these cross-cousins, who are termed *anak makain* and address each other as *kau*. The unilateral asymmetric marriage grouping, of

---

[51] Schadee, 1915, pp. 129 ff.; Willer, 1858, pp. 7 ff., 20 ff.
[52] Tauern, 1918, p. 184.
[53] Schadee, 1915, p. 134.
[54] Willer, 1858, p. 20.
[55] Tichelman, 1925, pp. 668, 678.

which exclusive cross-cousin marriage is a consequence, appears from the following still to be in force. The husband's family is called *malameit,* and the wife's family is called *tauli.* The *malameit* may not marry the *tauli.* As the terms are based on an affinal relationship, however, the meaning of this report can only be that women of the *malameit* cannot marry men from the *tauli.*[56]

The populations which inhabit the inferior of *Buru,* and which, in opposition to the coastal peoples, have safeguarded their traditional character, call themselves *gib'emliar,* i.e., original people.[57] They are divided into a number of *uli* (tribes), each of which contains several *nòro* (patrilineal clans),[58] which in their turn are segmented into *màrah* (apparently sub-clans).[59]

As a rule, a man takes a wife from the *nòro* or *màrah* of his mother; such a *màrah* is called the *mar'benima,* one's own *màrah.* To judge by the examples given by Schut, this closely approaches exclusive cross-cousin marriage. It is true that he does not say explicitly that the marriage relationship is unilateral, but from his entire description it seems, with a probability verging on certainty, that this is the case. In order to be sure that it will be possible to contract a marriage of the desired type, a lien is secured on a child who is yet unborn (*sihih engàlit*), or at any rate a betrothal is arranged with a girl who is as young as possible (*ipik,* to take as security). It appears from the following that the approach is always made to a particular *màrah* of the other *nòro.* If a man cannot find a wife in his *mar'benima,* the *màrah* of his mother, he has to make a *sihih engàlit* marriage within his own *uli.* It happens quite often that a man who is already adult brings up his prospective spouse himself, and carries her about everywhere with him in a cloth sling. Such an affinal link with a new *màrah* is acompanied by sacrifices and prayers to the ancestors, in order to avert possible ill consequences for the husband, for to take a wife from another *nòro* will not please the ancestors or the *mar'benima,* and the gift-exchange between *sànat* (husband's family) and *etkori* (wife's family) will be completely disrupted by such an irregular marriage.[60]

A *màrah* other than that into which the mother was born is called

---

56 Van Schmid, 1842, pp. 583, 596 ff.; Duyvendak, 1926, p. 128.
57 Schut, 1918, pp. 17 ff.; 1921, pp. 615 ff. Van der Miesen, 1902, p. 431, distinguishes between *gib masin,* beach-dwellers, and *gib fuka,* mountain people.
58 Schut, 1918, pp. 22 ff.; 1921, p. 617.
59 Schut, 1921, p. 618; 1923, p. 331.
60 Schut, 1918, p. 18.

mar'dikat (other *màrah*), and a *màrah* from a different *uli* is called *mar'méyet* (strange *màrah*).[61]

Exclusive cross-cousin marriage does not occur in Halmahera and Celebes. Although the social structure of these regions is, with a few exceptions, hardly at all known, this fact seems to be certain. A couple of reports, taken from two far-separated parts of Celebes, might be taken to contradict this conclusion and will be considered here.

The former relates to the To Laki, on the southeastern peninsula of Celebes. They are divided into a number of groups, each of which comprises several villages, spread out over a sometimes very extensive territory.[62] Treffers speaks of an aggregation of small "tribes or families",[63] and further reports a "family consisting of fathers, sons, nephews, and sometimes brothers-in-law" inhabiting a complex of dispersed houses. According to Kruyt,[64] marriage is matrilocal, so the complexes referred to are apparently not exogamous. The few kinship terms with which we are acquainted denote patrilineal and matrilineal relatives identically. The marriage of cousins, whether parallel or cross, is forbidden. Brother-and-sister exchange (*mesila wua*, to exchange areca nuts) is not strictly forbidden, but is much disliked. The parties must be thoroughly "purified" (*mosehe*), and it is still expected that there will be all sorts of ill consequences for the first couple.[65] The prohibition of this type of marriage is naturally of considerable significance in connexion with the question of the presence or absence of unilateral groupings on Celebes.

The second of the reports which we are considering concerns the area of the Sadan Toradja in the southwestern part of central Celebes, on the upper course of the Sadan River. In this area the composition of the group of consanguineous kin varies from one place to another, but it is always a bilateral kin group. In the western districts, on the other side of the Masupu and Mamasa rivers, and thus particularly in Mamasa among other places, the situation is different. In this region, according to Kruyt,[66] only cross-cousin marriage in its exclusive form is permitted. This is described in a note by Van der Miesen, who lived for a long time in the upper Binuang district, as absolutely incorrect.

---

61 Schut, 1918, p. 25.
62 Van der Klift, 1922, pp. 68 ff., 71; J. and A. C. Kruyt, 1921, pp. 693 ff.
63 Treffers, 1914, pp. 198, 201, 210.
64 Kruyt, 1922*b*, p. 445.
65 Kruyt, 1922*b*, pp. 429 ff.
66 Kruyt, 1923*b*, p. 104.

Marriage between "cousins" of any sort is quite forbidden. Directly after the reference to exclusive cross-cousin marriage, Kruyt states in addition that *sampu penduan* and *sampu pentalun* (cousins of the second and the third degree) may always marry. Such an unrestricted range of marital possibilities is of course not compatible with exclusive cross-cousin marriage. A very important fact in this connexion is the report by the same author that brother-and-sister exchange is forbidden in Balusu (Rante Pao) and Makale. This is said to be *sisura* or *sisula sirin*, i.e., higgledy-piggledy. The whole family is thought to die out, and crops and cattle to suffer severe harm.

It is true that exclusive cross-cousin marriage entails such a prohibition, but the prohibition does not necessarily indicate, conversely, the existence of exclusive cross-cousin marriage. It is indeed reported from Rante Pao and Makale, where it is certain that exclusive cross-cousin marriage is unknown. The two forms of marriage in question have, however, one essential point in common: they both require a more or less explicit form of unilateral alliance group. The following is particularly noteworthy in this connexion: marriage with the wife's brother's widow is absolutely forbidden, for she is the man's *sangrara sangbuku* (of the same blood and the same bones) or *sanglalan* (going on one path). Those who break this prohibition are drowned.[67] We thus have the peculiar situation that, although brother-and-sister exchange is forbidden, a man and his wife's brother's wife are nevertheless "of the same blood and the same bones". Such a prohibition is an implicit consequence of a system of unilateral alliance groups: if the brother-and-sister pair is taken as the ego-group, then the man referred to above belongs to the wife-taking group and the widow in question to the wife-giving group.

---

[67] Kruyt, 1923*b*, pp. 107, 108.

CHAPTER II

DUALISM AND TRIPARTITION

In the foregoing chapter we have seen that an asymmetric arrangement of marriage possibilities need not be accompanied by an organisation of the clans into two phratries, though an asymmetric system may very well be integrated into such an organisation. In order to arrive at a better understanding of the interrelations of the two types of structure, let us first take a closer look at the division of a tribe into clans and potential phratries.

On *Sumba* a district is always occupied by a number of named patrilineal clans called *kabisu*. In central and eastern Sumba the clan possesses its own territory, and the head of the clan is at the same time head of a village. It is his task to organise feasts, and to take care of the objects connected with the cult of the *marapu* (ancestors) of the clan. Some of these *kabisu* may not eat or kill certain animals, usually of two kinds. For the *kabisu* Ihi Wawang in the Tarimbang district, for example, such were the crocodile and a snake. Their ancestor I Boku, or I Ratu, had married a crocodile, and had received the *marapu*-objects from his father-in-law. It still sometimes happens that crocodiles come in the form of human beings to visit "their aunt on land". The name of the *kabisu* is often that of an ancestor.[1]

In the most westerly district, Kodi, we encounter a quite different form of organisation. The descent group is not patrilineal but matrilineal. The population of the district is divided into 49 *wāla* (matrilineal clans), the number of which is supposed not to change. Six of these 49 *wāla* occupy a specially prominent place. The *wāla* are intermingled with each other. So long as the payment of the bridewealth (*wali*), which is matched however by a counter-prestation (*lipoko*) of equivalent value, is not complete, marriage is matrilocal. The husband's family possesses authority over the children. Daughters do not inherit

---

[1] Kruyt, 1922a, p. 474; Wielenga, 1913, pp. 163, 165, 184, 186; *Mac.*, 1909, p. 170.

from the father. Marriage between nephew and niece (i.e., children of brother and sister) is completely forbidden, whereas brother-and-sister exchange is said to be permitted.[2]

Valuable information is available on the number of *kabisu* in any district. It should be kept in mind, in this connexion, that a district (i.e., the territory under a *radja*) forms a bounded whole, and that we find any single *kabisu* in only one district.[3] At present the situation seems to be that the number of *kabisu* per district can vary considerably, but from other sources we have been able to a certain extent to reconstruct the original situation. In the districts of central and eastern Sumba we find a number of functionaries, known as *ratu*, whose significance will be discussed below. In most districts there are four of these dignitaries, and since they are descendants in the oldest *kabisu*, those which first occupied the land in ancient times, we can conclude with practical certainty that originally there were four *kabisu* in a district.[4] This is indicated, too, by a tale reported by Lambooy,[5] in which it is said that the first ancestor of the aristocratic house of Tabundung found men already on Sumba, namely four *ratu*, who married among themselves (which means, naturally, that their *kabisu* did so) on an equal footing. A story from the locality of Massu tells of eight grandsons of the first human couple. These eight individuals were the first *ratu* in Massu and its surrounding area. In Kambera also the four great *kabisu* are descended from the four oldest ancestors.[6]

In the west, the chief village of a district is inhabited by members of all the *kabisu* of that district. The chief village there is called, as Wielenga puts it, the "residence of the different *marapu*".[7] Thus in the main village of Lamboja there are four *kabisu*, and in Tarung (Lauli) there are three, one of which is divided into two so that here also we find a total of four.[8] From a number of indications it may be inferred with confidence that the four-clan systems in question originated in a dual organisation of society. The evidence to this effect is abundant from western Sumba, and for the eastern part of the island as well there are a number of valuable data. Napu, for example, is divided into two "*marapu* lineages", the *ana matjuwa* and the *ana ma'ari*, older

---

[2] Kruyt, 1922*a*, pp. 499, 603 ff.
[3] Wielenga, *Mac.*, 1909, p. 335.
[4] Wielenga, *Mac.*, 1909, p. 372.
[5] Lambooy, *Mac.*, 1927, p. 233.
[6] Wielenga, *Mac.*, 1909, pp. 333, 335, 373.
[7] Wielenga, *Mac.*, 1909, p. 373.
[8] Kruyt, 1922*a*, pp. 498, 573.

brother and younger brother. We are not told whether the term *marapu*-lineage refers to a *kabisu*, or whether it is a larger unit. In Lakoka, which was established by emigrants from Napu, there is a *kabisu* called Lakoka in addition to the two *marapu*-lineages. This dual organisation is not only social, but socio-religious. The *ratu* of the *ana matjuwa* watches over the *marapu kabala*, who stay in a stone somewhere in the wilderness. He controls the lightning, and during thunder-storms people come into his house. He also protects the crops against vermin, and receives the first bundle of rice when it is harvested. The *ratu* of the *ana ma'ari* is guardian of the *marapu tolu mata wai maringu* (raw meat, cold water). He makes rain, he purifies after adultery and incest, and he removes pollution from returning warriors. It is evident that the former functionary stands in contact with the sky, and the latter with things of the earth.[9]

In Melolo also there is a dual organisation, but unfortunately we are less well informed about it. We have to rest content with the report that Melolo is divided into Watu Pelitu and Palai Malamba, and that the *radja* of Watu Pelitu is the inferior or the younger in relation to the *radja* of Palai Malamba. The information on Tabundung is even more summary, namely that it is divided into two parts which in effect are independent. The *radja* of Watu Pelitu has to take his chief wife from Palai Malamba, while the ruler of Palai Malamba must take his chief wife from the aristocratic house of Tabundung.[10]

Laura is divided into two, viz., Lètèna, the older branch, associated with the mountains, and Marādana, the younger branch, associated with the plain. Both parts have a common origin in the hinterland; their tribal ancestor came from Tanggéba, in Wadjewa. When the Lètèna people came down from the mountains under their leader Riri Bano, the latter called upon his younger brother, Buka Rera, leader of the Marādana people, to drive out the original inhabitants, who belonged to the Lombo tribe. There is a myth which tells of the outbreak of war between Lètèna and the Lombo or Lumbung. Once, when the Lètèna were hunting in the lowlands, they were having a meal with the Lombo, and one of their dogs ran through the rice. For this offence the Lètèna were fined a buffalo and a horse, but instead they paid only a goat and a cat. This led to the strife between the two peoples.[11] Riri Bano remained the legitimate ruler, but Buka Rera

---

[9] Kruyt, 1922a, p. 477.
[10] Kruyt, 1922a, p. 467.
[11] Kruyt, 1921b, p. 552; Wielenga, *Mac.*, 1916, p. 34.

grew beyond his control. Marādana thus possessed the right to rule,
while Lètèna considered themselves to be the more important. Within
Marādana itself two leaders disputed between themselves over who
should rule, and the Dutch government, says Wielenga, thus found
itself dealing with three rulers in Laura.

Here we should turn our attention to a discrepancy in the reports
of Kruyt. Although he translates Lètèna as mountains, or at least
equates it with mountains, and associates Marādana with the plains, he
represents Lètèna as living on the coast and Marādana in the interior.
The main village of Laura is divided into two parts, which are separated
by a ravine. The left-hand part, where the Léténa live, is called Bondo
Kapumbu, and the right-hand part, that of the Marādana, is called
Buka Rera. This perhaps provides an explanation of the above discrepancy. Since it is plain that Lètèna and Marādana inhabit one
village, even though it is split into two, we can take it that the
association of Lètèna with mountain and Marādena with the plain is
purely traditional.[12] Further instances of dual organisation are found
in Lauli, which is divided into Lauli Bondo (above) and Lauli Wawa
(below), and in Wadjewa, where Bali Omba or Lewata, the central
village, is opposed as the oldest and as "owner (or holder) of the
land" to Bali Loko, the half of the ruler. Kruyt adds the comment
that these rulers may not eat mice, a prohibition which they explained
to him by saying: "We should be eating our own flesh". The division of
Kodi into Kodi Bokul and Kodi Bengedo is said however to be a local
one. Lamboja is divided into the real Lamboja, considered as the older
and senior, and Lamboja Patijala. On the right bank of a certain river
lies the village of Sodan, where a younger brother of the ruler is
guardian of the sacred objects. The village of Wunu Wuluta, on the
left bank, is the residence of the ruler himself.[13] Anakala is divided
into Anakala in a strict sense and Makata Kiri. The headman of the
village of Anakala, where the marapu-objects are kept, stands in the
relationship of elder brother to the ruler, who lives at Makata Kiri.
Anakala is the more important village of the two.[14]

A myth which reflects the antagonism of the halves runs as follows:
The original populations of Laura, Wadjewa, Lauli, and Lamboja,
comprised two groups, the Mangu Tanah (owners of the land) and the

[12] Kruyt, 1922a, p. 468; 1921b, p. 538; Wielenga, Mac., 1910, pp. 7, 8.
[13] Kruyt, 1922a, pp. 499, 468; 1921b, p. 538; Wielenga, Mac., 1916, pp. 34, 543,
   549.
[14] Kruyt, 1921b, pp. 536, 538, 549.

Bali Loko (from overseas). The latter were driven back to the east through the cunning of the Mangu Tanah. The purely traditional character of the antagonism in this myth appears perfectly clearly from the fact that Bali Loko still remains one of the halves of Wadjewa.[15]

Finally, there is yet another type of dual organisation to be discussed, viz., that of the *kabisu*. In Tarung (Lauli), one of the three *kabisu* is divided into two. One part is *goba kado* (literally, enemy buffalo horn) to the other. If a buffalo is killed, the horns cannot be kept as ornaments but have to be given to the other party.[16]

At the head of the tribes (i.e., districts) stand rulers called *maramba*. The clan to which the ruler himself belongs is the most important *kabisu* in the district.[17] We have seen how in the western part of the island, where a division of the tribe into halves is a phenomenon of general occurrence, the head of one of the halves has completely outstripped his counterpart in the possession of real power, whereas the latter nevertheless continues to be recognised as the older and the more eminent of the two. This dual organisation is often accompanied by a differentiation of spiritual and worldly power. In central and eastern Sumba also this division of labour has been effected, but in an entirely different way. Everywhere in this region there are two categories of holders of power: the guardians of the relics of the *marapu*, and the rulers. The task of the former, the *ratu*, consists chiefly in the performance of priestly functions; they also decide questions of inheritance and relationship, and all decisions by the ruler require their sanction. Furthermore, they are actually the *mangu tanah* (owners of the land), and they are thus invested with the dignity which is usually denoted by the Malay term *tuan tanah*.[18] The *ratu* is addressed as: "Mother who possesses the river, father who possesses the land". Ruler and *ratu* are never united in one individual. In the course of wars and annexations real power may at any time pass into other hands, and new holders of power repeatedly arise.[19] As we have already observed, in most districts there are four *ratu*, who are descendants of the oldest *kabisu*, those who in olden times first laid claim to the land. Evidently, therefore, the *ratu* is to be seen as having

---

[15] Lambooy, 1927, p. 234.
[16] Kruyt, 1922a, p. 498; Roo van Alderwerelt, 1890, pp. 578, 590.
[17] Wielenga, 1926, p. 39.
[18] Kruyt, 1922a, pp. 467, 469, 474.
[19] Wielenga, *Mac.*, 1909, pp. 370, 371.

been originally the head of a clan. The office of *ratu* has become an entirely spiritual one, providing few material advantages. If a *ratu* were to display an inclination to turn his official rights and authority to his own purposes, or if he were to be afflicted by what the source refers to as "megalomania", the clan heads would secretly decide, under the leadership of the ruler, to *hāpi na ja ratu* (literally, to pluck off the *ratu*); he would be murdered and be succeeded by his eldest son, and his wives and other children would be killed or made into slaves. When a *ratu* became too old to perform his duties, also, or when the people had suffered too much from sickness or other calamities, he was murdered so that he might be succeeded by a younger man. In western Sumba the ruler is at the same time the most important *ratu*, *kabundi ratō*.[20] We read in Kruyt, however, that the head is called *ratu*, and that the custodian of the tribal gods, on the contrary, is called *aru* (younger brother) *marapu*. But it often happens that the ruler himself is guardian of the *marapu*, and the *aru marapu* then lend their aid in order to assure the favourable influence of the *marapu* on agriculture.[21]

It may be inferred from the myth reported by Lambooy that the opposition ruler/*ratu* is to be found in the dualistic complex which we have been able to establish in the western part of the island. The founding ancestor of the ruling lineage of Tabundung met four *ratu* who were already there when he descended from the sky. What we see here, therefore, is an opposition between elder and earth on the one hand and younger and sky on the other, with actual power residing in the younger.[22]

The unilateral type of marriage, the existence of which we believe ourselves to have shown to be very probable, is explicitly reported to apply to the rulers. We have already mentioned the affinal relationships among Watu Pelitu, Palai Malamba, and Tabundung. Only the sons of such marriages can be considered for succession to the ruler. Our information on these interesting relationships is extremely brief. Tabundung is one of the oldest houses on Sumba, and only Kanatang and Rendeh [23] are also allied to it in such a way. We have to be satisfied with these vague indications of an intricate system of connubial relations which appears to cover a large part of Sumba. A striking

---

[20] Wielenga, *Mac.*, 1909, pp. 371 ff.; cf. the "rex nemorensis".
[21] Kruyt, 1922*a*, pp. 468, 477.
[22] Lambooy, 1927, p. 233.
[23] Kruyt, 1922*a*, p. 467.

feature is that the group from which the wife comes always possesses a considerable ascendancy over the wife-taking group. Lakoka, i.e., the ruling *kabisu*, has to take its senior wives from Napu (naturally, from the ruling *kabisu* there), on the ground that Lakoka was established by emigration from Napu.[24] It is worthy of mention, finally, that Wielenga reports that a ruler must always take his senior wife from a particular house. Only a son from this marriage is *ana maramba landung*, full-blooded son of the ruler. *Maramba* who acquire sovereignty by force, and are not of noble ancestry, cannot obtain such a wife, i.e., they cannot gain admittance to the system.[25]

From information provided by Van Hoevell it appears that on *Tanimbar* the most important social unit is formed by the complex (Van Hoevell refers to it as "negory") of several villages (*kampong* or *soa*). The complex consisted of three or four villages, each with its own name.[26] Thus Krawain, in the region to which most of Drabbe's publications relate,[27] is one of the villages of the "five-village area of Alusi" on the east coast of Jamdena.

It is reported from only the three smaller northern islands of Larat, Vordate, and Molu that such complexes existed, without however any precise information on the nature of the interrelationships. Three of the six complexes on Larat formed an alliance with one on the opposite coast; similarly, three of the six on Vordate and two of the five on Molu contract such alliances. Each of these small islands seems thus to be divided into four. On the island of Maro there were three complexes, two of which were inhabited by strangers; there were nine in northern Jamdena, thirteen in the south; Sera had five, and Selaru had ten.[28]

The following description of the most important village officials relates especially to the village-complex of Lauran, on the east coast of Jamdena. The terms are given in the language of the east coast.[29] The three most important functionaries of the village are the *pnuwe nduan*, owner of the village, the *mangaf wajak*, announcer, and the *mangsombe*, sacrificer.

The owner of the village is a direct descendant and heir of him who

[24] Wielenga, *Mac.*, 1916, p. 10.
[25] Wielenga, 1913, p. 234; *Mac.*, 1916, p. 35; Pos, 1901.
[26] Van Hoevell, 1890*b*, pp. 160, 162; 1890*a*, p. 146.
[27] Drabbe, 1925, p. 31.
[28] Van Hoevell, 1890*a*, p. 146; 1890*b*, pp. 160, 162, 164.
[29] Drabbe, 1927, pp. 181 ff.

by tradition first settled in the place where the village was built, i.e., the founder of the village. The term "village" is to be understood here merely as the place where people live together, not the lands which are the property of the village community or of individual landowners (*ambat ndunir*). In a village there may be not only many *ambat ndunir*, but a number (e.g., two or three) of owners of the village, according to the number of men who first took possession of the place. The *pnuwe nduan* has the right to permit anyone to build his house in the village, and thus to make use of the communal lands and property. Once he has bestowed this right he cannot revoke it. Whenever there is question of a general removal to another place, it is his right to decide what shall be done, but only after first hearing what the people have to say and then getting their consent. The *pnuwe nduan* is also called *riribun réréngjar*, which is the term for the plank beds of a large communal boat used in festivals or in war. The village community is often called *sori*, the common word for a boat; the village "square", the dancing place, where all important affairs are carried out, was often shaped like a *sori*. One of the most important parts of the great ceremonial boat mentioned above was the four plank beds, on which people felt as much at ease as in their own homes.

According to Drabbe, the *pnuwe nduan* was apparently in former times the *mangaf wajak* as well. He was able to renounce this right in favour of another, but as owner of the village he still had to approve the decisions of the announcer.

The present-day *mangaf wajak* is usually the lineal successor to the first announcer, but the community and the *pnuwe nduan* together could in the past confer this dignity on someone else. This was not done easily, however, for once a right had been inherited it could not with impunity be taken away unless there was good reason, and very often the consequence of such an action was virulent sickness and death. The function of the *mangaf wajak* corresponded for the most part to that of the modern office of *orang kaja*.

The *mangaf wajak* was the father of the village (*pnuwe dalam amnir*), and the sacrificer (*mangsombe*) was the mother (*pnuwe dalam ennir*). Although the status of the *mangsombe* was almost as high as that of the *mangaf wajak*, in situations of general interest the latter was the bigger man. The main such situations were wars, the conclusion of friendship, and the exchange of valuables with other villages. It was the *mangaf wajak* who decided, after communal deliberation and with general assent, whether or not there would be war. The *mangsombe* would then offer a sacrifice to the supreme being, in case the decision was to go to war, and the aortic arteries of the animal were examined to see whether they foretold a successful war. At this point there was another decision, and this was the final one. Heads which had been taken, and spoils of war, were brought ceremonially to the father and mother, who safeguarded them as common property. The house of the *mangaf wajak* was called *kmberre*, loft, i.e., the place where valuables are kept. The *mangsombe* had to stay in his house throughout the hostilities; this was called *nsombe*, to sacrifice.

Father and mother were in theory supreme, but they could decide nothing without the approval of the community, and this often went against them. In private affairs they had no authority; if one or both of them got into a quarrel the other party would often settle the dispute out of respect for their person, but just as often this did not happen and in this case there was no punishment or fine.

Fines could only be imposed by the community and on the strength of a communal agreement. A common verdict would be worked out, and it would be stipulated that another time a fine of a certain amount would have to be paid.

These dignitaries occupied no special position in everyday life, and their influence was largely dependent on their personal qualities or abilities and on the support of a large or influential family.

The most prominent among the *mel'angkir* (lesser functionaries) were the *mangatanuk* (speaker) and the *sori luri* (prow, bows). Like the *mel'silaiar* (the three higher functionaries), these had their allotted place (*totobat*, a large flat stone) in the village square (*natar*). The *natar*, as said above, frequently had the form of a boat and was always regarded as such. The *sori luri* sat on the foremost part of the *natar*, and slightly further up sat the other two dignitaries, the *pnuwe nduan* to his left and the *mangsombe* to his right. At the other end sat the *mangaf wajak*, on the left, and the *mangatanuk*, on the right. The *mangatanuk* had always and everywhere to convey the words of the *mangsombe* and the *mangaf wajak*, in their name and by their authority. The *sori luri* was also called *snjomb'luri* (beginning of the sacrificial feast), *mangbaluan* (he who goes before), *mangkei* (dragger), and *manglair* (precursor). He opened every sacrifical rite, when the village moved he had to be the first to erect a new house, his rice was the first to be planted and the first to be harvested; in these ways he played the part of the first in all village events. Both the *sori luri* and the *mangatanuk* might well possess power by virtue of their personal influence and the support of a powerful family.

In broad outline the above applies to all villages on Tanimbar.

Forbes [30] also mentions the great influence of the community. The *orang kaja* has only nominal power, and no more influence than that of any other adult man. The words of the older men weigh more heavily than those of the younger, but the latter can freely state their opinions, and so can the women. "The general voice is the law of the village community."

We should like to give a brief account here of the gift-exchange between groups standing in the relationship of *nduwe* and *uranak*, already discussed in the first chapter, in order to draw attention to the explicitly dualistic principles of classification which define the character of this gift-exchange. Additional observations will be made when we come to feasts.

Nduwe and *uranak* are obliged to lend reciprocal aid to each other. If I need anything in everyday life, or in *anggrijé* (affairs, important social crises, at which the intercourse of the clans assumes a very intense and emotional character), then I turn to my *nduwe* or *uranak*. But which of the two I shall approach is not indifferent, for the *uranak* will "tap palm wine for me" (*raflaīt*), and the *nduwe* "will bring me belt and sarong" (*ral umbin-teis*). The *uranak* brings (i.e., to his *nduwe*) everything appertaining to the man or which comes from the man, and the *nduwe* brings (to his *uranak*) everything that belongs to the woman or comes from the woman. The following are classified as masculine: fish, meat, palm wine, pigs, gold ear-ornaments, pieces of gold, antique swords, and elephant's tusks. The following goods, among others, are classified as feminine: tubers, rice, leguminous plants, cloths, shell arm-bands, necklaces, and women's ornaments. But it is not even necessary for me to ask, for if my *nduwe* has had a good harvest he will not forget his *uranak* and will bring him part of it unasked; the *uranak* behaves in the same way towards his *nduwe* after good fortune at hunting or fishing. Any exchange of gifts in the opposite directions, however, is completely out of the question.

The *Kei Islands*, like Tanimbar, are divided into a number of districts, each containing several villages. At the head of these village complexes stand rulers called *rāt*, a word derived from the alien *radja*.[32]

[30] Forbes, 1884, pp. 15, 21.
[31] Drabbe, 1923, pp. 547 ff.
[32] Geurtjens, 1921, p. 179.

The most important social unit is formed by what Geurtjens calls the family group, a patrilineal descent group called *fām* in the local language. The head of the *fām* is the *kapalla sowa*. A *fām* is characterised by a common name, which is also borne by women married into it and by slaves belonging to members of the *fām*. A woman who leaves the *fām* at her marriage, like a man who marries without paying *wilin* (bridewealth) and a slave who changes masters, acquires the name of the descent group to which she or he then belongs.[33] The *fām* owe their origin and their names to the sons, always seven in number, of a mythical "tribal ancestor of the family group". These seven sons married the daughters of other ancestors, and thus became the founders of a number of *fām*. Their descent is thus traced through their own forefathers from a common "patriarch". The *fām* descended from the oldest son retained supreme authority in its capacity as successor to the patriarch. The names of most of the *fām* are composed of the name of their founding ancestor together with *ubun*, which means "descendants". Words such as *rah jān* (oldest house) and *rah warin* (youngest house) denote rank-order. Several names are connected with the origin of the ancestors. These *fām* continually dispersed, usually because of dissension, lack of land or drinking water, and other difficulties. Commonly, however, the dispute arose because when a pig had been killed the stronger brothers took the fat pieces out of the pot for themselves and left only the bones and the liquid for the younger brothers. The latter, deeply shamed by such treatment, broke up the group and moved elsewhere.[34] It also happened, according to Geurtjens, that a number of *fām* would group themselves together in one village when they felt individually too weak in the face of possible enemies. In such a case the head of the original *fām* naturally assumed some degree of authority over the others. This is the explanation of the circumstance that at present many villages contain *fām* of very different origins.[35] Geurtjens endeavours to show that the common occupation of one village by a number of *fām* of various origins is in fact an exceptional case. In another place he says that each village is composed of different family groups, i.e., *fām*, each under its own head, who is called *kapalla sowa*. Members of the *fām* outside the village also remained under the jural authority of their *kapalla sowa*.[36]

---

[36] Geurtjens, 1921, p. 185.
[33] Geurtjens, 1921, p. 376.
[34] Geurtjens, 1921, pp. 17, 178, 302.
[35] Geurtjens, 1921, p. 179.

Van Hoevell similarly reports that a village is divided into *soa*, and that the *soa* sometimes coincides with the *rahan*, "family".[37] The word *rahan* appears in Geurtjens with the meaning of "house".[38] The *fām* or *soa* thus apparently consists of people living together in one house. According to Van Hoevell [39] the village is exogamous, and Geurtjens also reports that women leave the village when they marry.[40]

The following mythical relationship among a number of villages may be of some interest in connexion with the above matters. The villages of Raharing, Ohoi Nangan, and Wowr have one and the same line of descent, but the people of Raharing and Ohoi Nangan take a higher place at public gatherings because their ancestors beat those of Wowr in a bamboo-pulling contest. This game appears in another myth, in which the contestants are earth-dwellers and sky-dwellers. The bamboos were to be dragged to the beach, and the first to get there would be the winners. The earth-dwellers pulled the bamboos by the tips, and the branches continually got caught; but the sky-dwellers got hold of the lower ends and thus got their bamboos to the beach. Geurtjens also adds that the people of Raharing were let down from the sky by God.[41]

In village government there are five prominent functionaries. In the first place there is the *orang kaja* or *orang tu(wa)*, the village headman. Geurtjens says that each headman used to be a practically independent governor in his village. Most probably we should take this to mean that each village formed a practically independent unit, for in fact any tendency towards such independent rule was entirely alien to the office of headman. He was not permitted any arbitrary action, and for all important questions he had to call a meeting of the "elders" of the family groups; this usually took place in his house, and all interested parties would also be present. Women were not admitted, but this did not stop them following the proceedings from adjacent rooms and making their unsought opinions heard. It seems most likely that the *orang kaja* was the leading *kapalla sowa*, but Geurtjens nowhere states that this was the case.[42]

Then there is the *tuan tan*, the official owner of all village lands. In some localities the office is purely titulary, but in others he is still

[37] Van Hoevell, 1890*a*, p. 131.
[38] Geurtjens, 1921, p. 300; for the abbreviation *rah*, see p. 178.
[39] Van Hoevell, 1890*a*, p. 124.
[40] Geurtjens, 1921, p. 303.

recognised as having real authority. If anyone wishes to clear land
for new planting on land belonging to the village, they have to inform
the *tuan tan*, and he also divines whether or not the crop will thrive.
He is the supreme arbiter in disputes over land.

The third and fourth functionaries are the *mitu duan* (master,
attendant of the local tutelary spirit) and the *leb* (Malay *lebai*, religious
official). If the charge of some misdemeanour cannot be cleared up,
the offender is handed into the vengeance of the *mitu*. This is the task
of the *mitu duan*, whose powers include the administration of oaths
and the rendering of divinely inspired judgement. This official is often
the *leb* as well, and in that capacity performs sacrifices on behalf of the
community.

The fifth official is the *dir-u ham-wang* (precursor and carver), a
dual dignity. *Dir-u* (precursor) is a post of honour in the *bélan*
(ceremonial boat) which is the pride and showpiece of the village.
Each village has its own *bélan* and its distinctive *bélan*-name. The
ceremonial boat is the emblem of the village. *Bélan* connotes meta-
phorically "a supreme chief with his subordinates". Geurtjens also
writes that figuratively speaking the *bélan* stands for one or more
"family groups with the leader, especially in larger villages the subordinate heads with their followers". A *bélan* is beautifully decorated
with carving and flags bearing certain figures. These decorations
often lead to quarrels and fights because of real or supposed copying.
The arrival of a *bélan* is a festive occasion. The *dir-u* acts as pilot at
that time, and also when the boat departs. When other villages are
visited no one may go ashore before the voyagers have been cere-
moniously greeted by certain notables, upon which *sirih* and a couple
of gifts are offered. The *ham-wang* (carver) has the delicate task, after
a communal hunt of large game (manatee, ray, sperm whale, turtle),
of carving up the prize and dividing it among all the inhabitants of the
village.[43]

The number of clans which the tribe formerly contained is not known,
and just as little is reported on the number of "patriarchs" (clan
ancestors) whose descendants, the *fām*, contracted affinal relationships
among one another. Although Geurtjens says that the seven *fām* of a
clan traditionally lived together in one village, there is clearly no

---

[43] Geurtjens, 1921, pp. 187, 239, 249. This, together with the ceremonial boats
of Tanimbar which have already been described, may well be seen as a sort
of floating men's house. Cf. Nooteboom, 1932, p. 189, plates 93, 93*a*, & 93*b*;
Rassers, 1931.

connexion between the number of clans which formerly composed the tribe and the number of villages which today make up a district. It appears from information given by Planten and Van Hoevell that the number of villages per district on Kei Ketjil varies from two to fifteen.[44] There is no doubt that the district, headed by its *rāt*, is genetically related to the former tribe. Not much is known about the district, but it would seem to be the case that the district is the most important political unit, that in which a completely social life in all its aspects can be given full scope.

Dualistic tendencies in the social structure are not lacking here, either, as can be seen from certain incidental pieces of evidence. Thus in prayers, songs, and ceremonies all the men of the village are designated by a single name and all the women by another; this means that at the peaks of social and religious life the whole society is seen as two distinct homogeneous groups standing in opposition to each other. Geurtjens offers the conjecture that these two names, which are no different from ordinary ones, were probably the names of ancestors.[45]

	(men)	(women)
Somlain	Maibut Lestār	Did-il Tamhēr
Ohoidēr-tutu	Maibut Watnār	Did-Koran-Resok
Ngilngof	Maibut Wodil	Did-il Masnēw
Langgur	Maibut Watwāv	Ohoitib Ngimās

A Ngilngof chant goes as follows: Maibut and Wel-il (family groups of Ngilngof) shall proclaim themselves (i.e., go to war); the people of Did-il and Masnēw (Geurtjens wonders whether these are feminine family names) dance and prepare the victory celebration over that noble leader. It can be seen from this that Ngilngof is divided into four "family groups", and it appears from the division of their functions that two of them are classified as masculine and the other two as feminine. Did-il Masnēw and Maibut Wel-il, each taken as forming one word, are the names referred to above by which the group of women and the group of men are denoted. The opposing party Dulah is known by five names. Geurtjens thinks that three of these refer to

[44] Planten, 1892, p. 644; Van Hoevell, 1890a, p. 107.
[45] Geurtjens, 1921, p. 377.
[41] Geurtjens, 1924, pp. 237, 231.
[42] Geurtjens, 1921, pp. 184, 179.

the women of the various "family groups" of Dulah; the other two are said to be already trembling, and these are apparently the masculine groups.[46]

It is noteworthy that young boys' names are mostly animal-names, primarily fishes and birds and even less well-regarded creatures such as snake, scorpion, worm, and flying fox; and that girls's names, on the contrary, are chiefly taken from plants, flower-names being the most common. A few creatures are found among girls' names, viz., insects, shell-fish, and a number of birds such as chicken, parrot, and parakeet. Parts of the body are also to be found among these names, e.g., ear, hair, knee.[47]

Totemism has not declined on Kei to the same extent as among other peoples in this region. Practically every "family" has to deny itself certain animal or vegetable food because of a relationship between the ancestors and these animals or plants, e.g., that according to a myth they came to a certain mutual agreement.[48] Some families, according to their legends of origin, are related to certain kinds of animal and are supposed to respect them. Sometimes, for example, it is said that fish or shell-fish changed into the ancestors of these "families". Others may not eat the opossum, on the ground that their ancestors descended from the sky down the tail of this animal. To kill or injure such totemic creatures causes sickness.[49]

Often the relationship between an animal species and a "family" is expressed in precisely the opposite way, namely that the animal in question allows itself by preference to be caught and eaten by that particular family.[50] The two cases reported by Geurtjens relate to large marine creatures, and are based on a pact between them and human beings.

Langen relates a myth about three brothers, Hian, Tongiil, and Parpara, who lived in the sky with their sisters, Bikul and Meslaang. Parpara, who was always going fishing in the cloud-sea, lost the hook belonging to his elder brother Hian. The latter was very angry and ordered him to find the hook, which he succeeded in doing with the help of a fish. Parpara brought it about that his elder brother tipped over a bowl of palm wine belonging to him, and Hian could not pay

---

[46] Geurtjens, 1921, pp. 154, 377.
[47] Geurtjens, 1921, pp. 371, 372.
[48] Geurtjens, 1921, p. 170.
[49] Geurtjens, 1921, pp. 120, 74.
[50] Geurtjens, 1921, pp. 120, 74.

back the spilled wine. In order to find the palm wine he had to dig
a hole in the ground, and in doing so he discovered the earth lying
below him. The three brothers went down and called to their sisters
to do so too; Meslaang let herself down on the rope, and when the
brothers looked up and saw her pudenda they were deeply ashamed
and called to her to pull the rope back up. Langen adds that the place
where the three brothers, their sister, and four dogs landed is called
Wuat, a mountain on Kei Besar.[51] According to Planten, Bikēl was
already down when the incident with Meslaang took place.[52] Geurtjens
writes that the women were called Dit-il and Māslang, and that they
both turned back when their brothers looked up and laughed at the
sight of their pudenda. The brothers descended near Mastur, where
the people took them to be good-for-nothings who had been chased
out of heaven by God. A contest was arranged in order to determine
who among them were really such and who were good. This contest
(by dragging the bamboos) was won by the sky-people, who then
proposed another one, which was to hold back the tide. The earth-
dwellers strove unavailingly with their paddles. The brothers set to
work as the tide turned, and won the contest without difficulty. The
earth-dwellers now gave them women to marry. Seven sons were born,
who later dispersed to all parts.[53]

Geurtjens provides a pendant to this myth.[54] A hunter, Letwir,
comes upon an old woman in the underworld. She teaches him about
rice, and he acquaints her with the use of fire. They marry and decide
to go together to the upperworld. They quarrel about who shall go
first, and in the end the woman climbs up before the man. He looks
up, begins to laugh, and says: "I can see a little opossum hanging in
the fork of a branch." At this the woman angrily turns back. The
man succeeded in smuggling two grains of rice with him, concealed
in his scrotum, when he went up. He had first tried to hide them in
his nose, and then under his foreskin, but the woman had discovered
them and taken them back. He sewed these grains, and cooked only
the red rice, letting the white stand. The two kinds of rice then ran
away to the garden of a woman.

Finally, let us look at yet another myth, concerning the village of
Ngilngof. The village was first located at Ohoi-tum (literally, legend-

---

51 Langen, 1902, pp. 56 ff.
52 Planten, 1892, p. 280.
53 Geurtjens, 1924, p. 231.
54 Geurtjens, 1924, p. 277.

village, the place associated with the legend of the origin of the "tribe or the family group"), then at Ohoi-reinan (mother-village), and after that at Ohoi Idar. Here lived an old woman with great magical powers who was called "little mother Idar", after whom the village was named. The people treated her badly, so she made the village sink into the ground. The survivors fled everywhere, among other places to Reng-mās and Kelmanut. The old woman herself wandered about, giving names to all sorts of places, and finally changed into a rock. At Kelmanut an old woman called "little mother Kelmanut" found a mollusc, which changed into a man. His name was Tomel (sea-worm). The old woman obtained the princess Butri from Tetoōt, on payment of a large bridewealth, to be his wife. The people of Ngilngof said to the ruler of Tetoōt: "Your Majesty, Tomel and Butri are now married, and we therefore regard you as the father of us all; the entire lands of Ohoiwur are thus yours, and our land is also your land." At the present day this is denied, on the ground that Butri remained always in her own village.[55]

The little kingdoms of central *Timor* are divided into a number of districts, each with its own ruler. These rulers or districts are conceived as forming one family. One of them, the supreme ruler, who is of too high a status to concern himself with government, is the mother. The ruler who is next highest in rank after this passive figure, whose "right hand" he is, actually governs affairs; he is regarded as the father of the family, though he is usually referred to by the title of *fettor*. This is probably an indigenous term which originally was formed after the Portuguese *feitor* (governor). The remaining rulers, of whom there are usually an even number, are the "children" of the family; the senior of these children, as the "left hand" of the supreme ruler, is the commander-in-chief (*surik ulun*). These rulers were the official authorities of the kingdom.

The most important kingdom in north Tétun is Fialarang, the organisation of which we shall outline in rather more detail. Its social statuses and their arrangement are embodied in the following myth. In ancient times the whole of Timor was covered by the sea, and only the highest mountain in Belu, Lekaan, stood out above the water. The ruling house of Bauho originated on this mountain. The myth relating to this event could not be elicited on any conditions; it probably tells how the first woman came out of the top of the mountain, and that the man came from a far country. However this may be, the myth

---

[55] Geurtjens, 1924, p. 211.

continues with the second generation, a brother and a sister, who married and had two sons and two daughters. One of the sons, Atok Lekaan, went by boat with his sister Elok Loa Loro to the tip of Nenait mountain, which had emerged in the meantime, in Naitimu, where they became the ancestors of the rulers of Naitimu. Atok took the name Mauk Loro Lètèn Mauk Lali Wen. By this time several peaks had emerged out of the water in Lidak.

The other son, Taek Lekaan, and his sister Balok Loa Loro stayed on Lekaan mountain and had there ten sons and three daughters. In many situations the youngest of the sons demonstrated his superiority over his older brothers, and these then recognised him as ruler of the country. As such, he immediately knew the correct nature of all sorts of things which were seen for the first time on journeys through the new land. The older brothers, however, were ashamed to return to Lekaan mountain; five of them went off to the west and four to the east, where they became the ancestors of the rulers of these regions. The youngest brother established himself lower down the slopes of Lekaan, at Mainita. He was called Dasi Mauk Bauk, and married the daughter of the *meromak oa'n* (the ruler of Waihale, on the south coast), Dasi Lihu Aton, whom he bought from her father for some heads. Through this marriage he acquired the title of Loro (sun).

Two sons and two daughters were born to him. The elder son stayed at Mainita and married a daughter of the Loro of Lakékun (on the south coast); the younger brother became head of Klusin under the supremacy of his brother. The sisters married the rulers of Naitimu and Asumanu.

The ruler of Mainita had a son, who succeeded him and went to live lower down at Bauho, and three daughters, who married the heads of Lassiolat, Naitimu, and Lidak. The ruler of Bauho was not able to get a wife from the ruling house of Waihale, or from that of Lakékun, except with a high bridewealth; so he took a daughter of the ruler of Balibo, by whom he had six sons and three daughters. The eldest son succeeded his father, and the younger ones established themselves as heads of Lasaka, Dafala, Manuk Lètèn, Umak Laran, and Sorbau, all under the authority of their oldest brother.

One of the rulers of Bauho, on a journey through the surrounding areas of his territory, came to Asumanu. The ruler of this land was so frightened by this encounter that he began to make water (the place is called Mihun, from *mi*, to urinate, and *hun*, head, leader). After this, he followed the ruler everywhere. On the way, the ruler of Bauho showed the ruler of Asumanu one of his sacred regalia; the latter "was frightened almost to death" (the place is called Matèh Wain, from *matèh*, dead, and *wain*, very, much). Once he had recovered from his fright, the *radja* of Asumanu ran away, but in doing so he trampled a mouse to death (the name of the place is Lahokroën, from *laho*, mouse, and *kroën*, to kick, tread on). At this he abandoned further flight, acknowledged the ruler of Bauho as his superior, and placed himself under the latter's authority.

Continuing on his journey, the *radja* of Bauho met the ruler of Lassiolat, who at the sight of him cowered in fear (the place is Manuk Laën, from *manu*, bird, and *laën*, to pull out tail-feathers, to diminish). When Bauho showed him one of his regalia he began to weep with emotion (the place is Loloé, from *loloé*, to weep). From that moment Lassiolat also acknowledged Bauho as his overlord.

These two rulers, of Asumanu and Lassiolat, had made their appearance from out of the earth after their districts had dried up.

The three other districts, Tohé, Maumutin, and Aitōn, which stand under the sovereignty of Bauho, are apparently not related to it either by descent or by direct intermarriage. Tohé established a connexion by means of the marriage of its ruler with the daughter of the ruler of Lassiolat. The other two are said to have become subordinated entirely of their own accord, but Grijzen suspects that it may have been because they were too weak to remain independent.

All the districts together made up the kingdom of Fialarang, which thus consists of twelve divisions under the overlordship of the ruler of Bauho. Their respective rank-order corresponds to the greater of lesser importance of their place in the myth.

The myth formulates not only the structure of Fialarang itself, but also its relationship to other kingdoms. These relations will be dealt with in another context; at present let us merely mention the following points. Fialarang owes its special position to the mythical marriages of the ancestors of its ruling house with women from Waihale and Lakékun. The *meromak o'an* (son of a god) of Waihale is a mystical personage whose influence was felt throughout practically the whole of Timor. The relationships with Lidak and Naitimu, who married women from Fialarang, show that these two kingdoms belong to the sphere of influence of Fialarang.

The ruler of Bauho had himself named *astanara* (to look up high). His status was too high for him to be involved in affairs of government, and he delegated this work to the ruler of Klusin, who belonged to the next highest branch of the ruling house of Fialarang. The latter ruled and did everything on behalf of the ruler; only through his intermediacy might the sovereign ruler be approached. The decision or the advice of the *astanara* was called upon only in weighty matters. Bauho and Klusin were regarded as the mother and the father respectively of the family in which the ten remaining districts were the children. Lassiolat was the foremost of these, thanks to the marriage of its ruler with a daughter of an *astanara* from a lineage which was barely inferior to that of Klusin, and thanks also to the size of its population, which made it more powerful than all the other "children". Because of this the ruler of Lassiolat was commissioned as war-leader of Fialarang, and as such he was the "left hand" of the ruler. The rest of the children may have varied in power, but none of them occupied a specially important place with regard to the others.

All rulers possessed regalia which were repositories of great supernatural power and without which the kingship was inconceivable. Some of these had been received from the supreme ruler, and others had been inherited from the ancestors, who had usually obtained them by supernatural means.

Lasaka no longer exists as a sub-division; one of its rulers was murdered by the supreme ruler on account of his cruelty, and his land was annexed to Bauho.

Two main divisions can be distinguished in Fialarang: western Fialarang with Bauho, Klusin, Dafala, Manuk Lètèn, Umak Laran, and Sorbau (the last four are also called *umah hāt*, the four houses, or *rin besīn hāt*, the four iron pillars (i.e., of Bauho); and eastern Fialarang, comprising Lassiolat, Asumanu, Tohé, Maumutin, and Aitōn. The traditional relationships have been the better preserved in western Fialarang; in eastern Fialarang the connexions between Bauho and Klusin have largely disintegrated, and the ruler of Lassiolat occupies the position which was the right of Bauho in former times. Next stands the *mak o'an*, the speaker, the one who knows the stories and traditions, the right hand of the ruler and the man who gives the orders. At the present day, only the rulers of Bauho and Lassiolat are *dasi*, i.e., of pure noble blood; all the others have declined to a lower status, that of *datu*. The fact that they have remained rulers is the result of their possession of the regalia and other property associated with the office. They are only charged with the observance, as it were, of the status of ruler.[56]

---

[56] Grijzen, 1904, pp. 26, 36. On the *mak o'an*, see p. 129.

The kingdoms often take their names from the number of children:

Fialarang	*dasi sanulu*	the ten *dasi*
Maukatar	*kaluni nèn*	the six sleeping-places
Beboki	*kaluni sanulu*	the ten sleeping-places
Lamak Nèn	[means]	the six wooden plates
Lamak Sanulu	[means]	the ten wooden plates

Lidak is said to have consisted of a ruler, his right hand, and a third *dasi* as his solitary child. Today it is called *fukun lima*, after the five *fukun* (*tumukun*) who next to the ruler hold the reins of government.[57]

Djenilu, a small kingdom on the north coast, is said to have comprised originally two independent divisions. These were the coastal strip, the land of the *datu hitu*, seven *datu*, and the mountain part, the land of the *datu hāt*, four *datu*, each under its own ruler. The first *dasi* of Kabuna, the mountain part, came out of a hole in the ground which is still to be seen, together with three brothers and two sisters. The sisters were conveyed by birds to Lekaan and Vohotérin (south Tétun), where they became ancestresses of the house of Bauho and the rulers of Vohotérin. The oldest brother became supreme ruler of Kabuna, the second was his right hand, and the third the commander-in-chief. The youngest brother was thrown into the sea during a war with Balibo in order to bring about victory, and he changed into a crocodile.

After a number of generations there was only a woman *dasi* eligible to succeed as ruler. She married the ruler of the coastal region, and from them are descended the present rulers of the united kingdom of Djenilu. The ruler of Kabuna is now the right hand of the supreme ruler. The descendants of the three brothers are the present-day *datu*-heads of Kabuna.[58]

According to some, the inhabitants of Djenilu came originally from far-off regions, perhaps from Malaya; others tell that the population first lived in the mountains and then came down from there to the coast.[59]

A south Tétun myth reported by Grijzen runs as follows: some hundreds of years ago four tribes (*hutun rai hāt*, literally: tribes,

---

[57] Grijzen, 1904, pp. 33, 129.
[58] Grijzen, 1904, pp. 32, 129.
[59] Jansen, 1895, pp. 10, 11.
[60] Grijzen, 1904, pp. 18 ff.

countries, four) left their country, Sina Mutin Malakkan (China white Malaya) [61] in order to find somewhere else to live. In addition to the ordinary members of the tribes, there were on board some *buan* (sorcerers) who had lived among them in Malaya. The emigrants at first encountered all sorts of set-backs, which they barely survived. These reverses continued until one of the voyagers discovered that they had forgotten to bring the "dogs of the *buan*", screech-owls, with them. They turned back in order to repair this omission, and for the time being everything went well. They were shipwrecked at Ninobé Rai Hènèk (i.e., Makassar) and there made wooden vessels under the direction of two sub-chiefs, Datu Makérik (carved out, spotted, sly, cunning) and Datu Bédain. (Up till now they had used bamboo rafts.) Some of them stayed at Larantuka-Bauboin (Flores), and the *radja* and coastal peoples of Larantuka are descended from them. Most of them went further, to Amanatun (on the south coast of Timor), where they settled in the eastern lowlands.

Three of the four tribes had leaders, but the fourth had none. The three headmen, who were brothers, had brought various objects and goods with them from their homeland. Among these things there were three young trees, and each of the brothers planted his in the place where he settled. The oldest and senior brother planted *waringin* (*ai halé* in Tétun) almost in the middle of the area, and called his kingdom after it: Aihale, or Waihale. The second brother planted in the western part a tree called *ai biku*, after which his kingdom was called Waiwiku; and the youngest planted a *katimu-* or *hatimu*-tree to the north of this, and named the area which he settled Hatimu or Haitimu. The fourth group established themselves in the hilly region to the north of Waihale, and later obtained a son of the ruler of Waihale as their leader; the latter went to live at Fatu Aruin, and there took the title of Liurai.

The colonists, because of their better weapons, were able to bring the indigenous population — wild, unhelpful, bad people, who showed not the slightest respect for the alien rulers — under subjection with little difficulty. There are still to be found settlements which are descended directly from the original inhabitants (*emma mélus*), though they are no different from the others. The ruling house of Waihale employed an indirect method of extending its sway, by founding new settlements and by marrying its daughters to the rulers of the first population.

---

[61] A substitute-name, such as is used in ritual language, for Malaya.

The ruler of Waihale, the *meromak o'an*, had brought from the homeland certain sacred objects from which he derived supernatural power and which he safeguarded in a house in the forest near his village of Pétun. This house was fire-proof, and although the roof was not covered the rain could not enter. It was guarded as a sanctuary by snakes. Among the sacred objects were a pair of elephant's tusks and some earth from the motherland. With these objects the *meromak o'an* had power over rain and drought, and over success and adversity in war; he could also cause and perpetuate epidemics among human beings and animals, and he could cause the crops to flourish or to fail.

The whole of the area of Waihale, Fatu Aruin, Waiwiku, and Haitimu is in fact called "the Liurai". The inhabitants consider themselves to be superior to the other *emma tétun*, and they regard even the Dutch as their younger brothers, though the latter are much cleverer.[62]

The structure of these kingdoms corresponds entirely with that of the north Tétun equivalents. Waikiku has four children; Waihale is under the *meromak o'an* and three "lesser radjas".[63]

Lakékun consists of two parts: Lakékun Aë (*aë*, grass), and Lakékun Alas (*alas*, forest).[64] Dirma has eight children, one of whom acts as the "left hand" of the ruler, who has his residence at Sanleo.[65]

The differences in social structure between the northern and southern populations of central Timor relate almost exclusively to the internal organisation of the descent groups. The division of the tribe, the structure of the kingdom — for this is the territorial unit within which the descent groups are congregated — is throughout almost the entire area the same as has been established above.

In south Tétun, by contrast to the north, the rule of descent is matrilineal, and marriage corresponds with it in being matrilocal. The mother is said to be the head of the family. After the husband's death one of the children is transferred to his descent group (in the case of chiefs this is two). Here there is none of the complicated system of gift-exchange by which a marriage is consolidated in north Tétun; usually the husband gives a small present, and receives in return a matchet and an axe, so that he can make himself useful.[66] The transfer

---

[62] Grijzen, 1904, p. 38.
[63] Grijzen, 1904, pp. 32, 129.
[64] Grijzen, 1904, p. 37.
[65] Grijzen, 1904, pp. 26, 31.
[66] Grijzen, 1904, p. 64.

of children is known in north Tétun also. If many children are born
to a marriage, and if few have survived in the wife's family, then it
often happens that the husband gives up one of his children to his wife's
family. The child no longer belongs to its father's descent group. The
converse happens when a marriage remains childless. Children born
before marriage generally belong to the woman.[67]

If a chief in the north desires to be a ruler in the fullest sense of the
word, and lay claim to all worldly and supernatural powers, which are
embodied especially in the regalia, he has to belong to the highest
class, i.e., that of the *dasi*. A *dasi* is someone who belongs to one of
the ruling lineages, and both of whose parents were similarly *dasi*. The
offspring of the marriage between a *dasi* and a woman of lower status
bear the title of *datu*. Marriage between a man of lower status and a
dasi woman is not allowed. If an unmarried *dasi* woman has a child
by a lower-class man, the child and usually the father are done away
with. An independent minor kingdom that has any regard for its good
name must always have a *dasi* at its head. In south Tétun the situation
is different; the children there take the class of their mother, whatever
or whoever the father may be.[68]

A ruler is succeeded by his son, brother's son, sister's child or by
an adopted child from his *umah manèh*. In the absence of a man, a
woman can also succeed. In default of anyone who would generally
qualify as eligible to succeed, the leading men under the ruler make a
choice among the candidates. It thus seems that in such situations
the district in question had the right of say, and not the other districts
in the kingdom.

Under the ruler stand the *datu ferikatua* (head-*tumukun*), each of
whom has authority over two or more *datu fukun* (*tumukun*). The latter
officials each head a *fukun*, i.e., a complex of several villages and
hamlets with the associated territory. The residents of a *fukun* are
originally of "one family, this being taken in its wider sense, and they
are still today generally of common origin". Thus the *datu fukun* is
really a family head, under whom there are the *mata*, who in company
with the village elders conduct village affairs. The *ferikatua* mostly
belong to families which are branches of the family of their ruler. The
datu fukun stand in a corresponding relationship to their *ferikatua*, and
the *mata* are frequently of the same origin as their *datu fukun*. This
very roundabout description of the descent groups to which respectively

---

[67] Grijzen, 1904, p. 64.
[68] Grijzen, 1904, pp. 126 ff.

the various leaders belong thus says, in a very wordy fashion, no more than that they all belong by origin to one and the same genealogical group, viz., that to which the ruler himself also belongs. It may be surmised that the members of a *fukun* similarly belong, or belonged, to one genealogical group; that the district in its traditional form included only one descent group, of which the ruler was the head; and that the kingdom united the genealogical groups which represented the former tribe.[69]

The occupation of uncultivated lands is not confined to the *fukun*, but must be kept within the boundaries of the district.[70]

The "lord of the land" whom we have repeatedly met as the performer of more or less important functions makes his appearance here also, under the name of *rai o'an*, children of the land. By this title reference is made to the descendants of the original occupants of the land, who must be present at sacrifices at the *voho* [71] of the kingdom in order to strew rice. It is not certain whether this sacrifice concerns the whole kingdom or else a number of districts, but Grijzen seems to have the latter case in mind. It appears from the evidence that the *rai o'an*-ship has not been functionally integrated, as it has been elsewhere, for there is continual reference to a group of *rai o'an*, the *emma rai o'an*. In general, moreover, the *rai o'an* have no special influence or importance.[72] The term "lord of the land" also occurs among the forms of address applied to a ruler. These are: *nai lulik*, sacred lord; *rai nain*, lord of the land; and *ata nain*, lord of the people (?). *Rai nain* are also earth-spirits, whose worship occupies such an important place in religious life.[73]

Sonnebait, the most powerful kingdom in *western Timor* (in the Dawan language area), is said to have been inhabited originally by a single people and to have been known as Labala. The eldest of the four sons of the ruler succeeded. These four sons had to flee before an invasion by three younger brothers of the woman ruler of Waiwiku-Waihale, and they established kingdoms elsewhere. The eldest brother among the invaders, Sonnebait, made himself master of the treasures and thus possessor of legitimate power, and later took the title of

---

[69] Grijzen, 1904, pp. 127 ff.
[70] Grijzen, 1904, p. 141.
[71] The offering-place for the local tutelary spirits (*rai nain*, lords of the land), the worship of which occupies an important place in religious life (Grijzen, 1904, pp. 74 ff.).
[72] Grijzen. 1904, pp. 143, 77.
[73] Grijzen, 1904, pp. 74, 86, 127.

Liurai. The second brother, Benu, appropriated two daughters for himself. The youngest, Foan, took the land, which was divided into three parts, from which the kingdoms of Sonnebait, Ambenu, and Amfoan originated.[74] According to another account, two brothers of the house of the Liurai of central Timor (i.e., that of Fatu Aruin) journeyed to the south in order to set up a kingdom; the elder became the ancestor of Sonnebait, and the younger became that of Amfoan. Whereas Sonnebait continually strove to become more extensive, Amfoan desired no more than to hold fast to its rights.[75]

We owe to Kruyt the publication of a very detailed myth on the origin and division of Sonnebait.[76] There were three brothers living in Belu: If Belek, Fai Belek, and Tai Belek. Two of them emigrated to the west, to the land of Kune. This Kune gave them his two daughters, Djili Kune and Djasa Kune, as wives. The two brothers decided to go back to their own country to bring their younger brother Tai Belek, and they agreed with their wives upon a point where they should meet. The wives, together with their younger sister Nika, met there a dirty and unsightly man. The elder sisters refused to give him a drink from the golden drinking-cup of their parents, or even from a leaf, but the youngest sister did do the latter. The man let the water run over his body, at which he changed entirely in appearance; his body and countenance became radiant, and his weapons turned into gold. The young women now competed for his favour, but his choice fell upon the youngest. He turned out to be Tai Belek, who proclaimed himself ruler and sat on the throne of Kune, and his elder brothers subordinated themselves to him. The ruler took the name Sonnebait for his lineage. The brothers obtained the major parts of the land: the oldest got Mollo, and adopted for his line the name Oimatan, spring, because water sprang forth in the place where he thrust his spear into the ground; the other brother got Mio Maffo and took Kono, right over, as the name of his line, because he was the only one able to cast a spear right over Kune's house.

Kruyt also relates the following myth.[77] Sonnebait is the brother of Liulai, founder of the ruling house of Belu, in which district they had both descended from heaven, at a place called Timo Liulai Biahale Oibiku (these names are clearly identical with Haitimu, Liurai,

---

[74] Müller, 1839, p. 196.
[75] Gramberg, 1872, pp. 191, 192.
[76] Kruyt, 1921c, pp. 777 ff.
[77] Kruyt, 1921c, p. 779.

Waihale, and Waiwiku). In order to force the people to submit to him, Sonnebait went to the Mollo mountains to dam the sources of the Noni river and then cause a flood. He himself had brought this river into being by shattering a mountain in two and pouring in a pot of water. Sonnebait's rule was cruel and harsh; every year, when the people brought the produce of the land to him, he had one of his subjects killed in order to cool the earth. Sabat Neno, a prominent man in the neighbourhood, then killed the ruler at the instigation of Kune. Hard years followed in which the rice and the maize would not grow. The *fettor* Manubait from Fatu Leo and Mela of Bidjeli went to the *liulai* of Belu to ask advice. On the way there they found a baby boy of three months with a golden navel-cord passed over his shoulders, from which it appeared that he was Usif Neno's child, a child of the sun. He was brought to the *liulai*, who at once recognised him as his younger brother. Mela, who was to bring the boy up, concealed him in a cave so that the other members of the tribe should not kill him. This place now had rain in abundance, but in other parts it remained as dry as ever, and people starved to death. From this it was concluded that it was necessary to have a Sonnebait as ruler. The *fettor* ("barons") promised to do the child no harm; they submitted themselves to him, and the rain began to pour down. This ruler was called Neno Sonbai or Neno Balik Sonbai. The house of Sonnebait was once more massacred, but its followers were sensible enough to recognise one of the offspring.

The rulers lived in succession at Bidjela, Bidjeli, and Kau Niki (in Fatu Leo or Manubait). Today the kingdom no longer exists. As early as 1831 the power of the *liurai* had much declined; he had withdrawn to a high cliff where he lived alone, at enmity with the ruler of Kupang (in the extreme west), who bore a large part of the guilt for the disintegration of Sonnebait. Moral authority was all that the *liurai* still possessed.[78]

The second myth has for its subject the division of the kingdom of Sonnebait into the districts of Sonnebait (in the narrower sense), Mollo, and Mio Moffo. Among the older ethnographers, Müller also mentions a division into three, viz., Oinama, the *liurai*'s own territory, Mollo, and Amakono (i.e., Mio Moffo). Mollo and Amakono are said to have been each divided into two, the heads of each half being the offspring of a pair of brothers. The descendant of the elder brother

---

[78] Francis, 1838, p. 355; Müller, 1839, p. 145.

was charged with defence, and that of the younger brother with administration of the district which they shared. The two functionaries responsible for these duties are said to stand to each other in the relation of elder and younger brother.

Another report by Müller gives a division into five districts: Mollo, Amakono, Manubait (i.e., Fatu Leo), Pitai, and Takai. Another author similarly reports that the following belonged to Sonnebait: Mollo, Mio Maffo, Fatu Leo, Bidjoba, and Takaip. The kingdoms of Amfoan, Ambenu, Beboki, and Insana, which are also named in the source, perhaps originally belonged to the sphere of influence of the *liurai*, but they formed no part of the actual kingdom.[80]

The third myth represents the *fettor* Mela of Bidjeli and Manubait of Fatu Leo as being extremely closely associated with the *liurai*, whereas the places where the *liurai* lived are given as Bidjela, Bidjeli, and Kau Niki in Fatu Leo. Probably, therefore, Fatu Leo is the ruler's own district. Bidjoba, which is listed only by Kruyt, perhaps also belongs to this district, for it is referred to elsewhere by him as the domicile of the Sonnebait lineage and its three *fettor*-lineages Sunaf, Paut, and Betin. It is also the place where the first ancestor died and was buried; the children of this ancestor were Sunaf Bidjail (buffalo horn), Pauh (to stab, thrust), and Bitin (vagina). The name Bitin was later changed to Mela.[81] These four lineages are named together in another place as well. At the burial of anyone from the lineages of Sonnebait, Sunaf, Paut, or Betin no heads were taken, but a slave was killed. The *fettor*-lineages of Sunaf, Paut, and Betin reckon themselves to be of equal birth with Sonbai. These four clans were related by marriage, Kruyt saying that the Sonbai married daughters of the *fettor*-lineages. These nobles were allowed to take slaves from among the people, something which was not the custom anywhere else on Timor.[82]

Next to the districts of Mollo and Amakono (Mio Moffo) we thus find Pitai and Takaip. Taking into account the postulated dual division of the former districts, it is not inconceivable that Pitai and Takaip may be halves of Mollo and Amakono (or vice versa). It is not possible to say much with certainty about this, but the following may be of some significance. When Mollo had practically detached itself

[79] Müller, 1839, pp. 146, 197.
[80] Kruyt, 1921c, p. 780.
[81] Kruyt, 1921c, p. 783; 1923a, pp. 430, 413.
[82] Kruyt, 1923a, p. 430.

from Sonnebait, Pitai refused to make submission to the former but remained faithful to the *liurai*.[83] We should not like to leave this subject without mentioning an event in which the Pitai play a part. The Pitai once brought to Toklua, *liurai* of Sonnebait, a young woman who was later abducted by someone from his entourage. The Pitai, displeased by this, did not come to bury their ruler when he died, so the new ruler invited instead Amanuban, a kingdom on the south coast, in order to punish the Pitai.[84]

In addition to the real Sonnebait there was also a Little Sonnebait, a settlement in the western part of the lowlands. The *liurai*, who lived far in the interior, sent his brother to Uipura, which had been ceded by Kupang, in order to represent himself before the ruler of Kupang, but this representative made himself independent.[85] A certain D.B. has left us a report which undoubtedly also refers to this settlement from Sonnebait: when the Dutch came, he says, "half of the kingdom, or the sister-tribe" left for Kupang, where they remained under an independent ruler, while the people of Kupang moved to Semau.[86] Clearly, therefore, Kruyt's account, according to which the sphere of influence of Kupang was originally known as *suba fatu fetto* and called Little Sonnebait,[87] cannot possibly be correct.[88]

The kingdom of Amfoan is divided into two. The real Amfoan is in the mountains, and its ruler enjoys primacy at feasts and other special occasions over the ruler of the other part, Sorbian, which lies on the north coast. Sorbian is the more powerful of the two; the real Amfoan consists of no more than the village of Naklio and its estates.

This dual division is said to have originated in an earlier division of power between two brothers, by which the elder controlled the extra-territorial politics in the coastal regions and the younger ran the internal administration in the mountains. The residence of the elder brother on the coast was Naklio (*nai*, land, *klio*, crayfish); the territory of the younger brother in the interior was called Solebian (*soleh*, to divide, *bian*, in two), from which comes the name Sorbian. The name of the place where he lived was Suleo (wood-flute). The ruler of

---

[83] Kruyt, 1923a, p. 432; "the Pitai lineage" is mentioned on p. 433.

[84] Kruyt, 1923a, p. 432.

[85] Francis, 1838, p. 357; Müller, 1839, p. 145.

[86] D.B., 1852, pp. 206, 207.

[87] Kruyt, 1921c, p. 780.

[88] *Fetto* = woman, sister. *Suba fatu fetto* would thus seem to correspond to "the sister-tribe" of the other report.

Naklio has great moral influence, but does not concern himself with affairs of government.[89]

Clearly there is some confusion here. On the map which accompanies this report Amfoan lies in the interior and Sorbian on the coast. Amfoan, the inferior, is socially superior and has great moral influence, but in real power it is subordinate to Sorbian, the coastal territory. The functional division between elder and younger brother with regard to "extra-territorial politics" and "internal administration" has apparently led the ethnographer on to the wrong track. As we have seen, this division of labour exists in Mollo and Amakono as well; the elder brother looks after "defence" and the younger runs the "administration". No particular value can be assigned to the suggested etymologies of the place names, for such inferences, as so often in the older ethnographic literature, are no more than rather arbitrary guesses; e.g., the word *nai*, for land or earth, occurs neither in Tétun nor in Dawan.

Kruyt reports that the populations of the kingdoms of Amanuban and Amanatun, on the south coast, came from Mollo.[90] He relates also certain myths of origin concerning the ruling houses of these lands.

The following myth was given to Kruyt by Tua Isu, *fettor* of Malenat (Amanuban). There was once a feast in the land of origin, and it happened that the ruler got drunk and in his intoxication lay down naked. His two elder sons were amused by this, but the third son covered his father. When the ruler was later told of this he praised the youngest son, but he was so angry with the two others that from fear they fled from their fatherland in a boat. The two brothers, Isu (which must mean to seek ways of turning back) and Nope (cloud), landed in Amanatun and went to Sahan. Nope went to sit on a hill called Sae Nam, but Isu, whose real name was Sopo Bilas (Isu is the lineage name, which still exists today), went to stand in a hole in the ground, with his head covered by a *lontar* (palm)-leaf. They were found by a man called Nomlene, who was out hunting, and were taken to the village of Sahan. There they stayed with the ruler of Nunkolo, and each married one of his daughters; Sopo Bilas married Bitai Kolo, and his brother married Bi Fnatun. Every year they were to give their father-in-law some of the produce of their fields and a pig. The first year they brought young maize cobs and a sucking-pig; the ruler got angry with his sons-in-law and ordered them to go and

---

[89] Gramberg, 1872, p. 178; Francis, 1838, p. 356.
[90] Kruyt, 1921c, p. 792.

find something better. They went to Lunu, near Oi Uki, from where
they brought back cobs so old that the kernels had all been eaten by
beetles, together with a skinny old pig. The ruler did not want these
gifts; he asked them whether they could not find any good food, and
gave them two small gold figures, representing a man and a woman,
to take with them as talismans. This time they went to Tumbesi. The
people there complained to the strangers about their distress: every
year two of their children were seized and killed by a certain Kesnai,
from the village of Manela Ane, who had large ricefields and sacrificed
a boy and a girl in order to ensure rich harvests in the following year.
The strangers went to fight against Kesnai; they lay in ambush as a
cat lies in wait for a mouse (from which a champion is called *meo*,
cat), and whenever anyone from Manela Ane came by they cut off
his head.[91]

The myth of the two strangers is known in Amanatun also, and was
told to Kruyt by the *fettor* of Sahan. Before their arrival the *fettor*
of Sahan was the most important man in the country. One day he met
somewhere a man called Banu Nai Nano Senan, decked out with
beads and gold ornaments, who had come from the west. He married
the two daughters of the *fettor*, Tae Walan and Bikut. This stranger,
who taught the Timorese how to make fire with flint and steel, was
elevated to the position of ruler. Not long after this, the *fettor* of Sahan
found a second stranger; he was unclothed, did not know the language,
and was sitting between two stones under a lontar palm. He was given
the name Ulak Mai, after this spot. He was given clothes and was
taught to speak, and was then brought before the ruler, who gave him
his daughter Bifnatun for wife. The ruler also gave him a small pail
made of palm-leaf, with some earth, a spear, and a sword, and then
charged him to journey to the east. At Niki Niki he found a certain
ruler, Nuban, whom he drove out and replaced as lord of the land.
Whenever a member of one of the two lineages dies, the other must
be represented at the funeral.[92]

Yet another myth about the two strangers is known from Amanuban.
Two strangers, Sopo Bilas and Bilbanu, who came from Banam, were
made into rulers. The younger, Sopo Bilas, became *radja*, with the
lineage name Nubatonis, after which the land was called Amanuban.
The elder became *fettor*, and called himself Natu, from which the

---

[91] Kruyt, 1923*a*, pp. 427 ff.
[92] Kruyt, 1921*c*, pp. 796 ff.

associated land received the name Amanatun, the sister-land of
Amanuban.[93]

When Kruyt visited the district the ruler of Amanuban was called
Pae Nope, popularly known as Banam Tua. The most important lineage
was Nubatonis, which was located at Tumbesi. The narrator of the
first myth was Tua Isu, *fettor* of Malenat. In the narrative itself there
is also a *fettor* Tua Isu of Nopal, and a *mafefa* Tua Isu living at
Malenat. That these three Tua Isu may be identical can be inferred
from Kruyt's report that there were three districts or *fettor* in Amanuban, and that one of the *fettor* had acquired his title only a short
time previously, before which he had been called *mafefa* (spokesman),
i.e., the man who knew most about the *adat*. Malenat was not far from
Tumbesi, and there still existed an old settlement of the rulers in the
area of the *mafefa*.[94] Whereas we have no reports from Belu to indicate
that head-hunting was demanded by certain circumstances, Kruyt reports that in the rest of Timor heads were taken for the burial of a
ruler, and that Amanuban and Amanatun repeatedly went head-hunting
on such occasions; members of the latter ruling houses might not be
absent from each other's funerals. He had earlier said, however, that
when a ruler of Amanuban died head-hunters were sent to Mollo,
Oimuti, or Insana, and that when a ruler died while a war was in
progress between Amanuban and Amanutan the hostilities had to
stop.[95] One of the older authors writes in similar detail about Amanuban. This is said to have been formerly an undivided kingdom under
the ruler Niki Niki. Because of his cruelty a number of *fettor* broke
away from him; these all became dependent upon one of the four
foremost *meo* (champions) of the country. This leader bore the lineage
name Nagasawa and lived at Lassi. People went out from Lassi to
hunt heads in Niki Niki, and vice versa. Kruyt tells us nothing about
any partition or fission of Amanuban. Perhaps the author in question
refers to the division into Amanuban and Amanatun. But Kruyt
himself also provides some information which indicates a division of
Amanuban into four, viz., a reference to four men, Lenana, Nubatonis,
Neno Hae, and Namo Nafa, who are said to have been the first inhabitants of the earth.[97] It appears, too, that present-day Amanuban

---

[93] Kruyt, 1921*c*, p. 792.
[94] Kruyt, 1921*c*, pp. 791-3.
[95] Kruyt, 1923*a*, pp. 431, 397.
[96] D., 1851, pp. 166 ff., 169 ff., 174.
[97] Kruyt, 1923*a*, p. 474.

is still divided into four; the kingdom comprises, namely, "three fettors or districts", and as we know from elsewhere the ruler always has a right to his own district. The *mafefa* is one of the three *fettor*.[98]

Finally, let us note an obligatory marriage to which the ruler of Amanuban is committed. In olden days a sister of this ruler went to live at Pene (a region in the north of Amanatun); her descendants are called *usif fetto* (lords of the sister), and those of the ruler are called *usif mone* (lords of the brother or man). The ruler at Niki Niki must always take a young woman from the *usif fetto* at Pene as his head wife.[99]

Amabi (which lies further to the west) is said to be governed by two rulers: the more powerful is charged with "reigning", and the other with "waging war".[100]

According to Müller, Amarassi is under three rulers, one of which is pre-eminent;[101] but all other writers know only of a division into five districts, which are under, respectively, a *radja*, a *fettor*, a *kapitan*, a *seninti*, and an *amtiran*. The ancestors of the *fettor*, who stands next to rather than under the *radja*, came originally from Harneno (central Timor), and those of the ruler from Waiwiku-Waihale.[102] This division into five was, it appears from Bruynis,[103] perpetuated by the Dutch government, so that the people now have a ruler and four *temukung besar*. In former times the *temukung besar* stood in name only under the ruler.

We are very badly informed as to the internal organisation of the districts(the component parts of the kingdom). Steinmetz, as reported by Kruyt,[104] says that a number of "families in the wider sense" (*sukun* or *fukun* in Insana and Beboki, *kanan* or *loppo* in Mio Moffo) are united into one "district" (*klune* in Beboki, *nakaf* in Insana and Mio Maffo), the head of which takes the title of *fettor*. Such a "district" thus corresponds to the unit which in central Timor comes under a *datu ferikatuan*. In Amarassi the ruler and his *temukung besar* have under them a number of village heads (*nakaf*). The *nakaf* was

---

[98] Kruyt, 1921c, p. 792.
[99] Kruyt, 1921c, p. 790; 1923a, p. 412. At p. 362 in the latter article, however, Pene is described as being located in Amanuban.
[100] Müller, 1839, p. 144.
[101] Müller, 1839, p. 145.
[102] Francis, 1839, p. 536; Anon., 1892, pp. 231 ff., 219.
[103] Bruynis, 1919, p. 175.
[104] Kruyt, 1923a, p. 369.

originally head of a family, namely the head of the oldest family in the
village, thus someone who held a privileged position. The office of
ruler is hereditary in the Koro family; usually the designated successor
is the son of the deceased ruler, but the family heads (*temukung*) can
choose another Koro as ruler.[105] There is little to be related about
the connexion between *temukung* and *nakaf*. According to Kruyt,[106]
the *loppo* constitutes a local community ("settlement").

There remains the question of what precisely we are to understand
by the perpetually recurring terms "family", "family in the wider
sense", and "lineage", Krayer van Aalst [107] says that everyone, however modest his station, has a family name (*kana luan*) which is written
with a special sign (*malak*). His progeny will safeguard this name and
the associated sign as being something of value, and cannot imagine that
there was ever a time when they did not exist. People with the same
name may not marry, but if the family connexion is no longer close
the priest (*mnane*) can break this link by means of a sacrifice so that
the marriage may take place. It can happen that a man takes the *kana
luan* of his grandfather if the latter's *kana luan* group is threatened
with extinction. Since the rule of descent is patrilineal, the men sharing
one name form an exogamous patrilineal descent group. These descent
groups (such as Sunaf, Paut, and Betin in Sonnebait, Isu and Nope in
Amanuban) often trace their descent directly from the most distant
ancestors, and thus almost certainly include many individuals whose
relationship cannot be traced. It is thus very probable that at the
present time the society is still divided into a number of patrilineal
clans, though the ease with which the rule of clan-exogamy can be
suspended indicates that the clan system has already begun to weaken.
Amanuban has ten or eleven "lineages", and Amabi has nine. These
lineages are thus patrilineal clans.[108]

Kruyt's survey of rules of descent and marriage regulations in this
region, which is practically all the evidence we possess, is so muddled
and superficial that only limited value can be attached to the facts as
reported in it. Marriage seems in general to be matrilocal until the
bridewealth is fully paid, and in those areas where there is said to be
no bridewealth a man can take his wife away with him only after

---

[105] Bruynis, 1919, pp. 175, 171; Anon., 1892, p. 214.
[106] Kruyt, 1923*a*, pp. 789, 790.
[107] Kruyt, 1923*a*, p. 351.
[108] Kruyt, 1921*c*, p. 792.

making a large gift or (and) leaving behind one or more of the
children born in the meantime.[109]

In Mollo, Mio Maffo, Amanuban, and Amanatun the payment of
bridewealth forms no part of the contraction of a marriage. The ruler
of Mollo explained this by saying that the wife's family did not wish
to relinquish all rights over her. Kruyt remarks in this connexion that
although in this district "father-right is in full force, the mother's
brother also has a special authority".

In Amanuban the husband goes to live with his wife's family, but
if he wants to take her away to his own village he has to make a large
gift to her parents or undertake to cede an eventual daughter to them.
This payment must also be made if a man refuses to permit his wife
to go and help her parents at feasts and other such events. In Amanatun
a present must be given if the wife dies childless; this is compensation
for the child which would otherwise have been surrendered to her
parents. In other words, a child is handed over because no bridewealth
has been paid. In Fatu Leo a girl who has been transferred to the
wife's family bears the lineage name of her mother.[110]

In Amarassi, according to Kruyt, the bridewealth was formerly
very high,[111] but if a man married his brother's wife's sister no bridewealth was paid and the children of the marriage bore the *malak*
of the wife. Bruynis reports that no bridewealth is paid, and that the
man goes to the family group of his wife,[112] yet he also mentions a
fairly extensive exchange of gifts at the contraction of a marriage.

Let us conclude on this topic with Kruyt's observation that throughout Timor there is a mixture of matrilineal and patrilineal systems.[113]

In the whole of Timor we find the *pah tuaf* (lord of the land), but
the information on this official at our disposal is, sadly, far from
satisfactory. In Amarassi there are a number of *pah tuaf* in each of the
five districts. They have tasks to perform at the making of gardens,
the collection of wax, and the cutting of sandalwood; they have to ask
for rainy or dry weather, and are the custodians of traditions relating

---

[109] Bruynis, 1919, p. 172 (Amarassi); Kruyt, 1921c, p. 799 (Annas); Heymering,
    1845, pp. 123, 126 ff.; Kruijt, 1923a, pp. 356 ff. (Mollo, Mio Maffo, Amanatun,
    Amanuban), 357 (Amarassi), 358 (Lotas), 367 (Steinmetz: Beboki, Insana,
    Mio Maffo).
[110] Kruyt, 1923a, pp. 356, 358.
[111] Kruyt, 1923a, pp. 357, 352.
[112] Bruynis, 1919, p. 172.
[113] Kruyt, 1921c, p. 790.

to the land.[114] According to Kruyt,[115] each *radja* and each *fettor* (by which he apparently means district heads) has a *pah tuaf* or *baer tuaf*, who makes his appearance only at great ceremonies of general importance.

In the "district of Mollo in the territory of Mollo" the ruler is the only *pah tuaf*, but he has delegated his rights to the village heads.[116] Kruyt also remarks that the *fettor* are the *pah tuaf*, and that the village heads serve as their replacements.[117] Kruyt means by this, it can be inferred, that the heads of the largest units into which a district is divided are the real *pah tuaf*, and that these have handed over the function to the village heads underneath them. It is clear, though Kruyt does not say so explicitly, that here he refers especially to the districts of the kingdom of Sonnebait.

Where the rulers are thought to be of alien blood, as in Amanuban and Amanatun, they are not the *pah tuaf*, but this office devolves upon the heads of certain lineages (patrilineal clans).[118]

The *pah tuaf* generally conducts the agricultural ceremonies for the whole of his society. Everywhere on Timor he receives a share of the produce of the land, the *poni pah* (also called *pah sufan, pah boton,* or *pah nakan*).[119]

All the older authors agree in reporting the posture of inferiority which is adopted towards the rulers.[120] Their high status is seen also in the names by which they are addressed, e.g., *usif neno*, lord sun, *neno ana*, child of the sun, *usif leu*, sacred lord.[121] *Koko leu*, sacred snake, is one of the titles of the ruler of Amanuban. Persons of noble rank may never kill a *koko*-snake, and certain "baronial lineages" are said to be descended from such a snake.[122] The Nomlene clan, of Sahan (Amanatun), is decended from two dogs who came out of the sea, and hence they may not keep dogs. The clan Neno Li'u, of Lakufin, are the descendants of a cat which emerged from the sea, and they therefore show special respect to cats.[123]

---

[114] Anon., 1892, p. 214.
[115] Kruyt, 1923*a*, p. 475.
[116] Kruyt, 1923*a*, pp. 475, 480.
[117] Kruyt, 1921*c*, p. 783.
[118] Kruyt, 1921*c*, p. 783; 1923*a*, p. 475: the clan Tunu at Niki Niki, the clan Tanis and in part the clan Talain at Supul.
[119] Kruyt, 1923*a*, pp. 478, 475.
[120] D.B., 1852, p. 207; Francis, I, 1838, p. 392; II, p. 29.
[121] Müller, 1839, p. 147; Gramberg, 1872, p. 185.
[122] Kruyt, 1921*c*, p. 798.
[123] Kruyt, 1923*a*, pp. 461, 466.

The island of *Savu* is at present divided into four districts: Timu, Liai, Seba, and Mesara, each under a ruler. The ruler of Seba reigns over the whole island.[124] A district includes several "lineages" which are said not to be exogamous. The number of such lineages varies from one district to another: Seba has nine, Mesara seven, Timu ten, and Liai seven.[125] It used to be customary to marry within one's own district, except for rulers, who often married women from the ruling lineages of the other districts.[126] Van de Wetering, finally, states that the "tribe" is called *udu*, which also means "place of sacrifice"; it takes its name from the "tribal ancestor", and is the owner of the land. This *udu* is probably the same as the group referred to above as a "lineage". We are told by one of the older ethnographers that a district is associated with "one family group".[127]

In each of these four petty states there are three prominent officials. In the first place there is the *deo rai*, "lord of the land". The lineage to which he belongs is the oldest in the district. In Mesara the lineage of the *deo rai* is said to have been that of the ruler, but another lineage is supposed to have usurped this office.[128] In one of the older sources he is called *douwaai kapuh-èh* or *mounèh kapuh-èh*, which is said to mean "origin of the *douwaai*" or the "source". He was lord of the land and supreme priest. At his death he was buried in his garden by his son, who immediately took his place, and the death was not mentioned.[129] The *deo rai* performs the ceremonies (*udu nga'oa*) at the great feasts. He offers sacrifices on the occasion of drought, sickness, or general calamity. Just as the ruler has the people in his care, so the *deo rai* looks after the land. In any serious situation his advice is sought by the heads.[130] In Timu one of the lineages was charged with the duty of averting the danger of drought, by means of a sacrifice, when there was a lack of rain.[131]

The two other authorities are the ruler and the *fettor*. The former is called *do'ai* (man big), and the latter *wèto* (sister, woman). One of the lineages in Seba is divided into two: one half, Do Nataga Luluweo, is the lineage of the ruler, and the other, Do Nataga Djohina, is that

---

[124] Van de Wetering 1926, p. 488.
[125] Van de Wetering, 1926, pp. 488 ff.
[126] Van de Wetering, 1926, pp. 494, 490.
[127] Treffer, 1875, p. 224.
[128] Van de Wetering, 1926, pp. 488, 489.
[129] Esser, 1877, p. 164. According to Van de Wetering, *do'ai* means "great man" and is the title of the ruler.
[130] Donselaar, 1872, p. 310; Van de Wetering, 1926, p. 521.
[131] Van de Wetering, 1926, p. 489.

of the *fettor*. Marriages were permitted between the two. In Mesara the *fettor*-lineage was produced by the marriage of a girl from the ruler's lineage to a man from another lineage. In Timu the lineage of the *fettor* has at present the real power in its hands. We have no details from Liai in this connexion.[132] The relationship between ruler and *fettor* is said to be that of elder and younger brother. The former has the title Douwaai Padji or Mouneh Padji (flag-master), and the latter Douwaai Tungkut or Mouneh Fettor (staff-master). The supremacy of the former is said to be the result of governmental influence alone.[133] The *fettor* exercises unlimited authority in his own territory.[134]

We have already mentioned the dual division of the *nusak* Ti on *Rote*. As we have said, this tribe was divided into two exogamous halves by the two first ancestors; each of these phratries comprises eight clans. That which is descended from Sabanara (or Sabarai) is the ruler's phratry, and the other (descended from Sakunara or Taratu) is that of the *fettor*.[135] The heads of the clans are called *temukung*, *mane sio* (the nine men), or *sio ai* (possibly, the nine trees).[136] Members of different clans live among one another, and there is no exclusive relation between the villages and genealogical groups.[137] In former times genealogical and territorial groupings are said to have over-lapped.[138]

Next to the ruler and the *fettor*, whose indigenous designations are *manè* (masculine) and *fèto* (feminine, sister), we find once more "the lord of the land".[139] The data, however, are extremely scarce and summary, so that we shall have to leave many questions unanswered. Van de Wetering, to whom we owe the most detailed reports on this people, says nothing whatever about this functionary, even though he knew of his existence. He mentions, for example, that the ancestor of

---

[132] Van de Wetering, 1926, pp. 488 ff.

[133] Esser, 1877, p. 164.

[134] Donselaar, 1872, p. 301.

[135] Van de Wetering, 1925, p. 8.

[136] Van de Wetering, 1925, pp. 10-14, 630; 1922, p. 325. At p. 12 in the former article *mane sio* relates particularly to the heads of the "divisions" (*nggi leo*?) of the "tribe" (*leo*?) of the *fettor*.

[137] Van de Wetering, 1925, pp. 35, 605; Graafland, 1889, p. 362; De Clercq, 1874, p. 309.

[138] Kruyt, 1921a, p. 269; Jonker (1905, p. 456) gives a text relating to the division of the land by the three ancestors of Baä.

[139] Van de Wetering, 1925, p. 605; Graafland, 1889, pp. 362, 368; Jackstein, 1873, p. 351; Kruyt, 1921a, pp. 274, 270: *fèto* = sister (m.s.). At p. 605 in his 1925 article, Van de Wetering speaks of "distinctions which have crept in, such as *manèk* (king), *fèto*, *manè sio* ..."

the *tuan tanah* (lord of the land) of Keka was Inoama Leki, i.e., mother-father Leki.[140] Graafland refers to the existence of a "supreme priest", *dae lama tuwa*, in each petty state.[141] Kruyt speaks of a *dae langgak*, "lord of the land".[142] According to Jackstein, the head of the oldest village in a "negorij" (i.e., the district) is master of the land (*dae langgak*), and has a certain authority over the other village heads (apparently the *temukung*). He takes precedence at feasts bringing the whole district together, and makes sacrifices on the occasion of sickness, war, or the erection of a new house. In each "negorij" (district) there is one village (clan?) from which the ruler must come and another from which the *fettor* must come. The ruler is not supposed to embark on any undertaking without the consent of the "lord of the land".[143]

The following material is taken from an article by Van der Kam which appeared in the *Koloniaal Tijdschrift* for 1934 and came to our knowledge when the writing of this chapter had been completed:

The various *leo* are segmented into a number of *kita* or *nggitak*, which consist in their turn of *manu langgak* (chicken heads), which are small family groups made up of close kin. Slightly different designations for these social units are found in the *nusak* Dengka and in that of Ringgou. The latter tribe comprises four *leo*, each of which includes from four to seven *lutu*; in the former *nusak* several *leo* are frequently united into one *leo amba* (buffalo). In addition to *manésio* the heads of the *leo* are also called *manéleo*; latterly they have always been referred to as *temukung* (p. 587).

In order to characterise the relationship between *manèk* (rendered above as *mané*, man, masculine) and *fettò* (*fèto*, woman, feminine), Van der Kam cites a letter by Couvreur: "[They are like] two sides of the same authority, one aspect of which is the *radja*, the source of authority and the mystically-conceived but *also* decision-making power, while the other is the *fettor*, the part concerned with the administration of wordly affairs". Against Van der Kam, a local informant says that "the man is the head, the woman is the hand that works". Only three *nusak* possess no *fettò*, viz., Lelenuk, Oénale, and Della. The present-day Della originally formed a single *nusak* with Oénale, of which it formed the *fettò*-half. This *fettò* is thought to have split off and to

---

[140] Van de Wetering, 1922, p. 321.
[141] Graafland, 1889, p. 368.
[142] Kruyt, 1921*a*, p. 300.
[143] Jackstein, 1873, pp. 351 ff.

have founded the independent *nusak* of Della between 1800 and 1840 (p. 590). The modern Lelenuk, according to Jonker (p. 453), was set up by a number of families from the Bokai *nusak*.

In the government of the *nusak* the *manèk* is assisted by the *manéleo*; they regulate the internal affairs of the *leo* and settle minor disputes among its members. Important cases are brought before the *fettò*, who delivers his verdict in the name of the *manèk*. Later on, Van der Kam also says, however, that *manèk* and *fettò* often concern themselves each with the affairs of his own moiety. The advice of the *manédopé* (something like sword-bearer, i.e., of the *manèk*) is also taken into account. This person is familiar with all traditional situations, and at court-sessions he cites precedents from by-gone days and the pronouncements of wise and just *manèk* in the past. Although this office is not hereditary, it usually passes down from father to son, for a man first learns the ancient songs from his father (p. 595).

Although the *manèk* can act completely on his own ("when the *manèk* speaks," people say, "it is like the rolling of thunder"), he generally does his utmost to secure agreement (*dale èsa*, within one) in the *buau nusak* (people's assembly). This refers, to be precise, to unanimity, for decisions by a majority of votes are unknown. In addition to the above-named functionaries, the *lasi nusak* (the elders) and the *mané-anak* and *fettò-anak* (close kin of *manèk* and *fettò*) also formed part of the *buau nusak* (p. 596).

If a retiring *manèk* possesses a son suitable for the post, the latter almost automatically takes his father's place, though with a sort of recognition by the *mané-anak*, *mané-leo*, and *lasi-nusak*. Often a choice has to be made, which leads to much intrigue, but the choice always has to be limited to the *nggitak* or *kita* of the *manèk*'s *leo*. With certain qualifications this applies also to the *fettò* and the *manéleo* (p. 597).

In all *nusak* the *leo* are grouped into a *manèk*-half and a *fettò*-half. The members of these halves have to do certain work for their *manèk* or their *fettò*; those of the *fettò*-half sometimes have to work for the *manèk* (p. 594).

Van der Kam also contributes to our knowledge of the "lord of the land", the *daé-langgak* (*langgak*, head; *daé*, land, earth). He closely links this noteworthy figure to the *manasonggo* (literally, he who performs the rites, who sacrifices; cf. p. 586, n. 1). Each *leo* has its *manasonggo*, who only makes his appearance in important matters such as wars, epidemics, and harvesting; otherwise, family heads and individuals perform the necessary religious acts themselves. As the *manasonggo* acts on behalf of the *leo*, so the *daé-langgak* acts on behalf of the whole *nusak*. Van der Kam thinks that the office of *daé-langgak* developed from the involvement of the *manasonggo* in agriculture. Only in the *nusak* of Termanu is the *daé-langgak* explained as being originally "possessor or manager of the land"; this idea is apparently unknown in the other *nusak* (p. 589). On a later page Van der Kam expressly rejects the idea that *daé-langgak* should be translated as "owner of the land" (p. 590).

The *leo* is not a local unit, and the fact that here and there the *leo* lay claim to their own territories is ascribed by the author to modern influences, particularly the Dutch government. The single exception to this rule is the *nusak* Oépao, in which each *leo* has its own land (p. 594). Van der Kam also sees the *nggolok* (villages) as something new, and draws attention, in support of this inference, to the very dispersed pattern of habitation — in which case it might have been more exact to speak of districts. In former times there were settlements surrounded by high stone walls, called *kota*. According to Van de Wetering, there used to be three walls in a *nusak*: one round the kingdom, one round the capital, and one round the centre of it (1925, p. 608). The *langgak*, the head of the *nggolok*, occupies a fairly important position and has a part to play in all kinds of social events. In the course of his duties he has to deal with various *leo*. He is chosen from among the members of the *nggolok*, and his office is not hereditary (p. 597). Van der Kam's statement that *manèk* and *fettò* are the only territorial heads in the *nusak* is thus clearly incorrect (p. 594).

Finally, let us set down some evidence on a few individual *nusak*:

Nusak Loleh: The ninth *manèk* of Loleh, Mbesadai Lingga, was known as being quarrelsome, while his *fettò*, Lèbo Natu, was a peace-loving man. Since their time Loleh has consisted of the *leo-Mbesa* (twelve *leo* of the *manèk*) and the *leo-Lèbo* (ten *leo* of the *fettò*), and the members of these moieties are named respectively Mbesa-ana and Lèbo-ana (p. 594).

When Ndii Huan (on p. 591 there is a reference to a Ndii Hua, seventeenth *manèk* of Loleh) became *manèk*, though he was the youngest of five brothers, the three middle brothers joined themselves to him, and after a certain passage of time the eldest had to acknowledge him. Since then the descendants of Ndii Huan have always provided the *manèk*. The five brothers became the ancestors of twelve *leo* with twelve *manéleo*. The head of the *leo* of the eldest is the senior among these latter; he is the *manédopè Mbèsa*. The first among the ten *leo* of the *fettò*-moiety is the *manédopè Lèbo* (p. 597).

Nusak Ti: This *nusak* is said to have been divided in the time of *radja* Benjamin Messakh into Sabarai (fourteen *leo* of the *manèk*) and Taratu (twelve *leo* of the *fettò*). Ti already possessed a *manèk* and a *fettò* (p. 594).

Nusak Oépao: The two first ancestors of this *nusak* were named Léléré Séra and Léléo Daé. The *nusak* is divided into eight *leo*, which are said not to have formed any political entity until, at the instance of the Portuguese, a *radja* was placed over them. The choice fell on Léré Méra of the *leo* Ina Ai Dulu; the *nusak* was named Oépao after the ancestor of this *leo* (p. 589). We read on p. 590 that the *nusak* was made up of two groups of "related" *leo*. The head of the stronger group became *manèk*, and the head of the weaker became *fettò*, but there was no question of a strict subordination of the latter to the former. This division of functions is said to have been established after the arrival of the Portuguese. The territorial basis of the arrangement of the *leo* in this *nusak* is unique on Rote (p. 594). Before land is cleared the *manéleo* must be approached; no field may be cleared, or wood be cut, or any other such task be undertaken on the land of another *leo* without permission.

Nusak Keka: This *nusak* must have split off from the *nusak* of Termanu about 1770 (p. 593). In Keka the *manéleo* of the *leo* of the *manèk* and the *fettò* are at the same time *manédopè* (p. 597). Van de Wetering says that Inoama Leki, from Oénale, became "lord of the land", and that Malelak Belan, son of Bela Solu from Termanu, was the first *manèk* of the *nusak* (1922, p. 321).

Nusak Termanu: The land "where the group of Ma Bula (who came from Seran by way of Amfoan, Savu, and Loleh) lived in peace next to the group of Pada Lalais (who came from Seran via Amfoan to Termanu), the latter being acknowledged as lord of the land" (p. 592). "The descendants [of Pada Lalais] are the lords of the land"; the head of this group is *daé-langgak*, "the original owner of the land, at is were", and he always receives a portion of the harvest. The other group was under Ma Bula and his son Muskanan Ma, and from them the rulers are descended (pp. 587, 589).

Nusak Dengka: It is stated as a pure supposition that "the *manèk* must have been the manager of the land, and that he delegated the exercise of this responsibility to a certain person who then became known as *daé-langgak*; only later did this *daé-langgak* become at the same time the *manasonggo nusak*, religious leader of the whole territory, and eventually the title came to designate the religious leader alone" (p. 589).

Nusak Baä: Other authors have provided certain information on this *nusak*. According to Van de Wetering, Baä was already inhabited by the three "*suku*" (*leo*) of Kunan, Suki, and Modok when Loma Fuliha and Ola Fuliha, from Endeh, appeared on the scene. The first founded the fourth and ruling *leo* Ene of Baä, the second "took possession of the land" in Korbaffo (1922, p. 320). Jonker names three ancestors of the inhabitants of Baä as: Baï (grandfather) Suki, nicknamed Tanek or Lolena; Baï Mòdok, nicknamed Sèlek or Ndeë-ama; and Baï Kunak, nicknamed Mau. These divided the whole area of Baä among themselves (1905, p. 456). We read in Jonker, at p. 458: "when Ene moved from Korbaffo to Baä". According to Van Lijnden, Modo was the division of the *fettor* (1851, p. 396).

In connexion with this original tripartition, it may further be remarked that according to Van de Wetering the number three constantly plays a large part, and that it is an expression of completeness (1923*a*, p. 471).

On Savu,[144] as on Rote,[145] the children belong to the mother's descent group when the bridewealth is not fully paid. On Rote, "possessions" are inherited only within the patrilineal descent group, while "ornaments" pass down from mother to daughter.[146]

There is no evidence at all concerning the Bonfia, who live in the most easterly part of *Seran*. The allegation of general promiscuity among their western neighbours, the Seti, can be taken to be totally incorrect, and need not be discussed further.[147] The structure of the Manusela group of tribes, who live in the interior of Seran to the west of the Seti, is better known.[148] This group comprises four tribes, *ninia nia* or *amani*, each divided into a number of patrilineal clans, *uku, iba, ifa,* or *ifan*, and a number of hamlets, *lohoki*. These tribes are: Nisawele or Nusawele, with the *uku* Maoko (also called Lapilaitoto or Lelimina), Manutu, Lekeneh, and formerly Kaniki as well; Manusela (here in a restricted sense), with the *uku* Lilihata, Ilela, Amanokwam, and a few other small *uku*; Wai(ha)rama, with the *uku* Hapisoa,

---

[144] Van de Wetering, 1926, p. 494; Colenbrander, 1916, p. 44.
[145] Van de Wetering, 1925, pp. 15, 31.
[146] Van de Wetering, 1925, pp. 31, 37.
[147] Sachse, 1922, p. 61.
[148] Schadee, 1915, pp. 129 ff.; Willer, 1858, pp. 7, 20 ff. (on the *amani* of Wairama in particular).

Lihaya, Manusawa, Kopa, and Ituhunia; and finally the *amani* Hua Ulu, the internal division of which is unknown. The *amani* is called "district" or "negerie" by Schadee, and "district" by Willer. Schadee considers that the *amani* originated as an accidental and more or less arbitrary union of a number of *uku*, who then took their common name from the place where they lived. The following information refers especially to the *amani* of Wairama, on which our authority is Willer. A "native" is known as *rauhena manusia*, and a stranger as *manusia makasa*. A stranger can live for a time in the *lohoki*, but he must be handed over if his own head demands him. If a *manusia makasa* marries in the *lohoki*, he becomes a member of an *ifan* which he chooses, but never of that of his wife. Such a person is, however, liable to punishment by his own *amani*. A *manusia makasa* is thus someone from another *amani*, but it is not possible to say with certainty whether a *rauhena manusia* is a fellow-member of an *amani* or whether the term refers more particularly to a fellow-member of the *lohoki*.[149]

The *ifan* Hapisoa is also called Ifan Latu, because the *latu*, the head of the *amani*, must always come from this *ifan*. The other *ifan* are therefore referred to as *ifan rahekawasa*, those without office. It is also said that in the time before the choice of the first *latu*, there was already a distinction between noble and non-noble.

The *latu* governs the *amani* as a whole, and his own *lohoki* in particular. He is in supreme command of any warlike undertaking. The *latu*, together with the *makahitia*, heads of the *lohoki*, the *malesi*, "astrologer and champion (*kapitan*)", and two delegates from each *ifan*, form a council, *tuewe hapi hapi*, which meets in a building specially appointed for the purpose, *lofoa ira*, and deals with the different legal cases. The offices are passed from father to eldest son, and are also elective within the *ifan*.

The *lohoki* has no governing council such as the *amani* has. Very minor disputes are settled by the *makahitia*. The *amani* Wairama consists of two *lohoki*, viz., Amola and Tepu, which means that a number of *ifan* must thus be represented within one *lohoki*. The lack of correspondence between *lohoki* and *ifan* is also shown by the circumstance that heads of *lohoki* and delegates of the *ifan* take their places as separate officials in the *tuewe hapi hapi*. Since the *latu* is at the same

---

[149] Perhaps it should be translated simply as house-mate. *Ipia rauhena* are small sago-plantations of from 20 to 30 palms which are planted as close as possible to the house. In addition to these there are the larger plantations of the *ifan* or the *lohoki*.

time governor of his own *lohoki*, i.e., *makahitia*, it may be supposed that the basis of the office of *latu* lies rather in the *lohoki* than in the *ifan*. Marriage is apparently patrilocal, for Willer says that a woman goes for ever to the *ifan* of her husband. All land is the property of the *amani*, except for the ground on which the *lohoki* is built.[150]

Tauern also provides some particulars on this area: "Although it has long been customary in western Seran to live together in villages, the settlements in central Seran were mostly scattered. They provided a home, however, for a number of families which naturally were related to each other. Such family groups (*soa*) segmented, when they were large, into several houses, but these continued to maintain their close connexions, especially through the family elders, the *kapala soa* or *orang tuah*, who governed the *soa*... In central Seran, where the people have recently been compelled by the Government to live together in villages, the *soa* are divided into a number of villages, but each *soa* has nevertheless only one *kapala soa*." Concerning the *amani* Manusela he says: "The *latu* ... as ruler has under him all the villages in which his *soa* are scattered: Manusela, Makuala Inan, Illela Kita, Illela Botoa, Amanokwan, and Selimena." [151]

The word *soa* also occurs in composite terms in Willer's description of the *amani* Wairama. *Soa ira* are sago plantations of two hundred to a thousand trees in the planting of which everyone takes part. *Ipia rauhena* are clumps of from twenty to thirty palms, set as close as possible to the house.

The only social grouping of importance within the tribe which Tauern mentions, in addition to the *soa*, is the village established under pressure from the government. The members of a *soa* live scattered in more than one village, and Tauern may well have meant that in these villages there are no members of other *soa*. Several villages may thus be established within the territory of the *lohoki*. It should be mentioned, in this regard, that although Willer renders *lohoki* as "hamlet", the *lohoki* was not a village or a hamlet in any real sense. We should probably conceive it as a number of houses dispersed over a limited territory. The village names recorded by Tauern correspond in part to the names of the *ifan* of the *amani* as listed by Schadee. Villages which spring up within the *lohoki* thus perhaps coincide with the *ifan*, or segments of *ifan*, which traditionally belonged to the *lohoki*.

The structure of the Muslim villages on the north coast exhibits

---

[150] Willer, 1858, p. 20.
[151] Tauern, 1918, pp. 127 ff.

many points in common with what has been written above about those
in the interior. At the head of the "negorij" there is a *radja* or an
orang kaja (for whom the indigenous term is *latu*). *Bebatu*, or *tumato
latu*, are heads of the *soa*, "families or sections of the negorij". The
tumato latu are rather lower in rank than the *bebatu*. There is also a
council of minor heads which can only be convened by the *radja* or
orang kaja. The *kapitan* possesses no power in the "negorij", but is the
commander in war. The negorij thus corresponds generally to the
amani in the interior. As far as the *soa* is concerned, we encounter
the same wavering between genealogical and territorial criteria as we
have done in the case of the Manusela. The council which governs it
is familiar. In the *amani* of Wairama, Willer counts the *kapitan* among
its members.[152]

Among the peoples living to the west of the Manusela, the social
unit corresponding to the *amani* is generally referred to as "negorij".
Most of the reports lead one to believe that a negorij usually consists
of a single village, but other authors speak of village complexes. Thus
De Vries, for example, says: "a number of family groups congregate
around the *baileo* [a sort of meeting house]. These aggregations are
called *soa*, after the *baileo* (Wemale: *soane*). Several *soa* make up a
negorij".[153] This report applies more particularly to the Wemale.
Tauern complements this report with the statement that originally a
soa formed a whole village, but that at the present day a village is
lived in by more than one *soa*.[154] Concerning the Wemale, De Vries
adds that marriage outside the tribe is forbidden; a man from Honitetu,
for example, can never marry a woman from Ahiolo or from Walokone,
even though these three villages all belong to the Wemale and differ
from one another merely in dialect.[155] These descriptions amount to
saying that a village constitutes a tribe. This is expressly confirmed by
Tauern, according to whom the regents (the customary Dutch title
for negorij-heads had under them as a rule only one village. There
are, however, exceptions to this rule: e.g., the head of Uwin (Huene,
Wene) governs the whole of the Malowan group, and another negorij-
head with greater power is the *latu* of Honitetu (Nuetetu). It is extremely likely that these are examples of political expansion. Of more
importance in this connexion is the statement that sometimes villages

[152] Brumund, 1845, pp. 59 ff.
[153] De Vries, 1927, p. 132.
[154] Tauern, 1918, p. 127.
[155] De Vries, 1927, p. 107.

with too few inhabitants were united under one head.[156] Let us now turn to evidence which indicates that the negorij is a village complex. Each negorij has a *baileo anakota* where the governing council of the negorij meets. Sierevelt says that not all villages have a *baileo anakota*; those which do not have one come under the jurisdiction of the village where the *mauwene teman*, the supreme priest, lives, and where there is therefore a *bailo anakota*. A number of villages thus together form a negorij.

The governing council of the negorij is termed *saniri hena* by Sierevelt, and the village *baileo* is called *sisi hena*.[158] *Hena* can thus mean village as well as negorij. When the negorij consists of only one village, this goes without saying. At the head of the negorij stands a hereditary or elected official who is usually referred to as a "regent". These dignitaries are nearly always designated by the Malay titles *orang kaja*, *patih*, and *radja*, according to their rank. Their indigenous name is apparently *latu*.[159] According to De Vries, the Dutch Government appointed negorij-heads; where there were already hereditary heads these were continued in office.[160]

Next to the regent in each negorij came a "lord of the land". Tauern writes of "the Radja Tanah or Latu . . ., whose task it is to see to the maintenance of morality and customary law. He also has charge of matters of land tenure, and it is he who decides questions relating to the land. It seems that in general the Radja Tanah is the real ruler, whereas the Orang Kaja is the man who is appointed by the Government. This was repeatedly confirmed in western Seran".[161] According to Sachse, he has no official position.[162] Boot refers to him on one occasion as *latu nura*, and on another as *latu nusa*.[163] The latter author adds that the *latu nusa* is a *mauwen* (priest), and that in the negorijs which belong to the *kakehan* (men's secret society) he is also termed *masaloi*, i.e., leader of the youths at their initiation. The number of *latu nusa* is not fixed, at least according to Boot. Anyone who is brave and has taken at least fifteen heads is eligible. Both Boot and

[156] Tauern, 1918, pp. 127, 128.
[157] Sierevelt, in Sachse, 1922, pp. 110 ff.
[158] Sachse, 1922, p. 109; Stresemann, 1923, p. 336; Tauern, 1918, p. 153.
[159] Van Eerde, 1920, p. 536; Tauern, 1918, pp. 44, 127; Sachse, 1922, p. 133.
[160] De Vries, 1927, p. 141.
[161] Tauern, 1918, p. 128.
[162] Sachse, 1922, p. 133.
[163] Boot, 1893, pp. 661, 1197, 1199.

De Vries [164] list the lord of the land among the functionaries of the negorij. Most of the accounts of his duties agree.

Boot's ethnographical material excels in the abundance of its details, but because of its apparent inaccuracies it can be used only with caution. For example, his statement about the number of *latu nusa* in a negorij conflicts with the evidence of practically all the other authors and can thus fairly certainly be set aside as incorrect.

As has been said above, there used to be a negorij-council, *saniri hena*, which met in the *baileo anakota* in order to debate various questions concerning the negorij. The members of the *saniri hena* sat on benches against the walls, and the person charged, in the case of a delict, stood in the middle. The *saniri hena* was composed of: the *mauwen*, priests, of whom there were six in each negorij; the lord of the land; the regent; and the various heads of the *soa* (see below). The *mauwen* were the designated persons in all affairs touching on the *kakehan*. One of them, the supreme priest (*mauwene teman*),[165] a personage surrounded by an air of secrecy, was reputedly far and away the most prominent person in the negorij, surpassing even the regent in power and respect. This comes from Boot; all the other sources limit themselves to the statement that the regent is assisted by a council of *kapala soa*. Only De Vries and Tichelman mention a fourth category of officials in the government of the negorij, viz., the *alamanan*, spokesmen, composers of quarrels, and intercessors.[167]

The higher forms of organisation into which the negorijs were grouped were the river valleys with their *saniri*; these will be discussed later. Another inter-tribal relationship is constituted by the *pela*. This is an alliance between two or more negorijs, the chief obligations of which are not to take heads from one another, to lend support in everything, and not to refuse anything on the occasion of visits. This last condition applies to the extent that guests may take anything that catches their fancy, without asking.[168]

Only on the Wemale do we possess fairly detailed information concerning descent groups.[169] The tribe is divided into a number of matrilineal clans called *luma inai*, maternal house. Marriage is matrilocal. There is no bridewealth, and the husband is incorporated by

---

[164] De Vries, 1927, p. 140.
[165] Sierevelt, in Sachse, 1922, p. 110.
[166] Boot, 1893, pp. 1197 ff.
[167] De Vries, 1927, p. 140; Tichelman, 1925, p. 720; Tauern, 1918, p. 128; Sachse, 1922, p. 133.
[168] Sachse, 1922, p. 65; Stresemann, 1923, p. 414.

marriage into the *luma inai* of his wife. Marriage between nephew and niece, children of brothers or sisters, is regarded as incest.

The matrilineal rule of descent is qualified in one important particular: the eldest son does not belong to the clan of his mother but to that of his father. If no sons are born to a marriage, a son of one of the close matrilineal relatives of the mother is transferred to the *luma inai* of the father. The remaining children, needless to say, belong to the *luma inai* of the mother, says De Vries. If the mother dies before a replacement is given, the father returns to his *luma inai*, but otherwise not. The "substituted" son inherits all the property which belonged to his father before marriage, and the possessions of the mother are passed down to her daughters.

Kin are grouped around the *luma inai*, the "family temple", where heirlooms (chiefly porcelain) are safeguarded, and where the various rites are performed. The *luma inai*-bond is very strong, and forms the basis of the society. At the erection of a new *luma inai* the ancestors are repeatedly invited to attend.[170]

With the development of the ancestral cult, more and more family groups become associated with the *baileo*. These groups are called *soa*, after the *baileo* (Wemale: *soane*). Marriage within one's own *soa* is permitted. Several *soa* together form a negorij. The former family heads have been superseded by local functionaries: *mauwin, alamanan, radja tanah* and negorij-head, assisted by *kapala soa*, of whom there are always a number in the larger negorijs.[171]

Among the Alune there is a bride-price, and marriage is patrilocal. It also happens that two *soa* interchange women in order to obviate the payment of bridewealth.[172] In reporting the great attachment to the *luma inai* which exists among the Wemale, De Vries observes that this is not the case among the Alune, but that the latter have integrated the *ruma pusaka* and the *baileo*. It would appear from this that the *ruma pusaka* (the *luma inai* building) is to the matrilineal clan what the *baileo* is to the *soa*. The *soa* among the Alune seems to be a patrilineal group; and the more or less latent persistence of the matrilineal *luma inai* next to the *soa* may be inferred from the same source. De

---

[169] De Vries, 1927, pp. 106, 126, 132, 139.

[170] De Vries, 1927, p. 126.

[171] De Vries, 1927, pp. 132, 139. Sierevelt also mentions next to each other the *baileo soa* (consecrated house of the *soa*) and the *rumah pusaka* (house for heirlooms) (in Sachse, 1922, p. 110).

[172] De Vries, 1927, pp. 116, 128.

Vries says, for example, that "this *luma inai*-bond is particularly strong among the Wemale, where it is the basis of the society".

It is plain to see that the differing statements in the ethnography have to a significant extent been coloured by the writers' theories. It is not clear how far the *luma inai* still remains the "basis of the society", and to what extent it has lost influence to the emergent *soa*-groups. One wonders, too, what sort of group the *soa* is. And are the composite "family groups" whole *luma inai* or segments of *luma inai*? De Vries appears to ascribe a territorial character to the *soa*, in contradistinction to the *luma inai*, but living together was one of the features of the *luma inai* as well. The *soa* is said not to be exogamous, but several writers report the contrary, as we shall see below. It is possible that the relationship of *luma inai* to *soa* among the Wemale should be seen in the same light as among the Alune. Furthermore, the relations between the ancestral cult, the *baileo* (*soane*), and the *luma inai* building are very obscure. The growth of the *soa*, at the expense of the *luma inai*, is attributed to the increasing importance of the ancestral cult, but other reports make it seem indisputable that the *luma inai* house was intended largely for this cult. In the eyes of the people themselves ancestor-worship and the patrilineal groups are often conceived as originally related. Apparently this is the case in De Vries's reports as well, so that, as we indicated above, it is in this direction that the solution to the problem should be sought.

According to Stresemann, marriage within the *soa* is regarded as incest.[173] The indigenous term for *soa* is *nuru*. Tauern and Sachse write that the office of *kapala soa* passes down from father to son.[174] Tauern calls the *soa* a "family group"; Sachse refers to it as a "tribal segment" and also as a "family group possessing a common lineage name". The office of regent was hereditary in the masculine line; in default of a successor (in the person of a son?), the new regent was elected from among the *bangsa radja*, apparently the ruling lineage, or at least from the *soa latu*. The *soa* is thus quite certainly a patrilineal group.

There are also certain indications of a former totemism. At Honitetu (Wemale) it is said that the first human beings sprouted from a *pisang* (banana). They were two men, Jasua and Kapoli, and a woman, Apuwei. Jasua married Apuwei, and they had two sons,

---

[173] Stresemann, 1923, pp. 414, 336.
[174] Tauern, 1918, pp. 127 ff.; Sachse, 1922, p. 133.

Patetu and Kamoli, and one daughter, Isolai, who later met other human beings who had originated from the parrot, the flying-fox, fruit-trees, etc.

In Ahiolo it is thought that the people of Ahiolo, Honitetu, and Walokone are descended from the fruits of a *pisang kapok* which changed into human beings. The last fruit of the bunch was a woman, who imploringly called out to her brothers to wait for her. The blossom of the bunch, which she took with her, became a copper *sirih*-box, and the stalk she tied around her waist as a belt, which consisted of rings linked together. They settled on Solesiwa mountain, and people came there from all sides, among them the people of Lasabatai, who had originated from fungi growing on a "fallen *lasa*-tree" (i.e., *lasabatai*), and those of Kaluna, who had also sprung from a kind of tree. It is forbidden to eat of the trees, animals, and so on from which one is descended.[175]

In the village lying on the north coast of the Amahei sub-division (southern coast of middle Seran), the social unit which it is customary to refer to as a tribe, and which sometimes comprises a number of villages, is usually called a negorij. Tichelman gives some examples of a number of associated negorijs which are thought to have formed previously a complex of negorijs.[176]

The head of the negorij, who is usually referred to as the regent, comes as rule from the *bangsa radja* (which here apparently means a lineage) of a certain *soa*, the *soa latu*. The indigenous term in the Amahei language is *pu-u aja*; in the Elpaputi language it is *pu-u latu* or *upu latu*. *Pu-u* or *upu* is lord, head, grandfather; *aja* is *pemerintah* (Malay: government), regent; and *latu* is ruler.[177] Next to the head in each negorij there is a "lord of the land". Within the administration of the negorij, particularly with regard to customary law, he was the real authority above the head of the negorij, and he represented the negorij, as it were, to itself. He is thought to be a descendant of the first person who settled in the place where the negorij originated, and in the popular estimation he is nothing less than the owner of the territory of the negorij. He alone can allot land to the heads of families. At the present day he no longer possesses any power, but he is nevertheless treated with distinction, and is consulted on matters concerning customary law and land. Formerly his authority must have been very

175 De Vries, 1927, pp. 165 ff.
176 Tichelman, 1925, pp. 673, 697.
177 Tichelman, 1925, pp. 716, 717.

great, greater even than that of the head of the negorij. Decisions about land-usage rest with the negorij, represented by the "lord of the land". The indigenous title of this official is *uma-a hena* or *hena* (*amano*) *pu-uno* in the Amahei area, and *latu nusa* in the Elpaputi language. The word *hena* thus appears here with the meaning of tribe.[178]

Each negorij also has *kapitan*, a commander in war. Each *kapitan* is followed by a weapon-bearer called *malessi*. These offices are hereditary in the male line. In the village of Amahei, in the narrower sense, each *soa* has a *kapitan*, and the senior among them is called the *kapitan radja*.[179]

A negorij is composed of a number of *soa*, "genealogical jural bodies which were originally independent, not to be confused with the later *soa*, or wards, which are political groupings of a territorial nature". Tichelman goes on, however, to write about the *kapala soa*, who he says are "heads of family groups bearing the same lineage name and originally living together in wards". Marriage is patrilocal, at least when the bridewealth is paid.[180]

In the old coastal villages the negorij was composed of *dati*, under the jurisdiction of the *soa*. The *dati* are "family branches with their own rights in land". Tichelman gives on example in which a single *dati* had members in different negorijs. Formerly these negorijs made up a complex. Sometimes a number of *dati* are descended from a common ancestor. The *dati*-institution is strongly patrilineal. *Anak dati* are the members of the *dati*, and *tulung dati* are those who have become *dati*-members other than by descent. Strangers can be adopted into the *dati* if they request it, e.g., when they marry into the negorij. This is conventionally decided upon by a meeting of *dati*-heads, the lord of the land, negorij-heads, and the heads of the *soa*. In this case all rights in one's former *dati* are given up. When the bridewealth is not paid, or not completely paid, marriage is matrilocal, as we have seen above, and the husband then willy-nilly becomes *tulung dati* of his wife's *dati*. If a *dati* dies out, its rights in the land revert to the negorij.

Every *dati* has a *kapala dati*, who is elected for life by his fellow *dati*-members. In other negorijs this function is hereditary from father

---

[178] Tichelman, 1925, pp. 697, 716. The administration of oaths is also one of his duties.

[179] Tichelman, 1925, p. 685.

[180] Tichelman, 1925, pp. 716, 696, 697.

to son (as, for example, in Soahuku). The *kapala dati* are under the advice of the lord of the land.

The idigenous terms for *dati* are *uku-e nalani* (Elpaputi), i.e., *nama* or *fam soa*, and *nalano* (Amahei).[181]

Tichelman brings out the complicated nature of this form of organisation, and remarks that the people "constantly confuse *dati* with *dusun* (plantation), with family, and even with *pusaka* (heir-looms)".[182]

On the inhabitants of the Tala valley, who are Wemale, Tichelman adds that there the ownership of the *dusun* "passes down to the wife. The husband is presumed, by the fact of his marriage, to be in a position to obtain the *dusun* with which to supply the necessities of life. If bridewealth is not paid, the children belong to the *fam* (Amahei, *nalano*; Elpaputi, *nalane*) of the wife... Inheritance may go matri-lineally".[183]

Regent, *kapala soa*, lord of the land, *kapala dati*, *tua-tua negri* (negorij-elders), and *kewang* (forest-guards) together form a council, *saniri negri*, whose task it is, among other things, to proclaim *sasi*, prohibitions, governing planting.[184]

From the little that is known about the *Ambon Islands*, it would appear that ethnographically they are directly connected with the area of Seran just discussed. At the head of the negorij (*hena*) stands an "official" called *orang kaja, patih*, or *radja*. Each *hena* is divided into a number (two, three, or more) of wards, *soa*, under *kapala soa* or elders. The sago plantations of a *hena* are divided among the *dati*, of which there are a certain number in each *hena*. The *dati* are headed by *kapala dati*. This office passes down from father to son, but can also be occupied by a woman, e.g., by a mother in place of a son who is still in his minority, or by an unmarried daughter who has no brothers. The *dati*-divisions have nothing in common with the *soa*-groups. A *kapala soa* can at the same time be *kapala dati*. The *orang kaja* is head of his own *dati*. The members of a *dati* are known as *anak dati* or *tulung dati*. Plantations belonging to the whole *soa* are said not to have existed in former times.[185]

Every *hena* also has a *latu kewanno*, who exercises general super-

---

[181] Tichelman, 1925, pp. 696-7, 717.
[182] Tichelman, 1925, p. 698.
[183] Tichelman, 1925, p. 697.
[184] Tichelman, 1925, p. 699.
[185] Van Hoevell, 1875, pp. 19, 23, 180 ff.

vision over the cultivated and uncultivated lands of the *hena*. Van Hoevell refers to him also as *kapala kewang* ("village constable") and as *radja ewang*. *Iwanno* (Malay, *tanah ewang*) is the uncultivated land of the *hena*. This official thus corresponds to the "lord of the land", as he is known elsewhere.[186]

Certain information on *Nusa Laut* and its social structure is to be extracted from the Ambonese songs published by Van Hoevell.

Upu Latu (lord ruler) Lemese founded the *hena* of Lesiëla or Mula in the mountains. Latu Pikauli and Upu Latu Hehanusa divided the island in two: Inalohu, under Pikauli, and Inahaha, under Hehanusa. These two parts, the names of which mean "mother on (of) the lower side" and "mother on (of) the upper side", still exist today. It was decided that there should be two *latu* (*radja*) and five *pati*. Pati Manusama, with the *teun* (*soa*) Sialana, founded the *hena* of Kakarisa, the present-day Abubu. Upu Latu Hehanusa and his brothers (or kin) Luhua Tanasala and Upu Nunua (lord of the waringin) Soselisa, and Upu Latu Pikauli and Upu Wael (lord of the water) Patinala with their brother Sama Tahapari, each with their own *teun*, founded six *hena*. The heads and the *soa* (*teun*) of the various *hena* still bear the names listed in the myth.

These rulers populated Nusa Laut. In the song the question is posed as to who, among the Siwa or among the Rima, is more powerful than they. The answer is that they are the most powerful. Lemese now begins a war against the coast-dwellers, but he is beaten and retreats to Boano. For years after, slave-taking expeditions went out from Boano against the Uliasa, especially Nusa Laut.

Exactly the same structure is found on the island of *Amblau*, near *Buru*. Here there are seven negorijs, called *bena*, each divided into from two to five *nuru*, "wards or hamlets", which in their turn contain a number of *dati*, "lineages". Both the *nuru* and the *dati* are exogamous groups. Marriage into another *bena* is permitted. The total number of *nuru* comes to 22, and that of the *dati* to 59, the population as a whole being set at 802 by Willer [188] and 1048 by Bleeker.[189]

The *gìb'emliar* (the more original population groups) of *Buru* are divided into a number of tribes (*uli*). These *uli* owe their existence to the ancestral pairs who were "formed" by the supreme being and

---

[186] Van Hoevell, 1875, pp. 187, 196, 46.
[187] Van Hoevell, 1882, pp. 71 ff.
[188] Willer, 1858, pp. 204 ff.
[189] Bleeker, 1856, vol. II, p. 47.

who made their appearance at the origin of the various rivers. The *uli* lives in the valley of the river with which it is associated. These *uli*, four of which are named by Schut, are not related to each other. The names of the pairs of tribal ancestors are well known, but are only pronounced in case of need.

The tribe is divided into a number of *nòro*, patrilineal clans, who are descended from the sons of the pair of *uli*-ancestors. The members of a tribe are always named after the number of clans belonging to it, e.g., *nòro pitu*, to which the *nòro* Gìb'Hain belongs, among others. In three other cases, the number of clans totals three in one instance and five in the two others. According to some, the ancestors married their sisters. Each *nòro* has its own "lineage name" (*leit*).[190] The tribal ancestors of the *nòro pitu*, Lawan Dìtan (man) and Poteria Dìtan (woman), came into being from the sources of the river Wà Apu or Wà Kàbu. This couple had seven sons, from whom seven *nòro* are descended. The *nòro* (in order of birth) are:[191]

(*nòro*)	(*leit*)
Gìb'Hain	Selìki
Gì'Wàget	Behuku
Wà Tìmun	Nur'Làtu Wael
Wà Gìda	Tàsane
Wà Hidi	Tu Wael
Wà Lua	Nur'Làtu Bual
Gàeli	Wael

The Gìb'Hain take their wives from the *nòro* Gì-Wàget. When the offspring of a stranger and a Gìb'Hain woman took the name Behuku, the Gì'Wàget in Mesrète were very offended and changed their *leit* to Hukunala. Those in the Wà Sàma region still called themselves Behuku.[192]

The *nòro*, according to Schut, is itself segmented into several *màrah*, but the significance of the *màrah* is not at all clear. Various remarks made by Schut [193] point in the direction of sub-clans. Thus he writes: "The oldest male descendants in the tribal segment (= *màrah*) of the oldest *taplawa* (*màrah*-ancestor) are the foremost representatives of the

---

[190] Schut, 1918, pp. 17 ff.; 1921, pp. 615 ff.
[191] Schut, 1921, p. 617.
[192] Schut, 1918, p. 23.
[193] Schut, 1918, p. 17; 1921, pp. 617, 618; 1923, p. 331.

entire tribe (= *nòro*) descend in a direct line from the first ancestors".
In exceptional circumstances transfer to another *nòro* is possible, by
means of adoption, at the discretion of the elders of the *màrah* which
parts with the individual in question.[194] A differentiation which is
never lost sight of is that between the *nòro* and *màrah* which are descended from the elder and from the younger clan- and sub-clan
ancestors.[195]

After the pairs of tribal ancestors had been created at the sources
of the major rivers, their *nòro* settled in the river-valleys. Each of
the *màrah* built its hamlet, *hum'lolin*, i.e., collection of houses.[196]

Strangers and coast-dwellers use the term *fèna* for *nòro*.

Marriage is patrilocal.[197] According to Van der Miesen, the man
goes to reside with the wife if the bridewealth is not fully paid.[198]
Part of an address at the marriage ceremony runs: "Greetings to the
ruler ... Our regulations are those of the earliest times, from the time
when the three trees sprang up." [199]

In *Endeh* (middle Flores) [200] either the *raki pu'u*, clan head, or the
raki, lineage head, can function as *kolu*, lord of the land, and as such
they manage the uncultivated lands in the territory of the clan or the
lineage. The head is assisted by a *ria bewa* (= *wiwi ria rema bewa*,
moon great tongue long) and a *ndetu au* ("major domus"). At the
present day the *raki pu'u* is still head of a group, though it feels itself
to be more genealogical than territorial. Various districts are named
after the oldest clan-ancestor. Formerly, the village is said to have
been inhabited by a single lineage; it was headed by a *raki*. No *raki
pu'u* are met with in the coastal villages. The nobility here is called
ata nggaeh, and *mosa raki* in the interior; in addition to them there
are the common people and the slaves. Only if the bridewealth is paid
do the children belong to the lineage of the father, and the same
qualification applies to patrilocal marriage. The district of Wolo Wae
is exceptional, for here children are named after the mother.[201]
Adoption (*ndueh*) has already been discussed in an earlier chapter.
Van Suchtelen lists in the first place the adoption of a daughter's son,

---

[194]   Schut, 1921, p. 618.
[195]   Schut, 1918, p. 18.
[196]   Schut, 1921, p. 619.
[197]   Schut, 1918, p. 301.
[198]   Van der Miesen, 1902, pp. 443, 446.
[199]   Van der Miesen, 1902, p. 441.
[200]   Van Suchtelen, 1921, pp. 69, 88, 90, 102.
[201]   Van Suchtelen, 1921, p. 103.

and it thus appears that this form is the most frequent. Such youths are henceforth reckoned as belonging to the generation of their mother.[202]

A myth tells how a man, Roru, and a woman, Modo, descended from the sky on to Nusa Endeh. They had three daughters and two sons. One of the daughters disappeared on a cloud when her mother once wanted to punish her.[203]

Three men, Boro Kanda, Rako Madenga, and Keto Kuwa, who were busy eating fish on Nusa Endeh, saw a man called Ambu Nggobe, who was "lord of the land" and came from the coast opposite. He invited them to go with him to the mainland, where one of them should marry his daughter, since they were so clever as to be able to catch fish. Until this time, in fact, Ambu Nggobe had never seen anyone eating. An elephant's tusk and a gold chain were given as bridewealth, "to make the boat slide on the ground" and "to drag the boat". The region of Noa Roondja was named Noa Endeh, after the island that had been left. A son of Roru married a daughter of Ambu Nggobe. Their daughter married a man who had come from Madjapahit on a whale. Another daughter of this line took as her husband a Chinese who had been shipwrecked. The *ata nggaeh* (heads) are descended in a direct line from these four ancestors, chiefly from Roru and from the man who had come from Madjapahit. If a whale appears in the bay, offerings are regularly made to it.[204] According to Van Suchtelen, Djari Djawa, the ancestor of the rulers of Endeh, left Madjapahit after a quarrel with his elder brother.

There are two "lords of the land" in Endeh, one descended from Ambu Nggobe, the other from the people of Gunung Roondja. The former lives in the interior and is said still to possess the elephant's tusk and the chain referred to above.[206]

The following myth is reported by Van Suchtelen.[207] Sanga Kula, the first inhabitant of Pulau Endeh, came from Dori Woi and married a woman who had been driven across the sea from the coast opposite in the form of a *lontar* (palm)-leaf. One of their offspring, Radja Redo of Kerimando, adopted as his son Ambo Roru, who had emerged from a hole in a dry river-bed. With the rains there came a *lontar*-leaf from

[202] Van Suchtelen, 1921, pp. 107, 115, 122.
[203] Roos, 1877, pp. 481 ff.
[204] Roos, 1877, p. 489.
[205] Van Suchtelen, 1921, p. 164.
[206] Roos, 1877, pp. 507, 483.
[207] Van Suchtelen, 1921, p. 161.

Dori Woi which changed into a beautiful woman. The latter, who was called Puteri Nuru Laila, became the wife of Ambo Roru. From this marriage two daughters were born, Ambu Modo and Puteri Samasa. The former married Ambu Nggaeh, *radja* of One Witu, and the other put on the dress of her mother at a feast, upon which she ascended into the sky and then came down in Luwu (Celebes), where she became ruler. Here she waited for the appearance of a husband, who came out of the depths of the Luwu river. From their marriage are descended the present rulers of Luwu. Mosa Pio, son of Ambu Modo, married a woman from Nggela and had two daughters by her, Toni and Soru. The rulers of Endeh were born from the marriage of Toni, while Soru married the ruler of Sikka.

The central area of the kingdom of Larantuka (in eastern Flores) is, according to a myth which we shall examine elsewhere in more detail, divided into five parts.[208] The heads of these five parts — one of whom is the ruler himself — have a common mythical ancestor named Pategolo. The eldest son became radja of Lokea, and the others became the radjas of Bebalon or Waibalu, Balela, Lanama (the older name for Larantuka), and Lewerang. Lewerang is said to have come under the ruler of Lokea by "inheritance". So much for the stories; let us now see what the situation really is. Larantuka is governed by a radja and three main *kapala*. Each of these four officials has a complex of villages under him. In addition, the radja has eight villages directly under his hand, three of which belong to the former capital of Lewerang. The ancestral house of the ruler used to be at Lokea, but it was moved from there to Lanama (Larantuka). The area under the direct control of the radja is called the *rumah radja*, and the other village complexes are known as *po*. The heads of such village complexes, to whom Heynen refers as main *kapala*, are similarly descended from Pategolo. The village complexes are Balela and Bebalon. The fourth complex, Lanama (Larantuka), is under the *tuan tanah* (lord of the land), who because of his priestly functions in the administration has been replaced by a *kapala*. The *tuan tanah* or *radja tanah* is the spiritual counterpart of the ruler.[209]

It can thus be seen that the actual situation corresponds fairly well with that depicted in the myth, with the qualification that the head of Lokea has two of the five parts under his control, viz., Lewerang as well as Lokea, and that he is the radja of the entire area. The head

[208] Heijnen, 1875-76, pp. 75 ff.
[209] Heijnen, 1875-76, p. 81.

of the third part, Lanama (Larantuka), is the *tuan tanah*, and the chief village of his territory is at the same time the residence of the radja. The heads of the two remaining parts of the kingdom bear only the title of main *kapala*.

There is nothing more to be reported on the organisation of the village complexes and their interrelations. All that we can say is that, to judge from a sketch-map by Couvreur and the indications in his text,[210] the complexes have a fairly large extent. Couvreur also speaks of the village complexes as "separate entities". By his account the village complex of Lewerang is one of the "seven tribes", the *suku pitu*, to which Balela also belongs. We can only grope in complete darkness after the nature and significance of the *suku pitu*, for detailed information is entirely lacking.

A number of "*kakang*-ships" also belong to the kingdom; these are village complexes, each of which is headed by a *kakang*. It is said in the myth that the *kakang*-ship of Muda Kaputu consists of four indigenous villages and four stranger-villages.

Van Swieten states that marriage is matrilocal, and that bridewealth must be paid.[211] A man and his offspring acquire hereby the right to ask bridewealth for "all female children descended in a direct line from the bride".

We are indebted to Beckering for the few evidences at our disposal on the organisation of the social groups of the *Solor Islands*.

The *kakang*-ship of Horowura (on Adonara) [212] is divided into eleven *negeri*. A *negeri* is a mother-village with its colonies. The *negeri* of Horowura, which contains five villages in addition to the mother-village, comprises seven *suku*. A *suku* was a family in former times, according to Beckering. Each of the *suku*-heads has his own title; the senior among them, the *ataka beling*, is at the same time head of the *negeri*. In the other *negeri* this division into *suku* is more or less gone, and in fact each *negeri* has four *ataka beling*, "leaders at the sacrifice". Under the heads of the *suku* are the village heads. Feasts are celebrated by the whole *negeri* in the mother-village. In all the villages on the islands there are "lords of the land", *tuan tanah*.

In the kingdom of Adonara the radja has below him the village heads, *ataka beling* or *ataka laké*, and under these are the heads of secondary villages (*riang*) with the title of *temukung* or *orang tua*.

---

[210] Couvreur, 1908, pp. 564 ff.
[211] Van Swieten, 1897, pp. 7 ff.
[212] Beckering, 1911, pp. 172, 189 ff.

In the villages of Adonara and Sagu the *tuan tanah* was charged with the supervision of the cemetery.

On Lomblèm the secondary villages, or segments of the mother-village, are also called *suku*.

Kluppel states that in each village there is a small house which is consecrated, and a larger one in the village of the priest or *tuan tanah*.[213] It follows from this that not every village has a *tuan tanah*. The *kakang*-ship, like the territory of a radja, is an independent political unit.

[213] Kluppel, 1873, p. 393.

CHAPTER III

PRINCIPAL FEATURES OF THE
SOCIO-FAMILIAL SYSTEM

We have encountered the system of unilateral affinal relationships throughout a range of interconnected cultures in a large area stretching from Sumba and Flores in the west to the Kei Islands in the east, and including also the islands of Seran and Buru lying to the north. This island world comprises the whole of eastern Indonesia apart from Celebes and Halmahera. It is a remarkable fact that whenever we have at our disposal sources which are at all detailed and intensive, we find practically without exception that exclusive cross-cousin marriage and its associated type of social structure are reported. The gaps in our knowledge are nearly all the result of highly superficial descriptions or of sheer lack of data. For the chain of islands joining Timor and Tanimbar, for example, we possess no information which is of any real use for our purpose. It is beyond question that the fragmentary character of our material is to be ascribed in large part to this circumstance. The disintegration of the system, which appears everywhere to be already far advanced, if in varying extent, makes it difficult for our informants, nearly all of whom (particularly the missionaries and government officials) belong to the category of "casual ethnographers", to disentangle the original relationships. Under the influence of western culture this disintegration proceeds at an ever-increasing rate. It should not be forgotten, however, that in addition to external forces there are always tendencies within the culture itself which bring about changes in structural form. For example, it is quite certain that changes in the clan-organisation, and in everything connected with it, have taken place in this area, and these have necessarily led to a general alteration in the type of culture. Western influence, moreover, works rather to disintegrate the old than to construct anything new. Very little can be said at present about the possibility of regeneration, and as little about the way in which this might be effected.

The fact that we repeatedly find exclusive cross-cousin marriage and its organisational correlate, over an area of enormous extent, cannot be simply the result of fortuitous circumstances, or of borrowing on a gigantic scale, but indicates that this form of marriage is to be seen as an ancient culture-element known to all the peoples in the area. A culture is not just the sum of its component parts, a composite of all kinds of disjointed elements which can be of various origins, but forms a solid unity of thought and action. Its elements are the stones in a meaningful construction, and are only to be understood as factors in the cultural system of which they form part. It is not our intention merely to give an explanation of a particular marriage-possibility; we wish to furnish an insight into the totality of these cultures, and to this end we have chosen this culture-element as our starting-point.

In the first chapter we disengaged the structural type of exclusive cross-cousin marriage from its cultural milieu in order to see it function, as an isolated culture-element, in a better and truer way than would have been possible in the midst of the many other cultural forces which are activated by its operation. In setting to work in this way, however, we should not lose sight of the fact that it is not really possible totally to isolate a cultural factor. Each part of the culture is linked to the other parts by too many ties. The homogeneity of culture means that one part constantly stands in the closest connexion to another. Any attempt at an arbitrary isolation leads to distortion, and often to incomprehensibility. Here lies the explanation for the sterility of the writings of many of the older ethnologists, who, in dealing with a single cultural factor, collected their data from all parts of the earth and tried to explain these apart from any cultural context. Our method, which aims at synthesis, is intended to avoid this mistake. We have considered the structural type of exclusive cross-cousin marriage separately, by way of making a preliminary acquaintance with it, only in order to set it back in its proper place in the culture.

Cross-cousin marriage, in both its unilateral and its bilateral forms, has always attracted the attention of anthropologists. They have pointed especially to the connexion with phratry-exogamy, which does indeed make the marriage of parallel cousins impossible. But cross-cousin marriage also occurs among peoples who have no phratry-exogamy; similarly, dual organisation provides no explanation for the exclusive form of cross-cousin marriage. There has been a tendency to propose local-historical explanations for the institution, two of which have acquired special renown: these derived exclusive cross-cousin marriage from the transfer of marriage rights, from father to son in a patrilineally organised society, and from a man to his sister's son in a matrilineal society.[1]

The data which we have assembled show convincingly that cross-cousin marriage is not merely a popular form of marriage within a narrow circle of consanguineous kin, but is the logical expression of a systematic communication of women among larger social groups. These social groups were originally clans, a point on which the unanimity of the sources leaves no doubt. Although signs of disintegration are to be seen in most cases, we have nevertheless found here and there, e.g., on Sumba, systems which are still almost intact; and even in Endeh, where patrilineages have taken the place of the clans, memories of the latter have still not by any means disappeared. In spite of the fact that the system is constituted primarily by a number of relationships among groups, personal relations nevertheless play a large part. Marriage with the mother's brother's daughter is, as we have seen, a consequence of group-relationships with regard to marriage. But why, one wonders, is marriage with the mother's brother's daughter obligatory (Kei, Tanimbar, Buru, Sumba) or preferred (Flores, Rote, Seran) when this girl is only one of the many potential spouses that a man possesses? On Kei and Tanimbar obligatory exclusive cross-cousin marriage is restricted to the eldest son, and on Kei such a marriage is then actually forbidden for the other sons. Notwithstanding this contraction of the working of exclusive cross-cousin marriage, it is not to be denied that the personal relationship plays a large part. But there is little to be surprised at in this, for in the last instance it is of course individuals who maintain the relationships in question. It seems self-evident that once affinal connexions have been entered into by two families, they will not quickly be abandoned or broken off. What more in accord with the entire system than that these more individual relationships should from time to time be consolidated and renewed? This happens not only through marriages, but also through a continual exchange of smaller and larger gifts. The giving of a daughter to a sister's son is naturally one of the most effective means of strengthening and perpetuating the special relationships existing between these two men. Another factor is that as the clan system falls

---

[1] Gifford, 1916, p. 139; Rivers, 1914.

more and more into disuse, so personal relationships will proportionately come to occupy a prominent place.

The prohibition of brother-and-sister exchange is of even greater general significance than exclusive cross-cousin marriage as an index of unilateral tendencies in the social structure. Such a prohibition is entailed by exclusive cross-cousin marriage, but it need not be taken always as an indication of the occurrence of exclusive cross-cousin marriage. This is why the two reports which establish the existence of a prohibition on brother-and-sister exchange on Celebes are of such great importance. In both cases the reckoning of kinship is described as being absolutely bilateral. Parallel and cross-cousins are not distinguished in any single respect, and marriage among them is out of the question. Among the Sa'dan Toradja, it is said that all cousins of the second and third degrees are permitted to marry. The very positive statements about brother-and-sister exchange among the Sa'dan Toradja are particularly noteworthy. It is striking, too, that precisely here mention is made of exclusive cross-cousin marriage. But it is certain that this discovery rests on a mistake; it seems not impossible that the indigenous informants misunderstood Kruyt, and that they intended merely to give a unilateral formulation of the prohibition on brother-and-sister exchange.

An integral system of affinal relationships based on unilaterality entails that all the clans of the tribe are linked to one another in a closed chain of marriage connexions. The number of clans involved is immaterial, i.e., so long as there are at least three: in this case, clan 1 takes wives from clan 2, this takes wives from clan 3, and the last in turn takes its wives from clan 1. If the system is to function regularly, each ego-clan will have one other as its wife-giving clan and another one as its wife-taking clan. Our factual material shows clearly that this must indeed have been the original situation. On Kei, no relationships of the traditional type can be brought about through irregular marriages; in Timor and on Buru no marriage which fell outside the system was willingly entered into. On Tanimbar, to the contrary, it appears that new alliances were purposely created.

Dual organisation of the tribe is not required by the system, but can very well accompany it. The number of clans must total at least four, and must always be even: clan 1 takes wives from 2, 2 from 3, 3 from 4, and 4 finally takes from 1. The pair of clans 1 and 3, and that of 2 and 4, constitute exogamous groups, i.e., exogamous phratries. If the number of clans comes to more than four, e.g., to six, the division into two exogamous halves is not so directly apparent but is still very probable.

The prohibition on marriage between sisters' children, similarly, need not be based primarily on a possible two-phratry exogamy, but it is certainly a consequence of the system of unilateral marriage groups. Under such a system women from any given clan always marry into one and the same other clan, and their children are thus ipso facto excluded as potential spouses.

The triad of ego-clan, wife-giving group, and wife-taking group forms a social element of great importance. As our investigation proceeds, we shall constantly find it associated with the most disparate cultural factors. From the stand-point of the ego-clan, these three groups form a complete social whole. Its entire social activity can be fully realised through the relationships with its two partner-clans. The remaining clans of the tribe appear to have no special significance for it. As far as the ego-clan is concerned, the triad is entirely self-sufficient. We have seen these relationships expressed in various social conceptions. The ego-clan occupies a position of authority over against the wife-taking group; it plays a subordinate role in relation to the wife-giving group. This duplex character of the ego-group is, as we shall see later in more detail, one of its characteristic features. The ego-group is simultaneously a wife-giving group, at once superior and subordinate, according to whether it addresses itself to the one or the other of its partners. We may recall in this connexion the conflicting evidence about the *maduan* on Kei. Geurtjens represented him to be wife-purchaser for a group, but also as representative of the wife-giving clan. If the latter is correct, we should perhaps see the *mang ohoi* in the first place as the ego-clan, with the *jan ur* on the one side as the wife-taking clan, and the *maduan* ("lord", cf. the Tanimbar *nduwe*) on the other as the wife-giving clan. This would be identical with the triad of *uranak-mirwan'awai-nduwe* on Tanimbar and that of *fet'sawa-alin maun-umah manèh* in Timor. If the system is combined with an organisation into phratries, then of course the ego-clan will belong to one phratry and its two partner-clans to the other.

In the light of these considerations, any attempt to explain exclusive cross-cousin marriage by special circumstances, particularly a potential transfer of marriage rights, can be accorded only a very limited value. The group-relationships are primary, not the particular marriage customs. A great difficulty, furthermore, is that anthropologists have set about explaining the institution in different ways according to whether it occurs in a society with patrilineal descent groups or in one with matrilineal descent groups. But the unilateral marriage system functions in exactly the same manner with either rule of descent. A matrilineal clan depends upon two other distinct clans for getting men and for "marrying them out". The chain-like system undergoes no change whatever. It is absolutely immaterial whether the principle of genealogical grouping is matrilineal or whether it is patrilineal. This provides no grounds for any increased confidence in methods of explanation which are necessarily heterogeneous. Some of these explanations are of a very hypothetical character, and others, to the extent that they are based on demonstrable marriage customs, are redundant, since the customs in question can easily be explained as variations on marriage possibilities created by relations between groups. If the marriage possibilities were primary, moreover, it would then be a very remarkable matter that nowhere do we find marriage with the father's sister's daughter reported as the exclusive form. Theoretically, such a form of marriage is entirely conceivable, but it makes a systematic ordering of affinal relationships between groups impossible; in fact, it brings these relationships into a state of total confusion. Ordinary and exclusive cross-cousin marriage are the representatives of two opposed systems of affinal relationships between groups, bilateral and unilateral respectively. In the former case brother-and-sister exchange is permitted; in the latter it is absolutely forbidden.

In the above-mentioned triads, for any individual a pair of clans form an exogamous group. For a woman under patrilineal descent, and for a man under matrilineal descent, these are the clans of the father and mother. Apart from their own clan, a man in the former case may not marry into that of his sister's husband, and a woman in the latter case may not marry into that of her brother's wife. These considerations indicate a mode of grouping in which account is taken of both unilateral-paternal and unilateral-maternal principles. Let us now see to what extent the system of unilateral affinal relationships is connected with such a double grouping.

If we take a patrilineal clan system with unilateral affinal relationships, and exclusive cross-cousin marriage as the obligatory form of marriage, then it will be noted that if a woman marries into clan A, her daughter takes a man from B, her granddaughter a man from C, and so on. As can be seen, women repeatedly marry into another clan in each succeeding generation. If there are four clans, a woman in the fifth generation marries back into clan A.

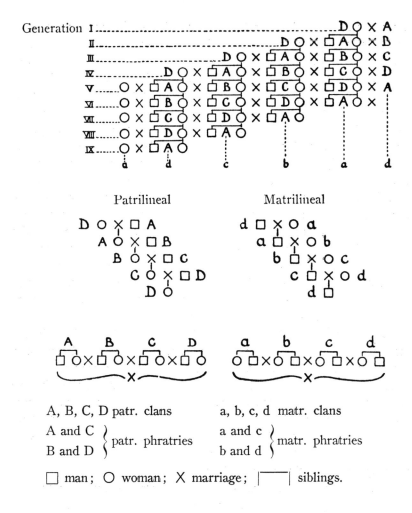

A, B, C, D patr. clans

A and C ⎱
B and D ⎰ patr. phratries

☐ man; ○ woman; ✕ marriage; |‾‾| siblings.

a, b, c, d matr. clans

a and c ⎱
b and d ⎰ matr. phratries

If this system is worked out for a complete society, the conclusion emerges that in addition to the four patrilineal clans there must also exist four exogamous matrilineal groups which are similarly connected by a chain of unilateral affinal relationships. That there are only four matrilineal groups (the same number as patrilineal) results from the circumstance that the two *A* men in the fifth generation must be identical, and must thus also belong to the same matrilineal group which marries women from matrilineal group *a*. There is no point in stating the particular features of a matrilineal organisation with unilateral affinal relationships, for we have already indicated above that for the latter system it is entirely immaterial whether the rule of

descent is matrilineal or whether it is patrilineal. In the case of matrilineal descent, a clan takes its husbands always from a certain other
clan and gives its sons to a third clan. Four successive generations of
men marry one after the other into four different matrilineal clans.
We have now brought to light a deeper reason for the fact that it
makes no difference to the system whether the rule of descent is
patrilineal or matrilineal. It is a consequence of the unilateral system
that both patrilineal and matrilineal principles of grouping co-exist
and are entirely equivalent, so that it might be called a double-unilateral
system. It is self-evident that the matrilineal clans also form moieties
by pairs of clans: a and c, b and d. It is not difficult to show that a, b,
c, and d really form exogamous matrilineal groups. The matrilineal
character of the groups is brought out simply by the figure, and the
feature of exogamy is also plain. An A man must always marry a D
woman; from group a, for example, only his mother and his sister's
daughter's daughter's daughter, together with fellow-members of their
generations, belong to D; he may not marry the former, and marriage
with the latter is practically speaking out of the question.

Such a system entails that the whole society is divided into sixteen
marriage classes (the product of the number of matrilineal clans and
the number of patrilineal clans), each comprising one generation.

The first and fifth generations (matrilineal or patrilineal) belong
to the same class. No peculiar marriage possibilities can occur, therefore, since it is naturally out of the question that the first and the fifth
generations should be alive at the same time. Marriage takes place
absolutely within the same generation, and exclusive cross-cousin
marriage is the single preferred form.

Because both the patrilineal and the matrilineal clans form exogamous
groups, pair by pair, a double two-phratry system is also entailed.
The entire society is divided into four main classes. The consequent
operation of the system is thus wholly identical with a simple four-class
system with reciprocal affinal relationships. One belongs both to the
matrilineal moiety x or y of the mother, and to the patrilineal moiety
I or II of the father. Class xI stands in a relationship of reciprocal
connubium with yII, and the children are xII or yI, which likewise
are related to each other by reciprocal connubium. The first and third
matrilineal or patrilineal generations belong to the same main class.
The difference between this system and a genuine four-class system
is constituted by the unilaterality of the affinal relationships between
the clans and by the feature of same-generation marriage.

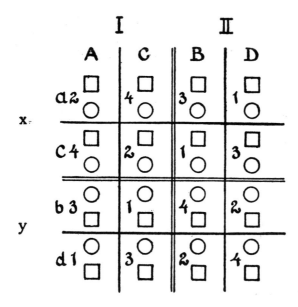

1, 2, 3, 4 consecutive generations
I, II patr. phratries
x, y matr. phratries

With an uneven number of clans (e.g., three) the system works in the same way, except that the phratry-grouping is lacking and there is no question of any correspondenec with a four-class system.

	A	B	C
a	1	3	2
b	3	2	1
c	2	1	3

In this case, the first and fourth generations belong to the same class, so that marriage possibilities here also are practically speaking confined to members of the same generation.

The system seems also to combine with patrilineal or matrilineal moieties which are not sub-divided into a number of similarly organised genealogical groups but which do contain a number of descent groups with opposite rules of descent.

	a	b	c
A	1	1	1
B	2	2	2

	A	B	C
a			
b			

Every matrilineal or patrilineal clan is divided into two classes, each of which covers more than one generation. With matrilineal moieties a man and his son's son belong to the same class, and the women-generations 1 and $n + 1$ (where n = number of patrilineal clans) belong to the same class. With patrilineal moieties, of course, the opposite obtains. Under this system peculiar marriage possibilities, between members of different generations, can arise. If the number of clans is even, then a double phratry-system once more makes its appearance. As for whether or not marriage possibilities are confined to the same generation, moreover, it appears that the system is not necessarily different from class-systems with reciprocal affinal relationships. In a certain sense the number of classes in these systems does not much matter, except in one respect, viz., whether the number of classes is a square or whether it is instead the product of two unequal numbers. In the former case same-generation marriage may be expected (with the exception of the four-class system), and in the latter case marriage possibilities between different generations.

We have seen above, however, that the unilateral system results logically in the same number of matrilineal as of patrilineal clans. It can be imagined that within the moieties other groupings may have a more or less latent existence. If there were, e.g., matrilineal moieties and four clans, then each moiety could contain two matrilineal groups, and this would be expressed by a same-generation rule of marriage. If the society is divided into an uneven number of clans (e.g., three), then such a situation is not readily conceivable.[2]

---

[2] Double clan systems have become particularly well known from Africa; cf. Luttig, 1933.

CHAPTER IV

MYTHS AND SOCIAL STRUCTURE
IN THE TIMORESE ARCHIPELAGO

The question of the number of clans into which the tribe was originally divided in Timor is more or less decisively answered in the myths. According to the origin-myth of Waihale the immigrant ancestors were divided into four "tribes" (*hutun*). Three of these *hutun* were led by brothers; the fourth had no leader. The number four also plays a great part in the Fialarang myth. The third mythical lineage, which sprang from the marriage of a brother and a sister, was made up of two brothers and two sisters, who married one another. The fourth lineage consisted of ten brothers and three sisters: the youngest became ruler of the land, five brothers went to the west, and four went to the east, of which regions they became the rulers. Nothing further is said about the three sisters. The supposition that the ruler and his three sisters were the four ancestors of Fialarang would thus seem not to be absurd. The next ruling lineage of Bauho consists again of two brothers and two sisters, and the one after this consists of one brother and three sisters. The last mythical generation is connected with the present-day order in the kingdom. The Djenilu myth, finally, tells how the four *dasi* with two sisters came out of a hole in the ground. The two sisters were carried away by birds to become the ancestresses of the ruling houses of Bauho and Vohotérin, while the fourth brother was thrown into the sea as a sacrifice. These myths thus indicate an original division of the tribe into four. This must therefore have been four clans, organised by the prevailing marriage regulations into two phratries. The concept of the triad of groups as the model of social completeness is also present in the myths. In Waihale, only three of the clans had heads; in Djenilu, the fourth brother, representative of the fourth clan, was thrown into the sea. This propensity for tripartition is not limited just to the organisation of one's own tribe, but can be seen in the myth to extend over a larger area, and inter-tribal relationships are also brought together within this framework. In the Fialarang myth the kingdom in question is centrally placed between the western lands of the second group, and the eastern areas of the third group into which the children of the ruling house were divided, namely the regions of Okkes and Vohorua. The Djenilu myth likewise recognises the following tripartition: one's own land (under the brothers), Fialarang (under a sister), and Vohotérin (under the other sister).

The present-day situation indicates almost everywhere a significant expansion in the number of clans (districts) per tribe (kingdom), and a number which, with only few exceptions, is always even. We have shown above that the kingdom divided into districts is genetically related to the tribe divided into clans. An indication in this direction is similarly to be found in the organisation of the kingdom of Lidak, which is called *fukun lima* because in addition to the principal ruler there are five *datu fukun* who also hold the reins of government. In this case, therefore, the largest component parts of the kingdoms are indeed descent groups. In the other kingdoms of north Tétun the situation is such that the district comprises various *fukun*, so that the kingdom has acquired something of the character of a federation. Practically nothing is known about the connexions between the marriage customs and the district, the territory under a *datu ferikatua*, and the *fukun*. The most that can be inferred from the little information available is that commoners usually marry within the district, whereas the traditional inter-relationships of the districts (clans) are perhaps perpetuated by the affinal relationships of the rulers. The federational character is most prominent in "the Liurai": Waihale, Waiwiku, Haitimu, and Fatu Aruin. The component parts appear here to be completely independent kingdoms. Waihale (the senior among them) is governed by a principal ruler and three "lesser radjas"; Waiwiku has four "children". This elevation of the status of the component districts (for this is what the development really amounts to) need not, of course, add by one to the step-wise internal division of the kingdom into social units of decreasing span. The six parts of Waiwiku, and the four districts of Waihale, can very well be identical with the districts, under one *datu ferikatua*, into which Fialarang, for example, is divided. As we have already said, what is at issue is more a formal raising of the status of the various segments than an actual expansion and growth. "The Liurai" is often denoted as Waiwiku-Waihale, and the absence of a distinctive name for the kingdom is perhaps a sign of a genuine federation. The idea of a federation is strongly contradicted, however, by the state of affairs in Fialaring, where eastern Fialarang and western Fialarang have more and more assumed the character of independent kingdoms, and where the idea of two earlier independent kingdoms is out of the question.

The kingdom of Fialarang is at present divided, according to tradition, into twelve districts: a father, a mother, and the children (the *dasi sanulu*). In reality, as we have seen, there are only eleven districts. It cannot be said with certainty whether the twelfth district, Lasaka, ever really existed, but doubtless the propensity for arriving at an even number of districts, as in all other kingdoms of the area, plays a considerable part. This gives expression to the structural tendencies to dual organisation which are characteristic of these kingdoms. A tribe consisting of an even number of clans is divided into exogamous phratries by the system of unilateral affinal alliances. The districts of the kingdom of Fialarang are split into two groups: eastern Fialarang and western Fialarang. It is plain from the role of their respective ancestors that this organisation goes back to a former phratry-dualism. The ancestors of the districts of western Fialarang (Bauho, Klusin, Dafala, Manuk Lètèn, Umak Laran, and Sorbau) are members of the same mythical patrilineage, whereas the ancestors of the districts in the other half of the kingdom (Lassiolat, Asumanu, Tohé, Maumutin, and Aitōn) came to belong to the kingdom in other ways. Lassiolat and Asumanu are related to Bauho by marriages with daughters of the Bauho lineage, and Tohé by the marriage of its ruler to a woman from Lassiolat. The two others are said to have made submission of their own will .The opposition is very clear in other respects as well. Whereas the Bauho moiety came down from the Lekaan mountain, the heads of Lassiolat and Asumanu emerged from a hole in the ground. The two halves are thus conceptually associated with sky and earth, an opposition typical of phratry-dualism. The inferior position of the rulers of Lassiolat and Asumanu is made abundantly clear in the myth: they are extremely pitiable and down-trodden beings who are struck with fear and consternation at the sight of the representatives of the other moiety — so much so that they piss themselves with fright. Such an opposition between an inferior earth-phratry and a superior sky-phrarty is a characteristic phenomenon of social dualism. Although the thirteen members of the third generation, who divide themselves into three groups, express rather more the opposition between the kingdom and the other kingdoms, there are certain particulars to be remarked which are of interest in this connexion. The ten sons and three daugh-

ters apparently represent the twelve-fold kingdom of Fialarang, to
which there is added a thirteenth which symbolises its unity. This is
a procedure which we shall repeatedly encounter. In the myth the
youngest brother seizes the kingdom for himself through his greater
ability and cunning and by his capacity for correctly assessing things
in nature which were unknown to him and his brothers, whereas the
stupidity and limited vision of the older brothers appear on the contrary in a glaring light. It is plain that this myth sets out a traditional
distinction in the abilities of the two phratries such as we are familiar
with from elsewhere. The reconnaissances of the brothers through the
new world, by which things are named and their uses defined, may be
seen as a sort of work of "transformation", the result of which
is determined by the activities, working in opposite direction, of the
"transformers" belonging to the two phratries. This co-operative labour
is at the same time a conflict. If the younger brother claims anything,
the older brothers are ready to deny it to him or to put a doubtful
cast on the issue. Thus when he showed that honey-combs could be
eaten, they wanted to show that they could not, and to this end caught
some bees by which they were severely stung. The youngest brother
then drove the bees away with a smoking piece of wood, and was easily
able to lay hands on the bees' nest. When another such case arose,
he stipulated that if he were in the right he should become ruler.[1] It
is remarkable that all nine brothers leave for other parts, while only
the youngest stays behind with his three sisters. One's own land is
thus associated with the feminine, whereas strange lands, on the
contrary, are associated with the masculine. The most esoteric part of
this myth is marked by the same opposition. It appears that the first
human pair were a woman who came out of Lekaan and a man who
came from a foreign country overseas. Here we may see the union of
two primal elements, the feminine earth and the masculine sky, from
out of which everything has been produced. The association of the
woman with the earth out of which she emerged is clear, and the
equation of "from a foreign country", "overseas", and "sky" will be
met with a number of times.

At the present, six districts belong to the Bauho half of the kingdom,
and five to Lassiolat. The twelfth district, Lasaka, was added to Bauho
after the ruler of that district had been murdered by the *astanara* because of his cruelty. In the myth also Lasaka is named together with

---

[1] Grijzen, 1904, p. 27.

Bauho. The fact, however, that the principal ruler took up arms against Lasaka would be more fitting if this district belonged to the other half of the kingdom, in which case, moreover, the districts would be more equally distributed between the two halves. In the myth there are at first only Bauho and Klusin standing in opposition to Lassiolat and Asumanu. It is not until the last mythical generation that Bauho is expanded by five districts. The three districts of Tohé, Maumutin, and Aitōn play no part whatever in the real myth; their existence is stated and explained quite separately. The conclusion forces itself upon us that Bauho, Klusin, Lassiolat, and Asumanu represent the four clans into which Fialarang was originally divided, and that only later did these increase to the present twelve districts. We have already pointed out that in the present day western Fialarang and eastern Fialarang have more or less assumed the character of independent petty kingdoms; perhaps the last generation in the myth reflects the modern division of western Fialarang into six, the so-called *rin besin hāt* or *umah hāt*. This would also explain the hesitation between six and seven districts. The six brothers represent the six districts of eastern Fialarang, to which there is added a seventh which stands for their unity. We shall meet elsewhere other cases of a six-seven division.

It should be pointed out that the value-contrast between Bauho and Lassiolat is purely traditional. Lassiolat, in fact, came to occupy an exceptional position, because of the size of its population, and over-shadowed all the other districts with its power. The rulers of Bauho and Lassiolat, also, were the only ones in the whole of Fialarang who still belonged to the *dasi*-class.

We have a rather more detailed myth also concerning Djenilu, which like Fialarang is divided into two halves: the coastal region, the land of the seven *datu*, and the mountains, the land of the four *datu*. The ancestors of the four *datu* came out of a hole in the ground, and the last woman ruler of this region married the ruler of the coastal part. Evidently, therefore, the half of the kingdom which lies in the mountains represents the old earth-phratry, and the other half the sky-phratry. Perhaps the tradition which makes the first inhabitants of Djenilu come from overseas refers more particularly to the coastal region. What we find, then, is exactly the same opposition as in the Fialarang myth: the familiar and indigenous is associated with the feminine and is opposed to what is strange, which is associated with the masculine. The myth of the man with seven heads who changed

into six white women and one man clearly typifies the exceptional position of the seventh as representing unity. The opposition between white women and black men, who marry one another, is undoubtedly connected with the classifications which always accompany phratry-dualism. The man fishing for his daughter, who has taken the shape of a fish, perhaps represents once more the union of those two beings from whom humanity derives its existence. It is quite clear that the daughter stands for the better half in this dualism, for it is her directions that the man must follow in order to obtain the desired result, whereas previously his attempts had remained fruitless.[2]

The three important functionaries in a kingdom — the principal ruler, his right hand (the *fettor*), and the war-leader — can readily be explained by reference to the marriage system with its central three-clan grouping. The position of the principal ruler as central figure in the kingdom is indisputable, and can also be seen from the titles of the two other dignitaries, who are his "right hand" and "left hand". It is highly likely that the ruler is the representative of the ego-clan, and that his co-officials are conceptually associated with the clans which are affinally related to the ego-clan. In the Fialarang myth, the head of Lassiolat owes his important office as left hand to his marriage with the sister of the *astanara*. There is a great obstacle in the way of this conception, of course, in the fact that *astanara* and *fettor* both belong to the western Fialarang group, which we have identified with the superior sky-phratry. According to the interpretation just advanced, the *fettor* and the *surik ulun* should in fact both belong to one phratry, and the *astanara*, as representative of the ego-clan, to the other. But we should not lose sight of the fact that this attribution of functions has no more than a purely traditional character, and is based on the classificatory principles which result from the unilateral system of marriage possibilities. The connexions and relationships in question no longer rest on actual affinal relationships or on a still-existing phratry-system. The forms are undoubtedly determined, however, by the same structural tendencies as were manifested in the former tribe with its probable division into four clans. In Djenilu, as a matter of fact, the ruler and his right hand seem indeed to have belonged to opposite dual divisions.

We have already stressed the duplex character of each group which forms part of a chain linked by unilateral affinal alliances. Seen objec-

----

2 Jansen, 1895, p. 10.

tively, the *alin maun* belong to one phratry and its *fettoh sawa* and *umah manèh* to the other. Subjectively, however, seen from the point of view of the ego-clan, *fettoh sawa* and *umah manèh* stand for opposed aspects of the social dualism. The arbitrary isolation of one triad from the series unavoidably leads to all sorts of hesitations, shifts, and ambiguities.

The inter-relations of *astanara*, *surik ulun*, and *fettor* are certainly determined by the more subjective view. The principal ruler, representative of the ego-group, should not be seen primarily in opposition to *fettor* and *surik ulun*, but as the central, more or less ambiguous, figure by reference to whom the opposed activities of the left hand and the right hand must be explained. From this point of view, the opposition of *surik ulun* and *fettor* is clear: the former belongs to the earth-phratry, the latter to the sky-phratry. Making war, therefore, is evidently a responsibility of the earth-phratry, whereas active control and administration is the task of the other.

Next to these two active figures, and in opposition to them, stands the principal ruler, who plays a completely passive role. The contrast between the ruler and his two co-officials in this respect is very striking. No special function is assigned to the *astanara* of Fialarang, and only exceptionally does he take any part in the government of his kingdom. He is supposed to be of too elevated a status to involve himself personally in the conduct of affairs. The only way in which this "rex otiosus" really makes his mark is by just existing. But he is not merely an unimportant ornament, in the structure of the kingdom. The supernatural powers which he possesses and manipulates are of the greatest importance for the survival of the kingdom. The myth depicts in bright colours the fear and consternation of the heads of Lassiolat and Asumanu, who are also very moved, at the sight of the ruler and his regalia, the bearers of his supernatural power. The subjection of these two heads is brought about more directly, also, by the display of the sacred objects. The sacred emblems of office possessed by minor rulers come in part from the principal ruler, and their holders owe their legality to the possession of them. In this way the powers issuing from the principal ruler pervade the entire kingdom and thus maintain the system. The ruler of Waihale, the *meromak o'an*, controls rainfall and drought, and good fortune or adversity in war, by means of the sacred objects brought by his ancestor from the mythical land of origin; he can also cause and continue epidemics among men and animals, and make the crops flourish or fail. By his simple existence he maintains the kingdom in order; he represents the religious powers of the entire society. The principal ruler is to be seen as the personification of the kingdom, particularly today the totality of the local communities from which the opposed powers of *surik ulun* and *fettor*, each of whom represents one of the local-cosmic phratries, derive their origin. He represents the higher unity in which both the heavenly and the earthly are conjoined. Each of his instruments, the *surik ulun* and the *fettor*, belongs to another phratry, while the principal ruler occupies a position between them. He is not only *nai lulik*, "sacred lord", but also *rai nain*, "lord of the earth". Perhaps the *rai o'an*, the "children of the ground", should be seen as his representatives in the earthly sphere. We know nothing about them except that they have a function to fulfil on the occasion of sacrifice to the local spirits of the kingdom or the district. Both the principal ruler and the *rai o'an* are thus associated with the religious powers of the local community, but the heavenly aspect predominates in the former, the earthly in the latter.

Together with this conception of the ruler as representative of a twofold unity there exists also that of the *astanara* as the "mother", the feminine, versus the *fettor*, as "father", the masculine. These persons thus compose the married couple of which the other districts are the "children". In connexion with this dualistic conception we should like to stress once more the difference between the attribution of a sexual character to social groups and the phratry-organisation in a society with unilateral affinal relationships. Membership of one or other phratry is absolute, whereas the ascription of a sex to a special group is relative and depends on the standpoint adopted. A group is masculine for its *umah manèh*, but the same group is feminine for its *fettoh sawa* (cf. the Tanimbar classification). This is unaffected by the circumstance that one phratry is regarded as feminine and the other as masculine. Thus from the standpoint of the "child" Lassiolat the Bauho group, as *umah manèh*, are feminine, and the Klusin group, as *fettoh sawa*, are masculine, which thus corresponds to the conception of the *astanara* as the mother and the *fettor* as the father of the family. For Klusin, however, Bauho are in fact masculine. The opposition between Bauho and Klusin corresponds perfectly with the triad which has been outlined, in which Bauho appears as the ego-group. We have already pointed out the remarkable anomaly that Bauho and Klusin belong to the same local-cosmic grouping, and we have made certain preliminary observations on the fact. Let us now go rather more deeply into the matter. We know that the ruler of Lassiolat was occampanied by a *mak o'an*, a "speaker". He appeared as the right hand of the ruler and was the one who gave out the orders. Grijzen refers to him as being knowledgeable in the traditions and customary law as well.[3] With this "speaker", therefore, a fourth official makes his entry in the polity of Fialarang. In the light of everything that we know about the structure of the kingdom of Fialarang, it seems not unlikely that this *mak o'an*, like the three other officials, is ruler of his own district. This district could in this case be no other than Asumanu, which plays an important part in the myths next to Bauho, Klusin, and Lassiolat. Here we see once more how an original fourfold division has been supplanted by a tripartition under the influence of a preference for triads brought about by the unilateral alliance system. It may be wondered, also, whether the *mak o'an* is a traditional dignitary or whether he only made his appearance when eastern Fialarang began to arrogate to itself the style of an independent kingdom. As far as the latter process is concerned, it should be pointed out that the links between the parts of the kingdom, which for the most part are of a merely traditional nature, have been considerably under-estimated by the ethnographers, who have overly directed their attention to actual relationships of political power. This, together with data from else-where (Kei, Tanimbar, the kingdom of Amanuban-Amanatun in Timor) which we shall discuss below, leads to the conclusion that the *mak o'an* was indeed a traditional functionary. This fourth dignitary is of great importance in connexion with the Bauho-Klusin opposition, which apparently conflicts with the local-cosmic phratry-dualism. The strong impression is given that the local dual division into eastern and western Fialarang is not yet expressed, and that we are dealing here, not with a single, but with a double dual division. On the one hand there is that of Bauho and Klusin in opposition to Lassiolat and Asumanu, a division which is perpetuated in the local groupings of eastern and western Fialarang. On the other, the rulers of Bauho and Lassiolat can be taken together in opposition to the *fettor* of Klusin and the *mak o'an* (of Asumanu?). Both groups possess more than enough common features to permit this procedure. Both Bauho and Lassiolat have a principal ruler, and at present these are the only *dasi*-rulers in Fialarang. The *fettor* and the *mak o'an* have in common an active character, chiefly in their governmental functions; each is the right hand of his ruler. Their titles are different, however, and

---

[3] Grijzen, 1904, p. 129.

also it is not explicitly said that the *fettor* is "speaker" or that he is repository of "customary law and traditions". Perhaps these latter functions belong rather to the earth-phratry, to which both Lassiolat and the *mak o'an* belong, whereas only the governmental function is reported for Klusin, which together with Bauho makes up the sky-half. This last dual division has mainly a local character; the dualistic ordering of the rulers in opposition to their *fettor* "right hands" is of more than a social nature. In this context, the opposition of Bauho and Klusin as feminine and masculine groups, even though they belong to the same (local) half of the tribe, is no longer surprising, and the classification into masculine and feminine also acquires a more positive character.

		Social	
		Astanara	*Fettor*
	Sky	Bauho	Klusin
Local			
	Earth	Lassiolat	Asumanu (?)
		Surik ulun	*Mak o'an*
		Feminine	Masculine
		Ruler	Right hand

An arrangement of this kind, placing Bauho and Lassiolat together in opposition to Klusin and Asumanu, answers entirely to the present situation, and the exceptional position of Lassiolat may be seen in the myth. This last point is not absolutely correct, however, for in the mythical genealogy Asumanu is named a generation earlier than Lassiolat, i.e., in the same generation which also produced the *fettor* of Klusin. The meeting between Bauho and Asumanu is thus placed before that of Bauho with Lassiolat. Asumanu ought thus to occupy a higher and more important rank than Lassiolat. Perhaps, therefore, we should view the supremacy of the latter district as a later development. In favour of this inference there is the circumstance that the preponderance of Lassiolat is generally ascribed to the size of its population and its power, i.e., to accidental factors. It is conceivable that the *surik ulun* of Lassiolat and the *mak o'an* (of Asumanu?) should exchange places in the figure, from which it would follow that know-ledge of customary law and traditions would be classified as a feminine good, and war-making as a masculine activity, which seems more probable than the reverse.

The social dualism of ruler and right hand seems better able to provide an explanation of the constantly even number of "children" than does the local dual division. The traditional conception of a kingdom as consisting of an even number of districts has its roots in the idea of a family with children, and thus in a dual division of social functions. That this grouping cross-cuts the local grouping is confirmed by the conception of western Fialarang as a petty kingdom consisting of a father, a mother, and four children. The local organi-sation conflicts, however, with the traditional symmetrical speculations; at the present day, eastern Fialarang contains five districts and western Fialarang six; according to the myth it is supposed originally to have counted seven of the twelve districts. We have found a similar uneven division of a number of districts between the two halves of a kingdom in Djenilu as well, where the coastal stretch, the land of the seven *datu*, is opposed to the mountain region, which is the territory of the four *datu*. We have already pointed out that a fifth or seventh group is often added to a society originally divided into four or six in order to symbolise the unity of the whole. In both Fialarang and Djenilu we find the same opposition between a four-five group and a six-seven group, in which the former represents the inferior and the latter the superior half in the local-cosmic dualism. We wish to make it abundantly plain that such divisions into four-five or six-seven groups are mostly of a purely traditional kind, and often do not at all correspond to actuality. The role of Lasaka as the seventh district of western Fialarang is particularly instructive in this regard, and once more throws a clear light upon the two-fold character of the principal ruler. Although he chiefly represents the sky-phratry in the religious context, he belongs to the feminine half in the dual division by social function and is the mother of the family. We have already drawn attention to the fact that such a conflict as that between *astanara* and Lasaka might rather be expected between groups belonging to different halves of the kingdom than between members of the same local-cosmic group. It now seems very plausible to connect the antagonism between the two groups with the dualism of social function which cross-cuts the local-cosmic dualism. But the relationship between Bauho and Lasaka is also of great importance in another way. Bauho, as principal ruler, and Lasaka, as the seventh district, both represent unity, the former with reference to the whole of Fialarang and the latter more particularly with reference to western Fialarang. This straightaway provides the explanation for the conjunction of the two areas. Lasaka-Bauho together stand for a two-fold unity conceived in strongly antagonistic terms. Lasaka is the malicious element, Bauho is the benevolent and beneficent element, and both factors are united in the person of the *astanara*. In a sense, it might be said that Lasaka has never existed and that it still continues to exist. It is the traditional mythical reflection of the two-fold unity. In the generation in which the ruler of Lasaka is named for the first time, he is really, as we have already remarked, a double of the *fettor* of Klusin. The opposition thus apparently refers back to the mother-father unity of *astanara* and *fettor*.

The four petty kingdoms of Waihale, Waiwiku, Fatu Aruin, and Haitimu are conjoined into a larger unity, "the Liurai", the structure of which is modelled in complete concordance with the ancient myth of the tribe. Three of them have parts to play, whereas the fourth, Haitimu, has sunk into unimportance and obscurity. Waihale, with its *meromak o'an*, is the superior in spiritual authority among the other three, but as far as the exercise of real power is concerned it plays merely a passive part. Actual power is divided between Fatu Aruin and Waiwiku: the former fills the well-known office of right hand to the ruler, but Waiwiku has arrogated to itself, by its own power, the foremost place in this little confederation. "Waiwiku is more of a burden than a pleasure for Waihale," says Grijzen.[4] According to the myth, the present Fatu Aruin was the anonymous fourth member of the set of groups; it and Haitimu thus seem to have exchanged their roles. Should we now see the peculiar structure of this confederation of petty kingdoms as the result of a culture-psychological process, or simply as the result of an historical process of development in which each of the kingdoms grew out of one of the former clans? The ethnographic evidence does not permit a definite answer, but even so it is clear that the organisation of the Liurai corresponds completely with that of Fialarang. The elementary four-fold division of the tribe or kingdom, which we have thought it possible to postulate, is expressly confirmed here by the myth and still continues to exist in the structure of the largest unit, as well as in that of the mother-kingdom Waihale.

---

4 1904, p. 24.

This grouping is largely overshadowed, both in the myth and in present-day reality, by a division into three. We have already demonstrated that the model for such triads is given by the system of unilateral affinal alliances. The two younger of the three tribal ancestors represent, with respect to the oldest brother, who occupies a central place, the opposed powers of the two phratries, the action of which stems from the presence of the ego-group, the two-fold unity. These two brothers are undoubtedly identical with the culture-heroes Datu Makérik and Datu Bédain, who initiated the building of wooden ships at Ninobé-rai-hènèk. The meaning of the name of the former (carved out, spotted, sly, crafty) clearly betrays the character of these two "sub-chiefs" as representatives of the two phratries; we merely point out the significance of the crafty younger brother, who plays a part in the Fialarang myth. Considered more objectively, the eldest brother and the nameless fourth belong to one half, and the two other brothers to the other. The close link between Waihale and Fatu Aruin appears from the fact that a son of the *meromak o'an* later became *liurai* of Fatu Aruin. The petty kingdoms of Waihale and Fatu Aruin, lying to the east, are thus opposed to Waiwiku and Haitimu, which are placed to the west.

W.	*E.*	
Haitimu	Fatu Aruin	*N.*
Waiwiku	Waihale	*S.*

Mythical division of the Liurai

Waiwiku, which came to the fore through its own power, thus occupies in this respect a completely analogous position to that of Lassiolat in Fialarang; only the title and the formal function are lacking. If Fialarang provided grounds for the inference that Lassiolat had supplanted Asumanu, here we find that Waiwiku in the myth already takes a higher position than Haitimu, since it has an elder brother as its head. "The Liurai" is often denoted by the double name of Waiwiku-Waihale. This undoubtedly expresses the conception of the kingdom as a dual unity with Waiwiku and Waihale as its component parts. The antagonism between the two kingdoms, reported by Grijzen, forms an essential element, as we shall repeatedly see, in the sphere of dual division. The use of the name Waiwiku-Waihale for the whole "Liurai" may be an indication that they are thought of together in opposition to Fatu Aruin and Haitimu. This would make the shifts of power within the latter group more understandable.

There thus exists in the "Liurai" the very same opposition of an eastern group and a western group as in Fialarang. In contrast to the situation in that kingdom, it is the eastern group here which enjoys the greater respect. That the division by east and west is primary, and not that by north and south, emerges incontestably from the myth, according to which the eldest brother settles in the east and the two others in the west. The Fialarang dual division by social function is also encountered in "the Liurai". On the one side stand the rulers of Waiwiku and Waihale, on the other side the *liurai* of Fatu Aruin and the unimportant Haitimu, the former in the south, the latter in the north. The various alterations in function and character are natural consequences of the conflicting elements proper to the triadic grouping. We should recall, finally, that Waihale is divided into four and Waiwiku into six. In the relationship between the two territories there thus appears the very same opposition, in this case of a four-group and a six-group, as in the local dualism of Djenilu and Fialarang, and one to which the relationship of the eastern group and the western group in "the Liurai" entirely corresponds. Unlike the situation in the two kingdoms of north Tétun, the part of "the Liurai" under the principal ruler contains the smaller number of groups.

There is a great similarity on a number of points between the structure of Sonnebait and the structures of the kingdoms described above. Sonnebait comprises a number of political territories, nearly all of which have now assumed the character of independent states. These, in their turn, include a number of districts. The reports of Steinmetz relate to parts of Sonnebait, and also to kingdoms (Insana, Beboki) which belong ethnographically, if not linguistically, to the northern Tétun area. This author calls the districts *klune* (Beboki) and *nakaf* (Insana, Mio Maffo), and defines them as complexes of several *fukun* (Insana, Beboki), *kanan*, or *loppo* (Mio Maffo), which are "families in the wider sense". The district is headed by a *fettor*, who thus indubitably corresponds to the *datu ferikatua* reported by Grijzen for north Tétun. As far as Insana and Beboki are concerned, such a comparison affords no special insights. But in Sonnebait there may be found a situation analogous to that in "the Liurai": the *fettor* in Sonnebait are the same officials as the "lesser radjas" who in Waihale govern next to the ruler. In discussing "the Liurai" we were unable to give any answer to the question whether this social unit was a genuine federation, one modelled on the old tribal myth, or one which was gradually built up from the parts of a single tribe. The information on Sonnebait points unmistakably in the latter direction. The emancipation of the larger territories was necessarily accompanied by a rise in the position of the district heads. The ruler and his *fettor* now occupy the same positions as did earlier (and still do today in central Timor) the ruler of the kingdom and his district heads. Although the reports of Krayer van Aalst apparently refer more especially to the southern kingdoms, his statements about the *kana luan* (patrilineal clans) seem to be applicable to Sonnebait as well. We do not know, however, whether these *kana luan* are identical with the *kanan* of Steinmetz. There is thus the same descending series as in central Timor, viz., kingdom-territory-district-descent group, which precisely as in "the Liurai" presents itself as a series: federation-kingdom-territory-district. This, however, is merely a question of nomenclature and, from the indigenous point of view, of social rank. Essentially, the corresponding units in the two series are completely identical.

The Sonnebait myth places in mythical prehistory a kingdom called Labala, the original four-fold division of which gave way to a division into three. In the myth this is the result of an incursion by three brothers from Waiwiku-Waihale, before whom the four brothers who first ruled the kingdom had to flee. All the myths recognise Waiwiku-Waihale as the land of origin of the rulers; this reflects the great influence of "the Liurai" in this part of Timor, which culminated in a sort of spiritual supremacy of the *meromak o'an*. The treasures which the eldest brother seized are of course the regalia with which we have become familiar, the bearers of the supernatural power of the principal ruler, objects to which his central position in the kingdom was irrefragably connected. Next to and under him there are two brothers, who, as we have seen, are the opposed aspects of the power of the central figure. The opposition of the two brothers is clear: one takes the women, and the other takes the land. The associations behind this are not so obvious as elsewhere. Perhaps the former should be seen as the masculine element, and the latter as the feminine. The tendency towards systematisation in the myth is most remarkable: Foan takes the land that must be divided among the brothers; he is associated with the land as a totality. Likewise, the presumption is readily suggested that one of the two women whom Benu appropriated has to marry Foan. The second version of this myth is confined to placing the two brothers in opposition to each other, and setting out their differently directed activities. The relationship of rivalry, which is one of the most typical features of the two-phratry system, makes an unmistakable appearance. This myth gives Sonnebait its paramount and central place in the inter-relationship of kingdoms conceived as a triple unity (at least in the first version), and so provides a basis for its external activities (both versions).

The next myth, on the contrary, deals with the internal structure of the kingdom of Sonnebait. The first point of difference between the two myths is that when Sonnebait sets about establishing external relations he is the eldest brother, but that in the mythical description of events within the tribe he appears as the youngest brother. The separate treatment of the other two brothers is perfectly clear from what we have learned elsewhere. The adventure of the youngest brother with the Kune girls can be seen as the mythical reflection of an ancient initiation-rite, such as has been convincingly demonstrated by Rassers.[5] The duplex character proper to the ruler is also indubitably expressed here. The mythical story depicts the relationship of Tai Belek both to what is of the earth and to what is of the sky; his nature partakes of both elements. These two conceptions, of initiation and two-fold nature, are not necessarily mutually exclusive. It has indeed been proposed that conferring an ambiguous character on a novice (in the sense of making him bisexual) may be seen as the central element of any initia-tion-rite.[6] Kune, who plays no part in this myth, sees the occupation of his place by Tai Belek as perfectly self-evident. In the last story he appears in the sharpest opposition to Sonnebait, but here he remains more or less in the background as the unknown fourth. The familiar conceptions which appear to be inherent in the sphere of dual division are again expressed in the names of the two brothers and the deeds on which they are based. The elder brother, If Belek, got the name of "spring" from the spring which came up where he stuck his spear into the ground. Fai Belek was the only one who could cast his spear right over Kune's house, and he thus acquired the name "right over". Plainly, therefore, the former is associated with the earth, and the latter with the sky. It further appears from the myth that the sources of the Noni river are to be found in the Mollo mountains (Mollo is the territory of the elder brother). This may of course have given rise to the association, but it furnishes absolutely no explanation of the mythical

---

[5] Rassers, 1922; 1925, p. 311. An account of these important works is to be found in De Josselin de Jong (1933, p. 174).
[6] Winthuis, 1928.

complex as a whole. We shall also see, furthermore, that the rulers primarily have the power to give and to withhold water and rain.

In the last myth two concepts appear to the forefront in a most explicit fashion, viz., that the ruler does not belong unconditionally to the good and superior, and that he is essential. The former is displayed by the way in which Sonnebait forces people to subject themselves to him, by damming the sources of the river, and thus acquires power over them. The myth speaks of the causing of a flood, but one would think rather of the contrary, the cutting-off of the water supply. If we are correct in our opinion that If Belek is associated with the earth, this should be seen as an indication of Sonnebait's two-fold character. His interference with the sources of the Noni river would then be an expression of his activities belonging to the earthly sphere. Sonnebait's government is said to have been cruel and harsh; every year, when people brought him the produce of the land, he had one of his subjects killed in order to cool the ground. The double character of the ruler is very clearly the central element in this myth. The damming of the sources of the Noni river, just in order to secure power for himself, is the chief sign of his base and egoistical aspect. We have seen in the Fialarang myth what sentence the *astanara* carried out on the ruler of Lasaka, whose rule was similarly characterised by these qualities. But the killing of a subject in order to cool the ground should apparently be seen as being essentially a non-egoistical act, intended to do good for the benefit of the whole society. He himself was then murdered, at the instigation of the former ruler, Kune, and the result was that the unfortunate land was visited by calamities. The myth thus contrasts deeds which are alike but which are perpetrated from opposite sides: one is a sacred act, the other is born of evil intent and causes disaster. In the two-fold character of Sonnebait, therefore, it is his superiority and indispensability which predominate. As maker of the Noni river he can be seen as none other than the beneficent "transformer". If, however, we compare similar events in this myth and in that of Fialarang, then the superior character of the *astanara* is clearly displayed in contrast to the inferior character of Sonnebait. We shall return to this question again below. Kune, on the other hand, is simply the personification of the power of evil, of which his phratry is the representative. Only in this light is the short-sightedness of Kune to be understood, when he misjudged Sonnebait's actions. That Sonnebait, in this chain of events, really represents the higher aspect of a dually conceived unity-in-duality may be inferred from the fact that, in opposition to the murderers Kune and Sabat Neno, the two *fettor* Manubait of Fatu Leo and Mela of Bidjeli appear as protectors of Sonnebait. In these four figures we should undoubtedly see, after all that we have already learned, the representatives of a tribe divided into four clans grouped into two phratries. Manubait and Mela stand for the superior phratry, and Kune and Sabat Neno stand for the inferior. Sonnebait, as the fifth figure, can only represent the unity of the tribe.

Practically nothing is known about the modern organisation of Sonnebait, and we can thus add little to the foregoing general considerations. The mythical tripartition of the kingdom seems to be confirmed by reality, in that next to the ruler's own territory there are the lands of Mollo and Mio Maffo. Since the two latter districts each contain two halves, the tripartition turns into a grouping into five. Both Müller and a modern writer give the names of five districts, but their conclusions are not wholly identical. It is therefore impossible to determine how far this is an existing division, and how far it is still only traditional. As far as Sonnebait itself is concerned, we can only guess. The connexion with Fatu Leo is plain, but the place of the four main clans, Sonnebait, Sunaf, Paut, and Betin, is very obscure. The myth postulates an elementary four-fold division of the kingdom in the beginning of things, a division which was later replaced by one into three. The four-fold division is further encountered in four mythical figures: *fettor* Manubait, *fettor* Mela (= Betin),[7] Sabat Neno, and Kune. Sonnebait appears as the fifth figure, standing for unity. This conception survives in the idea of a kingdom containing five districts, one of which is Sonnebait's own territory. In addition to this local order, there are four important named clans, to which the clan of *fettor* Manubait of Fatu Leo may be added as a fifth. There can be observed here the same hesitation between a fourth and a fifth clan (Sonnebait and Manubait) as there is in Fialarang between a sixth and a seventh district (Bauho and Lasaka). In essence this is the conflict between tradition and reality. We have no data at our disposal on the dual unity of Sonnebait-Manubait. The second mythical figure who is closely connected with the principal ruler is the *fettor* Mela of Bidjeli. This *fettor* is evidently the representative of the clan Betin (= Mela), for at the present day one of the members of this clan is still *fettor* of Bidjeli. The inference is plain that Sabat Neno and Kune, the enemies of Sonnebait, represent the clans Sunaf and Paut. These two would

---

[7] The name Betin or Bitin was later changed to Mela.

then form the inferior and lesser phratry, and Sonnebait-Manubait and Mela (Betin) would make up the superior phratry. In the district of Sonnebait two areas thus seem to play am important part, viz., Fatu Leo and Bidjeli, the areas in which the clans Sonnebait-Manubait and Mela (Betin) are dominant.

The division into districts is given in different accounts as below:

Müller (1): Oinama	Mollo Mio (Amakono)	—	—
Müller (2): Fatu Leo (Manubait)	Mollo Mio (Amakono)	Pitai	Takai
Kruyt : Fatu Leo (Manubait)	Mollo Mio (Amakono)	Bidjoba	Takai

Nothing is known about the connexion between the descent system and the local organisation. It can be presumed that Fatu Leo and Bidjeli formed one half, and Mollo and Mio Maffo the other half, of a tribe originally divided into four, and that the tripartition arose through the conception of Fatu Leo and Bidjeli as a unitary group under Sonnebait. The dual division of Mollo and Mio Maffo then once more stimulated the creation of the familiar four-five grouping and at the same time ran parallel to the dual division of Sonnebait-plus-Fatu Leo and Bidjeli. On the other hand, the four districts of Mollo and Mio Maffo can in fact be seen as the continuation of the former tribe, headed by Sonnebait as the fifth local group, comprising a four-five clan organisation which likewise reflected the structure of the tribe. The lack of evidence, however, does not permit a satisfying answer, and perhaps only field research can throw any light on the question. But we have indeed been able to form a sound judgement on the nature of this form of organisation. The former tribe, divided into four and into two halves, still survives in the four-five division of the kingdom, and is also to be found unchanged in the four most prominent clans. The status of the clans is determined by the affinal relationships, about which nothing is known, though we can certainly expect a unilateral system. The establishment of this form of organisation in the myth is unmistakable, while we have already become familiar with the triad of groups as a consequence of the unilateral affinal system. The ambiguous features in the nature of the ruler spring directly from his central position, representing unity, in the triad, as well as in the four-five grouping of the whole tribe.

The four districts which together form the territories of Mollo and Mio Maffo are opposed to each other in two different ways. They can be conceived as the representatives of two local groups, Mollo and Mio

Maffo; whereas, considered functionally, in each territory one district
is responsible for defence and the other for government. Over against
the local dualism there is thus a dual division based on social function.
In order to show that the postulation of the same form of organisation
in both territories rests on more than mere juggling with words, we
need only point to Fialarang, where an entirely similar structure is
found. The two districts of one territory stand to each other in the
relationship of older and younger brother. Since the two territories
also form the halves of a larger unit, we can simply state that the local
dual division is cross-cut by a social one.

The local opposition emerges from the myth which deals with the
history of the brothers If Belek, Fai Belek, and Tai Belek. The oldest
brother, If Belek, is probably associated with the earth, as we have
seen, and gets Mollo as his territory; the younger brother, Fai Belek,
is connected with the sky, and Mio Maffo becomes his region. It can
therefore be seen that the local halves, precisely as in Fialarang, are
linked with opposed cosmic phenomena, while in this case it further
appears that the earth is regarded as the older of the two and the sky
as the younger. The local organisation thus has its roots primarily in
a cosmic classification, whereas the functional opposition in Fialarang
was connected with a division according to sex. Concerning Mollo and
Mio Maffo, we learn only that the oldest brother was responsible for
defence, and the youngest for the government of the territory. In the
relationship between Fatu Leo and Bidjeli, however, we come once
more upon the relationship between the sexes. As we have seen, these
areas belong to the same group, which is associated with the sky. Mela,
the name of the *fettor* of Bidjeli, was formerly Betin or Bitin, which
means vagina, so he is plainly associated with the feminine. Manubait
and Mela might well indeed be considered as the father and mother
of Sonnebait, for it is they who find the child, and Mela who brings
it up. Manubait is extremely closely connected with Sonnebait, and
Mela is the important *fettor*. Apart from the fact that the association
with the sexes is just the opposite of that in Fialarang, this corresponds
entirely to the opposition between the ruler and the right hand.

The functions of defence and government, which we find referred
to Mollo and Mio Maffo, are of course identical with those of the
surik ulun and the *fettor* in Fialarang, and can be ascribed to Waiwiku
and Fatu Aruin in "the Liurai". As representatives of the opposed
powers originating in the ruler, their tasks can be seen to be coupled
with both the local dualism of earth/sky and the social dualism of

masculine/feminine. The shifts in position of Asumanu-Lassiolat and Haitimu-Fatu Aruin find their explanation here. We have already pointed out that such shifts are an essential and characteristic feature of the organisation into triads. Such displacement can also be remarked in Mollo and Mio Maffo. There is a division by social function, with reference to the older and younger brothers, in addition to the local organisation. As a consequence of the rise in status of these territories into more or less independent kingdoms, the dual division of each territory within itself changed in nature and shows a correspondence with, for example, the division into eastern and western Fialarang.

With regard to the distinction of older brother and younger brother, it is to be remarked that this, just like the association with masculine or feminine, is of a relative kind, and depends on the standpoint adopted by the observer. It is reported, for example, that in Amfoan the oldest brother is responsible for "external politics" and the youngest for "internal government". This is thus the same opposition as that between defence and government in Mollo and Mio Maffo. We read, furthermore, that the older brother has moral authority and the younger the real power. If we consider the position in "the Liurai", we see at once that Waiwiku is younger than Waihale, but older than Fatu Aruin:

Younger	Older		
Government	Defence		
Fatu Aruin	Waiwuku	Waihale	
	Younger	Older	
	Real power	Moral authority	

Fatu Aruin participates, however, in the moral position of Waihale, and the latter in the governmental function of Fatu Aruin. This intimate relationship has been brought out clearly in the myth. The oldest and the youngest of the four constitute a kind of unity, and the difference in age seems to be not only a relative distinction but also an absolute one. This may be seen in the first two Sonnebait myths. When it is a matter of formulating external relations, Sonnebait appears as the oldest of three brothers (the elder of two, in one version), but in the myth which deals with the internal organisation of the kingdom he is, on the contrary, the youngest. Correspondingly, in the third myth Sonnebait in a younger brother of the *liurai*, since in this inter-tribal context the latter occupies the foremost position. In the Fialarang myth, although the older brothers leave for other parts in order to set up kingdoms of their own, the beginning of it deals indubitably with the internal structure, and here the older brothers have to acknowledge the youngest as ruler of the kingdom. It is evident that no solution to the difficulty can be arrived at by explanations based on individual psychology. If it were argued that it is very plausible for the most important kingdom to be established by the oldest brother, then the peculiar superior position of the youngest brother inside the kingdom would remain extremely puzzling. To stress the psychological fascination of the unexpected intellectual superiority of the youngest brother would run up against the same incongruity. This remarkable ambiguity must have its origin in the social system. After everything that has already been said about the duplex character of the principal ruler, the conception of Sonnebait as being at once oldest and youngest can be explained without difficulty. But why, one might wonder, is he in fact the oldest in the inter-tribal organisation, and the youngest in the internal structure? We have been able to relate the story of the Belek brothers above to the local-cosmic organisation, namely to the opposition of sky and earth. The sky is regarded as the younger half, and the earth as the older. The myth of the brothers Sonnebait, Benu and Foan, on the other hand, takes place in the sphere of social function, and has to do primarily with grouping by sex. It is Sonnebait who takes the regalia, while Benu and Foan take the women and the land. We have proposed that Sonnebait may be seen as representing unity, Benu the masculine, and Foan the feminine. The antagonistic conception of Sonnebait as expansive, and Amfoan as conservative, also points in the same direction. It appears, therefore, that the feminine is regarded as the oldest, and the masculine as the youngest, element in the dualism of social function. This appeared to be the case in Fialarang as well. As far as social oppositions are concerned, the principal ruler is thus the oldest and is associated with the feminine, whereas in a local-cosmic context of oppositions he is linked with the younger and the sky. Inter-tribal relations are subsumed under the former mode of classification. Here we may recall the opening part of the Fialarang myth, where the first human beings come into existence out of the union of a woman from Lekaan and a man from overseas. Here, too, the indigenous is represented as pertaining to the feminine, in contrast to the alien, which is masculine. But we can also think, in this connexion, of the union of the masculine sky with the feminine earth. The two cross-cutting dualistic conceptions appear finally, in the most esoteric part of the myth, once more to constitute a unity. This question, however, may better be dealt with in a different context, as we hope to do in another place. For the rest, it is not always possible to explain every point of difference, and every displacement, down to the smallest particular.[8] We have already stressed that such displacements are a necessary consequence of the organisation into triads. Furthermore, this dualism has to be regarded as having reached a high point of evolution, for it has become almost entirely detached from its former foundation, the descent system. In the process many entirely new elements have come within its scope, but in spite of all the variations and modifications the old structural tendencies can still be clearly recognised. It should not be lost to sight, incidentally, that a general disintegration of the cultures in question has also come about. To sum up, however, we can assert that the contrasting conceptions of the ruler as the oldest and simultaneously the youngest are based on the cross-cutting social and local dualistic tendencies. In a social context the ruler is feminine and the oldest, whereas in a local context he is the representative of the younger sky-phratry. Relationships between the different kingdoms are evidently thought of under the social aspect, in opposition to the local character of the grouping within the kingdom. This makes clear the significance which should be attached to the land seized by Foan. "Land" and "earth", that is, must be distinguished as two contrasted concepts. "Land" is a social factor, whereas "earth", on the contrary, represents one of the cosmic primal forces. As we have seen, the local organisation, and particularly the local dualism, is classified under the opposition sky/earth. The notions of territory and area thus correspond to the concept of "earth". It is clear from a number of points that this order is primarily religious, as appears particularly forcefully in the worship of the local spirits of the district or the kingdom in north Tétun. What we have referred to above as the "land" is chiefly the ground as a social-economic object. As inter-tribal relations are identified by the classifications with the dualism of social function within the tribe, the whole area of the kingdom, when this is placed in opposition to the territories of other kingdoms, falls under this social

---

[8] Thus the structure of "the Liurai", for example, seems to conflict somewhat with these conclusions, in that there the principal ruler is the eldest of the four heads. If "the Liurai" were seen as a federation, this would be entirely consistent with our contentions; but even if this is not assumed, it can still be pointed out that the ruler's half of the kingdom contains both the oldest and the youngest districts, viz., Waihale and Fatu Aruin.

classification. This topic will be examined in more detail in another connexion.

In this part of Timor the clan system survives in a better state of preservation than in the central part of the island, but almost nothing is known about the relationship between descent groups and local groups. One wonders whether the descent groups which together make up a district are entire clans or parts of clans, and whether a given clan occurs in only one district or territory. The district of Pitai is in fact also referred to as the Pitai lineage, and there is constant mention of "the Pitai". It seems not improbable that the district head is primarily head of a clan (cf. Mela, *fettor* of Bidjeli). We read in Kruyt that the district heads are the effective *pah tuaf*, and that the village heads are their deputies. They seem to have a part to play only in agricultural ceremonies.

We should like to demonstrate, finally, that the confusion concerning Amfoan is more apparent than real. The report consistently places the older Amfoan-Naklio in opposition to the younger Sorbian. The two oppositions moral authority/real power and external politics/internal government are well known to us. These two contrasts do not run parallel to each other, but they cross, and as a result certain peculiar shifts in associations can appear. That the functionaries are first located in the mountains and on the coast, and then precisely the other way round, is not a mistake in the strict sense, but is to be seen as a shift of the kind in question. This can be seen at a glance from the structural scheme of "the Liurai":

Oldest   Youngest
Moral authority — Real power   Waihale (and Fatu Aruin) — Waiwiku
Defence   — Government   Waiwiku — Fatu Aruin (and Waihale)

On a superficial inspection it would seem as if the two groups of functions are assigned similarly to the halves of the kingdom, but in the reverse order. Which of the two parts of Amfoan lies on the coast, and which in the mountains, cannot of course be made out with any certainty, but a location of the oldest in the interior is very likely. In this connexion we can point to the case of Laura, on Sumba, where such a localisation appeared to be completely traditional.

The kingdoms of Amanuban and Amanatun, on the south coast, are so closely related to each other that the conclusion forces itself upon us that they must formerly have been the two parts of a larger political unit. The myth can also be understood in the same sense, when it speaks of the division of a former kingdom between the rulers of Niki Niki (Amanuban) and Lassi. The same myth features an elementary division of this former kingdom among four *meo* (champions). Kruyt refers to Amanatun as the sister-district of Amanuban. The latter is at present divided among the ruler and three *fettor*. The kingdom contains ten or eleven clans. We do not know whether any given clan appears in only one district, but it is self-evident that each district contains a number of clans. We thus meet once more the same social orbits as in Sonnebait and in central Timor. Amanuban and Amanatun together made up the "kingdom", and each corresponds to the "territory" divided into a number of districts, each containing several descent groups. Let us merely note that the emancipation from minor unit to independent kingdom has progressed even further here than in Sonnebait. The relationship between Amanuban and Amanatun is now expressed only in myths and in a few traditional ideas and customs.

The oppositions of Amanatun/Amanuban and ruler/*mafefa* are dealt with in completely analogous fashion in myths which are practically identical. In the myth given by the *fettor* of Sahan, the relationship between the two kingdoms is typified by that between two strangers. One of these, Banu Nai Nano Senan, was decked out with beads and gold ornaments; he knew the art of making fire with flint and steel; his ascendancy and superiority were so great that he was immediately made ruler. The second stranger, on the contrary, was in every respect a pattern of inferiority, and only after he had been clothed and taught the language could he be brought into the presence of the ruler. His sitting-place between two stones, under a *lontar*-palm, and the fact that he was named Ulak Mai after this spot, indicate his association with the earth. The first stranger is the representative of the superior sky-phratry, the second belongs to the stupid, inferior earth-phratry. We see here, therefore, as elsewhere, how a local dual division is associated with the opposition of sky and earth. In this myth there is once more a triad of important figures in the opening part of the story: the *fettor* of Sahan and the two strangers. The central place, however, can be assigned equally to the *fettor* or to the ruler. The *fettor* can be seen as the original authority in contrast to the two strangers, whereas in the mythical affinal relationships it is unmistakably the ruler, on the contrary, who occupies the central place in the triad, in that he marries two daughters of the *fettor* of Sahan and gives his own daughter to Ulak Mai. The ruler thus represents the ego-group, which both gives and takes women. The marriage of Banu Nai Neno Senan to two girls can be taken to show that actually each of the strangers should have married a daughter of Nome Niti Bani. In the tale recorded by Krayer van Aalst,[9] a stranger called Mnuke Kase (descendant of the ruler-stranger) got a woman called Be Kutu Balan, daughter of Nome Nitbane, a ruler of Amanatun, in exchange for fire. Mnuke Kase succeeded Nome Nitbane, and from his son Muti Banu Naek the present rulers are descended. In this story, therefore, there is mention of only one stranger, and Tae Walan and Bikut are correspondingly united in one person, Bekutu Balan. The antagonism between Amanatun and Amanuban is seen in the ruler's command to Ulak Mai to move away to the east, where he drives out the local ruler, Nuban, and becomes master of the country in his place.

The idea held in Amanuban about the relationship to Amanatun is that of younger to older brother, and of ruler to *fettor*. The conception of the younger brother as representative of one's own group belongs, as we have seen, to the local-cosmic dualism, in which he stands for the superior sky-half. We observe, therefore, that each of the two territories feels itself the superior of the other. A reciprocal conception of this kind is naturally not to be identified with phratry-dualism, for in the latter the oppositions and associations have an absolute character and are acknowledged by both groups. The phenomena in question at present should therefore be seen as having developed later. In this case the more detailed Sahan myth can be assigned a greater value than the shorter communication from Amanuban. The opposition ruler/*fettor* is quite incorrectly employed in this context, for it has to do with the dualism of social function and not with the local-cosmic dualism. We can take it, therefore, that in former times Amanatun was associated with the higher sky-phratry, and Amanuban with the inferior earth-phratry. This is confirmed by the detailed Amanuban myth told by Tua Isu, *fettor* of Malenat. The introduction to this myth so much resembles the tale of Noah's drunkenness that it is possible to ascribe it to Christian influence.[10] The attitude adopted by the brothers Isu and Nope towards the ruler of Nunkolo stamps them unmistakably as representatives of the inferior phratry. The

---

[9] In: Kruyt, 1923*a*, p. 460.

[10] It is entirely consistent with the above indigenous conceptions, however, that the Bible story has been modified to the extent that it is the youngest, and not the oldest, of the three brothers who is the good son.

childish tricks which they perpetrate are a familiar element in any phratry-opposition.[11] The relationship between Nope and Isu (Sopo Bilas) is completely identical with that between Banu Nai Nano Senan and Ulak Mai in the previous myth. The parallelism between the two myths is remarkable, however, in other respects as well. Two strangers are set in opposition to the original ruler, who gives them his daughters in marriage. In the Sahan myth this in the *fettor* of Sahan; in the latter myth it is the ruler of Nunkolo. The strangers are found by a man, Nomlene, who is out hunting.[12] We read elsewhere that at the present day there is still a clan called Nomlene in Sahan; probably this hunter is once again the *fettor* of Sahan. While in one myth it is the lesser of the two strangers who drives out the ruler, Nuban, in the second myth both of them represent the inferior phratry and go head-hunting in Amanuban among the people of Manela Ane. It is plain that the opposition between Nunkolo and the strangers is identical with that between Banu Nai Nano Senan and Ulak Mai, and thus reflects the relationship between the kingdoms. Although the *fettor* occupies a more or less central position in the Sahan myth, yet he does not play nearly so important a part as the ruler of Nunkolo in the other myth. He even retreats completely into the background as the unknown fourth figure.

The present ruler of Amanuban is called Pae Nope, and the *fettor* of Malenat is called Tua Isu. The opposition between the mythical figures of Nope and Isu is thus that of ruler and *mafefa*. The same myth which in Amanatun formulates the relationship with Amanuban performs the same service in the latter territory, but it also deals at the same time with the relationship between ruler and *mafefa*. Oppositions of the latter type have been found described in a particular fashion among the peoples discussed earlier. Perhaps these departures from the rule should be seen as a result of the extent to which the parts of the kingdom have become emancipated. The oppositions within the new "kingdom" seem in their turn to have been subsumed under the local-cosmic dualism. Since the Isu myth locates the beginning of the action in Amanatun, and represents someone from Sahan as having found the strangers, we may exclude the possibility that the relationship between the kingdoms was only later modelled after an existing phratry-dualism, which would be in contradiction to the course of development established for other kingdoms.

---

[11] Cf. De Josselin de Jong, 1929.
[12] Kruyt, 1923a, p. 428.

There is a certain confusion about the name Sopo Bilas. The Isu myth gives this as one of the names of Isu, the ancestor of the *mafefa*. Elsewhere it is the ancestor of the ruler of Amanuban who is called so. We do not know whether this is a mistake, but we need find nothing to be surprised at in this exchange of name, for we shall see that the two ancestors in question are very often named together. It is noteworthy that in both of the main myths the wife of the ancestor of the ruler of Amanuban bears the name Bifnatun. In both myths the ruler of Amanatun gives certain objects to the representative(s) of Amanuban, viz., a palm-leaf container with some earth, a spear, and a sword, in one instance, and two gold figurines, representing a man and a woman, in the other. Given that the former objects belong to the earth-phratry, the latter indicate the masculine and feminine character of the bearers. These gifts should undoubtedly be seen once more as the regalia which represent the power of the principal ruler, the power which through lesser units and officials pervades the whole social body and maintains it in existence. The male and female figurines stand for the opposed forces which, issuing from the principal ruler, are embodied in Nope and Isu. The journey of Isu and Nope to Amanuban may be equated with that of Ulak Mai to the east. These journeys, which are really war-like or head-hunting expeditions, are to be seen as expressing the antagonism between the two territories, a sentiment which according to report has still not entirely disappeared today. In the case of Nope and Isu the opposition Amanatun/Amanuban changes into that between Manela Ane and Tumbesi. Every year Kesnai had a youth from Manela Ane and a girl from Tumbesi captured and killed for the benefit of his rice-crop. Isu and Nope retaliated with head-hunting expeditions. This episode shows a great similarity to the conflict between Sonnebait and Kune in the Sonnebait myth. In the latter myth, the ruler is murdered by representatives of the bad phratry, a deed which brings the greatest catastrophes upon the land. In the case in question, we find nothing of the kind. Since Isu and Nope appear here once more together, we have to see them as representatives of the inferior half of the tribe, and their behaviour should be equated with that of Kune and Sabat Neno. The latter commit a murder, whereas Isu and Nope by contrast organise a head-hunting expedition. The disparate character of their deeds is also manifested in the myth; the former is an evil action which was bound to have consequences, whereas the latter seems to be regarded as completely normal.

Tumbesi is the place where the "lineage" of Nubatonis lives; this group, as appears elsewhere, is the clan of the ruler. Not far from this place is Malenat, the residence of the *mafefa* Isu, in whose area there used still to exist an old settlement of the rulers. It may therefore be supposed that the mythical Manela Ane is identical with the present-day Malenat, and that the conflict between Tumbesi and Manela Ane is nothing else than an expression of the antagonism between the ruler and the *mafefa*. These mythical events thus simultaneously reflect two conflicts, viz., that of Amanuban and Amanatun, and that between the ruler (Tumbesi) and the *mafefa* (Manela Ane — Malenat). This also explains the appearance of Isu and Nope in each other's company, and it certainly agrees with the vacillating character of the whole myth.

We therefore find in addition to a local dualism, based on a cosmic classification, a grouping within the territorial segment which has a more social character. The ruler of Amanatun has the *fettor* of Sahan beside him, and the ruler of Amanuban has a *mafefa*, a "speaker", i.e., a man who knows most about the traditions. In the myth the military exploits of the ruler of Amanuban call for particular notice. These four functionaries may therefore readily be identified with the four authorities who figured in the kingdom of Fialarang. Banu or Nunkolo is the principal ruler, the *fettor* of Sahan is his "right hand", Ulak Mai or Nope is the "commander-in-chief", and the *mafefa* corresponds to the *mak o'an*. That the *fettor* of Sahan must originally have been the foremost man in the kingdom is a conception which fits perfectly into this framework. We have already indicated that the cosmic opposition of Nope and Isu, ruler and *mafefa*, should be seen as a later development connected with the emancipation of the major territory. The male and female figurines given to Isu and Nope by the ruler of Nunkolo indicate the association of these persons with the two sexes, and we have seen elsewhere that the opposition by social function is chiefly linked with a grouping by sex. The mythical head-hunting expeditions were sent out from Tumbesi against Manela Ane, so perhaps Nope, the ancestor of the ruling lineage Nubatonis at Tumbesi, should be seen as the masculine half, and Isu, *mafefa* of Malenat-Manela Ane, as the feminine half. The *fettor* of Sahan, who appears in the myth as a hunter, evidently belongs to the masculine side of this dualism, since hunting is par excellence a masculine activity. The principal ruler of Amanatun is then necessarily associated with the feminine. It can thus be observed that the principal ruler and the *mafefa* together represent the feminine half in the functional dualism, and the *fettor* and the ruler of Amanuban the masculine half. This corresponds completely with what has been found in Fialarang. There the principal ruler and the *mak o'an* seem originally to have been a feminine group in opposition to the *fettor* and *surik ulun*, though at present the emphasis seems to fall more on the two rulers on the one side and the *fettor* and *mak o'an* on the other. The same phenomenon appears in Amanuban-Amanatun as well. The two great kingdoms both have in common a most explicit local dualism. The social grouping of the four most important officials also makes its appearance in the mythical affinal relationships. Banu, principal ruler of Amanatun, appears as wife-taking group vis-à-vis the *fettor* of Sahan, and as wife-giving group vis-à-vis the *fettor* of Sahan, and as wife-giving group vis-à-vis Ulak Mai, the ruler of Amanuban. We have already pointed out that this may not be simply the familiar mythical triad, in which two opposed figures take their origin from a central one, for in no single respect does a contrast between Nome Niti Bani and Ulak Mai find expression; both personages have to acknowledge the superiority of Banu Nai Nano Senan. Here the objective conception is dominant: they belong to one half, and the ego-group to the other. Also, the fact that the respective clans of these personages still exist argues for this conception. We thus find the very grouping, cross-cutting the local dual organisation, the plausibility of which has been more indirectly argued above: the principal ruler (and the *mafefa*, as the fourth figure) on the one side, and the *fettor* and the ruler of Amanuban on the other.

The divine character of the rulers, which we have constantly been able to discern, is shown not only by their great miraculous powers and the necessity of their presence for the continuance of the kingdom, i.e., not just the political order but human society in its entirety in its connexion with the cosmos, but is unmistakably declared by the terms with which they are addressed. The most remarkable of these titles is Usif Neno, lord sun. Usif Neno is the supreme being, so the ruler is to be seen as nothing less than the earthly representative of the high god. Koko Leu, sacred snake, a title of the ruler of Amanuban, is scarcely less important, for the dualistic nature of the supreme being is often conceived in the form of a snake.[13] Nagasawa, the lineage name of the ruler of Lassi in an old account, is one of the names used in this region to designate a similar dual being in the form of a snake-dragon. The sacred relics of the *meromak o'an* (son of god) of

---

[13] Cf. Locher, 1932.

Waihale are guarded by snakes. It seems indeed that all of the rulers participate to a greater or lesser degree in this sacred character of the principal ruler, independently of the place which they occupy in the system. Each of the lesser rulers is a duplicate, as it were, a replica of the principal ruler, whose powers are spread in this way throughout the kingdom.

Before leaving these myths we should say something about vegetation and agriculture, though such matters actually belong to another context. It is a well known fact that primitive classifications are based primarily on the social categories of society, and especially on those of phratry-dualism. Generally speaking, vegetation is classified in one group with the earth. This is seen here in the myth which tells how the daughter of Nubatonis, one of the first four human beings, was killed and the parts of her body scattered over the earth, from which there sprang the edible plants, including rice (see below).[14] As we know, Nubatonis is the clan of the ruler of Amanuban, and as such belongs to the earth-half, the old earth-phratry. The killing of a youth and a girl from Tumbesi, the residence of Nubatonis, by people from Manela Ane, must therefore be regarded as a ritual repetition of a sacrifice by the earth-phratry in mythical prehistory, when men were presented with an important part of their most valued possessions. In the ritual, this phratry repeatedly offers itself up in order to make possible the continued existence of the whole society. As the Sonnebait myth clearly shows, the killing had to be done by the sky-phratry. The work of agriculture itself belongs, however, as we shall see further, more to the sphere of the socially feminine half. If the Sonnebait myth is compared with that of Amanatun, it will be seen that the principal ruler in the one, and Manela Ane in the other, play exactly the same part. Both are rice-cultivators, and for this undertaking human sacrifice is essential. The two groups belong to opposite cosmic phratries, but to the same social half, namely the feminine. Sonnebait seemed to be aberrant as far as the attribution of sex was concerned, but the detailed myths concerning Fialarang and the two kingdoms on the south coast left no doubt on this point in the original situation. This also explains the shift in position of the principal ruler and Manela Ane. The former group participates in the feminine character of the latter, and the latter in the celestial character of the former. Given the evolved character of the system, which has more or less lost

---

[14] Kruyt, 1923a, p. 474.

contact with the original clan-arrangement, such displacements need occasion no surprise. The fact that rice is often conceived as having come from the sky or from the supreme being [15] is no longer to be wondered at, while the association with the below which was seen especially in Sonnebait's function as rice-cultivator is perfectly clear. His two-fold character is manifested in his simultaneous appearance as agriculturalist and as sacrificer. The former activity has to be explained by his relationship with the feminine social half, the group of the agriculturalists; sacrifice belongs to his task as representative of the sky-phratry. The exceptional position of rice in opposition to other food-plants is thus connected with the dual division into heavenly and earthly within the same social moiety. The great importance which is ascribed to the cultivation of rice, in contrast to other plants, is a general phenomenon. The people of the mythical Manela Ane were rightly agriculturalists; they owe their function as sacrificers to being grouped together with Banu in one social half. The emancipation of the local halves will also certainly have had its effects. In the present case, Manela Ane is associated with the sky, in opposition to Tumbesi, which is associated with the earth, which is just the other way round from the powers which are associated with Isu and Nope. The different origins of the antagonism between Sonnebait and Kune, and that between Manela Ane and Tumbesi, emerge however more clearly in various actions of the latter groups or persons. The inferior earth-phratry (Kune) commits a murder, and the masculine social half (Tumbesi) performs the head-hunting ritual.

Very little is known about the present relations between the two kingdoms. That the ruler of Amanuban always has to take his wife from Amanatun agrees with the mythical affinal alliances between the two kingdoms, but in the absence of more detailed evidence such a fragmentary report can be of little significance. The application of the terms *usif fetto* and *usif mone* is not clear. It is difficult to see them as terms for wife-giving and wife-taking groups respectively, for in all other reports they are used, in accordance with their literal signification, with precisely the opposite meanings. Compound expressions including the term for "sister" always denote the wife-taking clan, as in *fettoh sawa* (central Timor), *fetto son* (western Timor), *jan ur* (Kei), and *uranak* (Tanimbar). A term such as *usif mone* (master of the brother or husband), to indicate the ego-group, on the other hand,

---

[15] Kruyt, 1923*a*, p. 474.

is quite conceivable. Also, according to the ideas on which unilateral affinal relationships are founded, marriage with the female descendant of a sister is absolutely prohibited.

Head-hunting is mentioned over and over again by Kruyt, and is just as often controverted. It is also reported by older sources that the two halves into which the original kingdom split went head-hunting against each other. Apparently this has to do with a traditional conception which corresponds to the antagonism which is also expressed in the myths, and in which head-hunting appears as a ritual conflict between phratries. That members of the ruling houses could not be absent from each other's burials, and that at the death of a ruler a possible war between the kingdoms was called off, are facts which show that in spite of all actual and traditional oppositions the two kingdoms were regarded as parts of a higher unity in which their co-operation was essential.

In Amarassi the title of *fettor* is used for a special functionary, and not as a general term for district heads. The opposition of ruler and *fettor* is shown by their different origins. The various titles formerly borne by the district heads indicate a division of functions such as in, for example, Fialarang. We have already demonstrated that such a grouping into five goes back to one into four. In the present day, the district heads are known as *temukung besar*, and under them are the *temukung*, "family heads". The office of ruler is hereditary in the Koro "family". The kingdom contains nine "lineages" (clans), of which Koro is apparently one, and the *temukung* are thus clan heads. The terms "principal *temukun*" and *temukun* are also used in central Timor for *datu ferikatua* and *datu fukun*.[16] In its external structure the kingdom of Amarassi thus corresponds to a district in central Timor. In all of the kingdoms we thus find as the basis of the social system a division into local units, districts, each of which contains a number of descent groups. The petty kingdom of Lidak, in north Tétun, constitutes an exception to this rule; it contains, namely, only six *fukun* (descent groups), and appears to have no division into regions or districts. Perhaps this exceptional position is no more than apparent, and the three functionaries who are said to have governed in former times may possibly have been district heads, each with two *fukun* under him. Practically nothing is known about the nature of the descent groups which compose a district in central Timor and which

---

[16] Grijzen, 1904, p. 128.

in western kingdoms are clans or segments of clans. It is thus not quite exact to say, as we have done, that the kingdom of Amarassi corresponds structurally to the district in central Timor. All that can really be said is that in central Timor a new social entity has been inserted between the kingdom and the district, and that this is externally similar to the kingdom of Amarassi. Genetically, Amarassi represents the former tribe, just as does, for example, Fialarang. The same is true of Amanuban and Amanatun: superficially, they resemble districts, but in their origin they are identical with the halves of the kingdom of Fialarang, only in their case there is no intermediate territory between the half of the kingdom and the district. The structure of Sonnebait has not become so clear to us. We are particularly in the dark concerning the place of the ruler's own district in relation to Mollo and Mio Maffo. It seems not unlikely that the original situation was an opposition of two "districts" or territories, like Amanatun and Amanuban. On closer inspection, therefore, the differing degrees of emancipation in the progress from district to kingdom, though important, seem to be not so great as might at first be thought. The evolution concerns not so much the districts as the halves of the kingdom, and this process has been carried to a remarkable point in Fialarang. It seems therefore that we should regard the present-day kingdoms in the first place as the outcome of a society originally divided into two local halves. On Amarassi alone do we have no information in this respect. Both the indications in the myths, and certain particulars in the present structure, demonstrate incontestably that this must have been a tribe divided into phratries and apparently into four clans. The case of Lidak points similarly in the direction of phratries, each however with three descent groups. This six-fold division, which we have also met within the halves of Fialarang and Djenilu, and in contrast to the four-fold division of the other halves, will be discussed in more detail in conjunction with similar phenomena from elsewhere. The simplest units in the kingdom, as forms of local organisation, are the districts. These must therefore have been the original parts out of which the kingdom came into being. The larger territories could have been formed from them by a process of expansion and bifurcation. In many cases it seems possible to isolate four districts or territories as the oldest and most important. In Fialarang the number of territories has also undergone a significant expansion. It is, of course, not inconceivable that some of these districts are of alien origin, though this is not particularly likely. All the information points to a development from within. The readiest explanation is that of a segmentation of the major territories of Bauho, Klusin, Lassiolat, and Asumanu. The general agreement among the ethnographers on the matter of the division of the districts into descent groups is truly striking. We have thought it possible to establish the common origin of these genealogical groups in central Timor, but there is no question of such a determination for western Timor. In the latter area the number of clans is for the most part greater than the number of districts. Even Amarassi, which in structure approaches the simplest possible form, nevertheless has nine clans. The number of local groups has apparently not increased so much in western Timor as in the central part of the island. The postulate that a clan is found in only one district seems to be a fairly safe one.

In the government of the *nusak* on Rote there are four prominent officials, whose inter-relationships are very clearly determined by double-dualistic conceptions. Within this group of four there is the familiar triad of *manè*, *fèto*, and *daé-langgak*, and so prominently indeed that the existence of the fourth dignitary, the *manédopè*, has been overlooked by most of the ethnographers.

The most obvious element in the structure of this tribe is undoubtedly the dualistic arrangement of each *nusak* into a *manè*-half and a *fèto*-half. Curiously, Van der Kam says on the whole nothing about the true nature of the *leo* and the halves, nor about their significance in connexion with the marriage regulations. From the reports of other authors it may be inferred without any question that here we have to do with an explicit phratry-dualism; in no other instance have we found the halves so convincingly classified as masculine and feminine as here. In the *nusak* of Oépao one phratry was the stronger, the other the weaker. The figures of *manè* and *fèto* evidently correspond to those of ruler and *fettor*, principal ruler and right hand, in central Timor: the *manè* is said to be mystical and contemplative, the *fèto* exercises secular power, and the *manè* is said also to be the source of authority. The attribution of sex has been effected in just the reverse way as in central Timor, but in the same way as in Sonnebait. The opposition quarrelsome/peace-loving, which characterises their relationship in the *nusak* of Loleh, has likewise been encountered in the Timorese kingdom in question. The designations of ruler and *fettor*, which are generally employed in the literature, can of course only be used with caution, and in assessing such terms it is always necessary to take into account the possible influence of the Government.

The title *fettor*, in particular, is very often used in a highly arbitrary way. The word is generally taken to be a corruption of the Portuguese *feitor*. However this may be, the similarity to the indigenous designation *fèto* has surely played an important part in the possible adoption of the title. In the case in question this seems plain; foreigners have quite certainly taken over the word *fèto* and have corrupted it into the familiar *fettor*.

The opposition of *manè* and *fèto* is crossed by that between *manè*-plus-*fèto* on the one side and *daé-langgak*-plus-*manédopè* on the other. It appears from the name of the *manédopè*, "sword-bearer", that he corresponds to the *surik ulun* in Timor; to judge by his function, as expert in traditions, he is also identical to the "speaker". These officials thus seem to be united in one person on Rote; in Timor as well we were struck by a certain hesitation about these figures. It will be recalled, however, that in the *nusak* of Loleh and Keka each of the halves has its *manédopè*. As the fourth or fifth functionary there remains still the *daé-langgak*; he is in the first place the sacrificer for the whole *nusak*. In this respect he exhibits a great correspondence with the principal ruler in other parts. Apparently a striking shift-over in the tasks of the *manè* and the *daé-langgak* has taken place; such a process has even been incorporated in the indigenous traditions of Dengka. This argues that a situation such as in Termanu, where the *daé-langgak* is actually said to be "lord of the land", was formerly more general. The priestly functions which were originally assigned to the principal ruler seem to have pushed the relationship of the *daé-langgak* to the soil somewhat into the background. The *daé-langgak* today is primarily the *manasonggo* (cf. Tanimbar *mangsombe*) *nusak*. As the fifth official, he can stand for the unity of the tribe, and in this respect also he corresponds once more to the principal ruler. To judge by the name Inoama Leki, Mother-Father Leki, he also has the same kind of two-fold character as this figure.

It has seemed possible to subsume relationships such as those between *manè* and *fèto*, and between *manédopè* and *daé-langgak* (taking the two *manédopè* together), under a dualism of social function, and to subsume relationships such as that between *manè* and *fèto* on one side and the *mané-dopè* and *daé-langgak* on the other under a local-cosmic dualism. On Rote the former oppositions are coupled with an explicitly dualistic ordering of the tribe. There is some doubt concerning the local character of these groupings. The authors agree that the *leo*-order is not territorial, and Van der Kam looks upon the local *leo* of Oépao as a unique phenomenon; but this is controverted by the report of Jonker concerning Baä, according to which three ancestors established a territorial partition of the tribal lands. In addition, mention should be made of the *nusak* of Della and Oénale, which originally stood for the halves of a single *nusak*. Finally, Van der Kam calls the *manè* and the *fèto* the only territorial heads in the *nusak*. In spite of these difficulties, it seems in fact certain that the *leo* are not locally grouped; and since the opposition of *manè* and *fèto* is very clearly linked with the division into *leo*, this dualism seems to accord very well with the social-functional dual division with which we have become familiar elsewhere.

The other opposition must therefore be based on that of sky and earth. There are not many factual data in favour of this hypothesis, but the parallel with similar phenomena elsewhere makes it quite likely. The *daé-langgak* is firmly associated with the earth; and it is said of the *manè* that his speech is like the rolling of thunder. This opposition cuts across that between *manè* and *fèto* in a striking fashion. Whereas the latter is connected with the division into *leo*, the former finds its expression within the *leo*. Each *leo* has a *manéleo* and a *manasonggo*; in Loleh each half has a *manédopè* in addition to the *manè* and the *fèto*, and in Keka the *manéleo* of the *leo* of the *manè* and the *fèto* are *manédopè* at the same time. In the *nusak* of Loleh, the double dualism is clear and prominent. The twelve *leo* of the *manè* are descended from five brothers; the eldest brother is the ancestor of the *manédopè*, and the youngest is the ancestor of the *manè*. This fits well with what has been found in other places: the *manè* represents the younger sky, and the *manédopè* stands for the older earth.

Whereas it is in fact usually the dualism of *manè* and *fèto* that is connected with the dual division of the tribe, in Termanu the two original halves are associated with the *daé-langgak* and the regents, who can be none other than the *manè* and the *fèto*. The "lords of the land" are descended from Pada Lalais, and the *manè* and *fèto* from Ma Bula and his son Muskanan Ma. We thus find a division into two halves, while one of the halves is again dualistically organised in terms of an opposition which crosses the former. Something similar is apparently found in Keka also. Here the "lord of the land", Inoama Leki, who came from Oénale, and a father with his son, originating in Termanu, stand in opposition to each other. The local character of the dualistic order in which *daé-langgak* and *manè* have their places is very clearly stressed by their origins in two different *nusak*.

These double-dualistic conceptions appear to be expressed in the organisation of the clan system itself as well. The *leo* are everywhere divided into smaller units known by various terms such as *kita, lutu,* and apparently *nggi leo.* A possible inference, therefore, is that the *leo*-order belongs to the dualism of social function, and the *kita (lutu)*-order to the local-cosmic dualism. The grouping into *leo* is connected with the sexual dualism of *manè* and *féto*; the sub-division of the *leo* is connected with the cosmic dualism of *manè* and *manédopè.* It would of course be of great importance if we could ascertain whether the *kita* of different *leo* are constantly joined into groups. Such *kita*-groups would then have to be brought under a dualistic order of the Termanu type: one half would be that of the *daé-langgak,* and the other would be that of *manè* and *féto.* This type would also have to accomodate the strongly local Oépao system; Van der Kam's attempts to ascribe it to the Portuguese show that there we are dealing with a very special case. Let us recall, furthermore, the case of Ti, which according to Van de Wetering is divided into halves containing eight sub-divisions each, whereas according to Van der Kam it consists of halves containing respectively fourteen and twelve *leo.* Van de Wetering provides the names of four ancestors; Van der Kam mentions only two. The most obvious explanation of this is, of course, that one of the authors is mistaken, but given the postulated double-dualistic conceptions it seems not wholly unlikely that there is more to the matter than this, especially since Van de Wetering's figures indicate an original division into four and those of Van der Kam a division into six — and, as we shall further see, the opposition between a four-fold and a six-fold division plays some part in this context.

A grouping which is composed of heterogeneous *leo*-segments is the *nggolok,* a social group with which we have become familiar elsewhere under the name of district. We have postulated above that a possible division of the tribe into groups of *kita* would have to be of a local kind. The presumption now is that the *nggolok* and the hypothetical group of *kita* are one and the same social unit. The *kita* would then correspond to the heterogeneous descent groups of the *nggolok.*

In the combinations of numbers associated with the various social groups, tendencies towards division by three, by four, and by six make their appearance next to one another. We have already seen that the three-fold division is a logical consequence of asymmetric connubium; the four-fold division has been related to the earth-moiety, and the six-fold to the sky-moiety, in the local-cosmic of central Timor. In

Loleh, as we have seen, the local-cosmic classification is based on a five-fold division, and we have also related the eight-fold division of Oépao to this classification. In Baä, the original local tripartition is supplanted by a four-fold division. In the opposition between the numbers of *leo* in the halves of Loleh there can be seen the opposition of an original four-fold and six-fold division; and within the *manè*-half these two numerical divisions cross each other. In Ringgou, we find the number four in the *leo*-division, and numbers from four to seven in that of the *lutu*. We can thus affirm that the two principles of grouping occur together, and are often thought of in opposition to each other, either in a double-dualistic classification or in connexion with a division into phratries. In spite of all divergences, one gains the impression that the four-fold division is primarily local, the six-fold division is more one of social function, and that the former is the more important of the two.

We should like to run ahead of our results for a moment, and state that it seems possible to us that types of structure such as the *nggolok* may be related to a former patrilineal principle of organisation, and types such as the *leo* to a former matrilineal principle. It is most remarkable, in this context, that the opposition of regents among themselves is in two cases apparently viewed as one between father and son; and it is self-evident that only in a matrilineal group can such an opposition have any meaning.

The situation on Savu seems to be much the same as what has been described above for Rote. The fact that in Seba the division of labour between *do'ai* and *wèto* is linked to the dualistic arrangement of one of the "lineages" indicates once more the familiar double-dualistic concepts. That the *do'ai* is the elder, and the *wèto* the younger, who as in Timu possesses real power, agrees entirely with what has been found elsewhere. The origin of the *wèto*, as given in Mesara, is less clear. The opposition between "flag-master" and "staff-master" is perhaps to be ascribed to governmental influence; but we also find similar conceptions elsewhere, and these fit unusually well into the dualistic framework.

The *deo rai* here seems almost to be an even more important official than the *daé-langgak* on Rote. His "lineage" is said to be the oldest in the district, so he seems to stand for the older earth over against the younger sky. In opposition to the ruler and the *fettor*, he occupies a more or less central place; he is "the origin or the source of the *do'ai*".

It is particularly in his ritual function that he appears similar, in very important respects, to the sacrificer and the principal ruler of Tanimbar and Timor. In Mesara this shift in function is expressed in the opinion that the *deo rai* used also to be the *do'ai*, but that he had to surrender this function to another "lineage". This does not detract from the circumstance that he is likewise thought of in opposition to the ruler: "as the ruler cares for the people, so the lord of the ground cares for the land".

A four-fold division plays a considerable part on Savu and, as we have seen, on Rote as well. It is difficult to say with certainty, on the basis of the available evidence, whether the districts on Savu were originally tribes or whether they are units corresponding to the districts in Timor. Various facts argue for the latter conclusion. With regard to Rote, we have several myths which mention a higher social unit in which formerly several kingdoms are supposed to have been grouped together.

In the eastern part of Sumba, the original four-fold division is one of the most characteristic features of the social system. The four *ratu* of each tribe are socially the most important functionaries. This is the first time that we find the office of lord of the land indubitably ascribed to the heads of clans. In opposition to the *ratu* stand the rulers. The relationship between ruler and *ratu* is clearly characterised as that between sky and earth. We know very little about the rulers, and although the ethnographers lay particular stress on their purely political character it is nevertheless an undeniable fact that the superiority and sacredness of most of them is unchallengeable. They stand for the religious powers of the local community, and in this respect certainly have something in common with the principal rulers in other societies.

In the western part of the island the dualism appears with particular clarity. In spite of conflicting reports this dualism has in many cases an explicitly local character. Unfortunately, we possess only the most superficial information on the details of this dual division. We come across the well-known oppositions of older brother/younger brother, real power/moral position, ruler/lord of the land, which indicate that we are once more on familiar ground. As we have already demonstrated, however, these various conceptions and groupings mostly involve such complex questions that it is well-nigh unfeasible to arrive at definite conclusions on the basis of such casual information as we have. As far as Laura is concerned, we are rather better informed. Within each of the halves there appear once more a pair of officials, so we may surmise that here there is a form of organisation such as we have come to know of in the different kingdoms of Timor (cf. especially Amfoan). There is probably a further parallel with the forms of organisation in central Timor. It is reported in a quite general fashion that the ruler is considered the elder brother, and the guardian of the sacred objects the younger brother. In Lamboja and Anakala this division of labour is connected with the dual division of the district. Other districts, however, exhibit rather divergent arrangements. A very interesting situation is met with in Napu. The *ratu* of the *ana matjua* (elder brother) is associated with the celestial, and the *ratu* of the *ana ma'ari* is associated with the earthly. The former controls in particular the forces of the sky which influence the success of the crops. As we know, the principal ruler also had a task to perform in this respect. Just as the *ratu ana matjuwa* receives the first bundle of rice, so the offering of part of the harvest to the principal ruler is an important element in many myths from central Timor. In this respect the two activities are entirely identical: these persons are primarily religious functionaries. The *ratu ana ma'ari* has, on the contrary, an expressly social function. His task is to nullify the various influences which threaten to endanger the order of human society. We thus see here once more the well-known opposition between a religious and a social dignitary, closely connected with a dualistic grouping. This type of order, in which the activity of the elder brother is directed to the celestial and that of the younger brother operates in the social sphere, seems to accord very well with the postulated partition of functions between an elder brother as ruler and a younger brother as guardian of the sacred objects.

CHAPTER V

MYTHS AND SOCIAL STRUCTURE
IN THE MOLUCCAS
AND THE SOUTHEASTERN ISLANDS

After the rather lengthy discussion of certain mythological and social phenomena in the Timor archipelago, let us now turn to Tanimbar and Kei, where we shall encounter practically identical structural forms. We shall be able to check the validity of our results, and possibly deepen our understanding of them, by what we shall find in these seemingly more primitive societies. The parallelism between the Tanimbar "trias politica" and that of Timor is patent. The *mangsombe* stands as the central figure in opposition to the *mangaf wajak* and the *pnuwe nduan*, and here too the triad more or less overshadows an original four-five division. The significance of the *sori luri* as the fifth figure, representing unity, emerges from his task and also from his place in the *natar*:

mangaf wajak	*mangatanuk*
pnuwe nduan	*mangsombe*

sori luri

His role in any event of importance in the village, and his place in the bows of the *natar* (the village square conceived as a boat), stamp him from the first as the representative of the formal unity of the village. The four other dignitaries present themselves in pairs. The *mangaf wajak* and the *pnuwe nduan* belong to one half of this dual unity, and the *mangatanuk* and the *mangsombe* to the other. This can be seen in the first place from their sitting-places to the left and to the right in the *natar*. This inference is explicitly confirmed by Drabbe's attempts to derive the function of the *mangaf wajak* from that of the *pnuwe nduan*. In his consideration of the matter these two officials are brought into the closest relation with each other.

The *mangsombe*, mother of the village and sacrificer, is identical to the principal ruler in Timor. While the ruler of Bauho was the mother of the kingdom of Fialarang, we found in the Sonnebait myths that the sacrificial function was one of the integral characteristics of the highest personage in this social-political unit. The remarkable office of "rex otiosus" is as clearly as possible associated with the *mangsombe*. For as long as a war was in progress he had to *nsombe*, "sacrifice", i.e., stay in his house. This precisely typifies him as the woman who stays at home, and whose actions have an effect on the men who are away in strange parts. We have proposed earlier that in Timor the "speaker" and the principal ruler belonged to the same group; on Tanimbar there seems to be no possible doubt about it. The *mangatanuk*, whom we place with the *mangsombe* over against the *pnuwe nduan* and *mangaf wajak*, was the man who always and everywhere had to speak on behalf of the father and mother. Drabbe calls him indeed the speaker. The *mangsombe* has a mainly religious function, whereas the activities of the *mangaf wajak* and the *pnuwe nduan* take place chiefly in the social sphere. The *mangaf wajak* is a warrior, and is involved in gift-exchange; his present-day position as village headman similarly corresponds to his active character, in contrast to the passive character of the *mangsombe*. The *pnuwe nduan* had in the first place control over the settlement of strangers in the village. We thus observe that the activity of the feminine element is particularly directed towards the religious, and that the activity of the masculine element is especially concerned with the social. The opposition within each group is similarly unmistakable. Through his central place in the triad the *mangsombe* embodies the dual unity from which springs the opposition of *mangaf wajak* and *pnuwe nduan*. The latter member of this couple is very clearly associated with the earth, and the former with the sky. His house is called *kmberre*, loft, the place where valuables are safeguarded. These are goods taken as spoils of war from other villages, or which have been acquired by exchange. Furthermore, the conception of the *pnuwe nduan* as the older in opposition to the *mangaf wajak*, who is now the more prominent, is by no means an unknown idea. It fits perfectly into the dualistic framework. It is noteworthy that the functions of the *pnuwe nduan* seem to be especially connected with the ground as locality, with the territorial uniy of the village, and that we have not found him associated with cultivated plots. *Pnuwe nduan* means "lord of the village", not "lord of the land". His name *riribun réréngjar* also indicates that he is connected with the village. In Timor, as we have said, the local territory was subsumed under the cosmic classification. The relationship with agriculture, which elsewhere is regularly ascribed to the "lord of the land", here seems rather to pertain to the *sori luri*, to the extent that his rice is the first to be planted and that his harvest is the first to be brought in. As in Timor, the fourth figure, the speaker, plays a less important part, for the triad has a predominant position in the system. Nevertheless the same opposition is to be discovered in the functions of *mangsombe* and *mangatanuk* as between those of *mangaf wajak* and *pnuwe nduan*. The former is directed, with his requests and prayers, towards the supreme being and the celestial; the other is a mediator in the earthly sphere and speaks to men. Perhaps there is also a certain ambiguity or two-fold character in his function as earthly counterpart to the *mangsombe*, for he speaks in the name of the father and mother. We thus find the same dualistic principles of classification as in Timor, viz., sky/earth and social/religious. But the system of which these groupings form part is rather different. In Timor their character is mainly determined by the local dualism, which used to be extremely closely linked to a cosmic classification. This opposition, which had in the main a religious aspect, was crossed by the social one, which was primarily based on the opposition between the sexes. On Tanimbar the local dualism seems to be missing; here the religious/social opposition is directly related to the grouping by sex. As we have already said, the feminine is directed towards the celestial, and its task is religious; the masculine operates in the social sphere and is associated with the earth. In Timor the local dualism is very prominent, whereas on Tanimbar we see more of an interchange between the two cosmic forces and the sex-opposition. We should like to recall once more, however, that in Timor the ascription of sex to various groups was not carried out entirely consistently. On Tanimbar, also, the local dualism is not entirely lacking, as we have said. The fact that we are not dealing here with tribal officials, but with those of a smaller unit, is not foreign to this development, for the cosmic and the local dualism were, it seems, very closely connected.

The functions of the *mangaf wajak* and *pnuwe nduan* have their parallel in Timor in those of the right hand and the left hand. Evidently certain displacements have occurred. In Timor the "lord of the land" is not a member of the group of the four main officials, and his office is dispersed among a large number of persons. This fact is perhaps to be ascribed to the essential difference, remarked upon above, between the government of a kingdom (tribe) and that of a village. If the office is considered in its entirety, there are then once more the five important functionaries, just as on Tanimbar. The absence of the lord of the land from the supreme governmental body is accompanied by a differentiation of functions centred upon the *mangaf wajak*. The *mangaf wajak* is not only active in government, but he is also a warrior, whereas in Fialarang, for example, the former function falls to the *fettor* and the latter to the *surik ulun*. These phenomena are undoubtedly connected with the structural differences, indicated above, between Timor and Tanimbar. On Tanimbar the *mangsombe* and the *mangaf wajak* are opposed to each other as a religious and a social functionary respectively; in the Timorese system the principal ruler and the right hand, as representatives of the sky-half, are together opposed to the *surik ulun*, who stands for the earth-half. Warfare belongs not only in the masculine half of the functional dualism, but in Timor is counted as part of the work of the earth-phratry. At first sight the principal ruler and the left hand seem remarkably similar, especially since they both appear as principal ruler of their half, but in reality they are two diametrically opposed figures who have nothing whatever in common. In both the cosmic and the social dualism they form part of different halves: one belongs to the celestial and feminine group, and the other to the terrestrial and masculine group. It seems, therefore, that in a genetic respect two totally different types of ruler can be distinguished, according to which of the two figures in question they stem from. Originally the former has in particular a religious function, and the other a more social character. It is thus possible to find rulers who at first sight have much in common, but whose offices are of totally different origins. Without understanding the whole system, therefore, it is scarcely feasible to form a judgement on the exact value and significance of a particular rulership. For example, the office of *orang kaja* on Tanimbar and the status of ruler in Lassiolat can only be understood as elements in the systems of which they form part. The progressive development and accompanying structural changes in Timor seem to operate towards the levelling of the various rulerships, to the effect that they share equally in the superiority and sacredness which the system seems primarily to ascribe to the principal ruler. There will long persist in myths and traditions, however, features which are in direct conflict with these levelling tendencies. The coexistence of two categories of "supreme" ruler, as in Fialarang, is undoubtedly the result once more of the ambiguous character of the ruler.

The functionaries in question together make up the government of the village. Nothing is known about the precise nature of the group which lives in the village, but we do know that three to five villages may be conjoined into a complex of villages. The quite nominal power of the dignitaries, and the continual allusions to their descent groups as the basis of their greater or lesser influence, seems to indicate that the village is inhabited by several distinct descent groups and that the functionaries come from these different descent groups. The villages are thus the local units into which the complex is divided, and as such might be supposed to correspond to the Timorese districts, which similarly contain several descent groups. The division into 3 - 4 - 5 villages per complex, just like the organisation of the smaller northern islands, may indicate an original four-fold division. Almost nothing is known about the inter-relations of these villages. It seems probable that there will be affinal relationships between villages, even if only on the part of important people, for otherwise the village complexes would have no reason to exist. The villages eventually established further relations with each other because of war and though gift-exchange, but we do not know whether this report concerns villages in one complex or in a number of different complexes.

The five important governmental officials of a village on Kei can be identified without difficulty with their respective colleagues on Tanimbar. The *orang kaja* or *orang tu(wa)* is of course identical with the *mangaf wajak*, the *tuan tan* with the *pnuwe nduan*, the *leb* (official sacrificer) with the *mangsombe*, the *dir-u ham-wang* (precursor, carver) with the *sori luri*, and the *mitu duan* therefore with the *mangatanuk*. The *dir-u ham-wang* is the representative of the formal unity of the village, a function which emerges clearly from his duties. The four other functionaries are grouped by pairs in exactly the same way as on Tanimbar. While Drabbe lists the *pnuwe nduan* and the *mangaf wajak* of Tanimbar together, on Kei the unity of the other two officials goes so far that the functions of *leb* and of *mitu duan* are often performed by a single person. The familiar triad is thus probably made up of the *leb-mitu duan*, the *orang kaja*, and the *tuan tan*. The relationship between the last two is characterised by Geurtjens in exactly the same sense as that between the *mangaf wajak* and *pnuwe nduan* is described by Drabbe on Tanimbar. The function of the former is said to have evolved under influence from the Government at the expense of the latter, but we have seen that the relationship between the two officials entirely accords with indigenous tradition, and we have found this relationship where there can be no question of European influence. It is not of course inconceivable that European interference may have speeded up the process, though it remains an open question how far the indigenous tradition reflects an actual historical development. It is equally possible, and perhaps more probable, that the indigenous view incorporated the influence of the Government into its own framework. It emerges from a number of particulars, taken in connexion with what has been learned elsewhere, that the *leb* is the central figure in the triad, which makes understandable the opposed forces which are embodied in the *orang kaja* and the *tuan tan*. It is not improbable that these forces are associated with sky and earth. In contrast to ideas on Tanimbar, it is expressly reported of the *tuan tan* that he is involved in agriculture. It is also important, in this connexion, that the *orang kaja* always belongs to the aristocracy, whereas the *tuan tan* often comes from the lower *ren*-class. The grouping into the two classes, *mel* (aristocracy) and *ren*, is evidently connected with the cosmic dualism.[1] Curiously enough, the *ren*-class is called the "older or foremost", which is quite contrary to reality. We have already pointed out, in discussing similar phenomena in Timor, that the opposition oldest/youngest can arise in two ways. In the cosmic dualism the sky is the younger but superior moiety, and the earth is the older but also the stupid half which has to acknowledge the ascendancy of the sky-group. The opposition "defence/government" also seems to fit into this scheme. In social relations, the principal ruler, associated with the feminine, was the older and also the more prominent in opposition to the exerciser of government in the kingdom, who was thought to be associated with the masculine. This opposition was characterised as "moral position/effective power", and inter-tribal relationships were also subsumed under this conception. The opposition *orang kaja/tuan tan*, which is paralleled by that between *mel* and *ren*, is based on the cosmic dualism. The *ren* are quite clearly the older group, but they are also stupid and have to acknowledge the ascendancy of the *mel*. A conception of this kind may well be the foundation of the relationship between *orang kaja* and *tuan tan*, who often represent these two social classes. In the social dualism the older is also *really* the foremost, and there can be no question of this in the case of the *ren* or the *tuan tan*.

The same opposition seems also to be expressed between the *leb* and

---

[1] Cf. De Josselin de Jong, 1928.

the *mitu duan*. The *leb* is the official sacrificer, and apparently he is primarily concerned with the supreme being. The *mitu duan* is the lord or the minister of the *mitu*, which according to Geurtjens are tutelary spirits of the family or the village. Every family group, he says, has its own *mitu*, who usually reside in the village, either in a tree or a rock or in some valuable such as a piece of gold, a gong, or something of the kind.[2] From these few particulars there clearly emerges the different nature of the activity of the *leb* and of the *mitu duan*. The former is concerned with the supreme being and the celestial; the latter is devoted more to the local or differentiated spirits and to the terrestrial. Elsewhere we read: "These tutelary spirits and God are the only beings to which one stands in a religious relationship, and this is brought about by the *leb* (priest) or the *mitu duan* (guardian of the *mitu*)".[3] The conjunction of these two functions in a single person recalls once more the dual character of the corresponding dignitaries which we have found elsewhere.

The most important opposition is that between *leb* and *mitu duan* on one side and the *orang kaja* and *tuan tan* on the other. The religious character of the former pair, and the social character of the latter, appears even more clearly than on Tanimbar. The *orang kaja* is a functionary whose office is founded in the first place on the descent system; we see him as one of the *kapalla sowa*. The social function of the *tuan tan*, in his relationship to the ground as a social-economic factor, is also very clear. Although the associations of *leb* and *orang kaja* with the sky-half, and those of *mitu duan* and *tuan tan* with the earth-half, are unmistakable, it is the opposition of *leb* and *mitu duan* on the one side and that of *orang kaja* and *tuan tan* on the other which is the most important. This social-religious division of labour is further accentuated by the fact that the functions of *leb* and of *mitu duan* are often united in one person. This functionary controls, as it were, the religious forces of the whole local community. The contrast with the *tuan tan*, whose good offices are connected with the ground as an agricultural object, is very striking. We have pointed out such a distinction in Timor as well.

Just as on Tanimbar, a number of villages are united in a complex, at the head of which stands a *rāt*. We have no information on the function and significance of this *rāt*. Although Geurtjens writes as though a village is inhabited by only a single *fām*, it seems that most

---

[2] Geurtjens, 1921, p. 85.
[3] Geurtjens, 1921, p. 86.

commonly a village contains more than one *fām*, and that the component *fām* are often of very different origins. Geurtjens means by
this, of course, that these *fām* are not descended from a single "patriarch". Strangely enough, the village, in spite of that fact that it is
often inhabited by unrelated *fām*, seems nevertheless to be an exogamous group. On Kei Ketjil, the number of villages in a complex can
range from two to fifteen. In the former case there must necessarily
be a number of different *fām* in the one village; with so large a number
as fifteen there is of course no such necessity. There is no concrete
information on the affinal relationships of the *fām* and the village.
Geurtjens writes only in general terms, and examples taken from the
structure of a particular complex are entirely lacking. Structurally,
the village seems however to correspond to that of Tanimbar and thus
to the Timorese district also: i.e., a local unit divided among descent
groups of different origins, a number of such local units composing the
tribe (the complex).

Although more direct evidence on the organisation of the tribe is
lacking, we can form a judgement from the myths and traditional conceptions of various kinds. What we find is two principles of grouping:
on the one side there are the seven *fām* descended in common from a
single "patriarchal" ancestor, and on the other there is an opposition
by sex within the village. In addition to these features there are the
inter-connexions of related *fām*, and also those among the villages of
a district. The factor of class-division contributes further to the extreme
intricacy of this type of structure. Let us adopt the same method of
analysing these phenomena as in the case of Timor, and start with the
myths.

In the myth of Parpara and his brothers and sisters the opposition
of sky and earth, and that between the sexes, both play a part. The
conflict between sky and earth reveals the former as the superior, and
the latter as the inferior half, from the union of which mankind
eventually comes into being. This at least is the evident meaning of the
myth, namely that from the marriage of sky-people and earth-dwellers
are born the seven sons who scatter over the earth. Within the group
of sky-people the opposition between the sexes is played out in the
obscene incident of the descent from the sky to earth. The earth-
dwellers are also divided into men and women. We thus see here once
more the familiar double classification: that into sky and earth is
transected by that into men and women. The mythical affinal relationships are contracted between the two diametrically opposed classes,

masculine sky-dwellers and feminine earth-dwellers. We have already discussed the fact that the two conceptions can be conjoined into that of a masculine sky in opposition to a feminine earth, and we shall return to a closer consideration of it below. The third opposition, that between the youngest brother, Parpara, and the oldest, Hian, seems capable of being subsumed under both conceptions. Since they are members of the same cosmic group, their conflict is identical with that between the sexes, and forms part of what we have referred to above as the dualism of social function, that which is cut across by the cosmic dualism. The dominant position which is clearly ascribed in the myth to the oldest brother fits perfectly, as we have already said, into this framework. The intellectual superiority of the youngest brother, however, forms part of the cosmic speculations. The appearance of the representative of the masculine sky-class in the form of a fisherman likewise wholly agrees with what has been found in other parts, where this figure is represented as a hunter. In this connexion, furthermore, it seems not unimportant that Hian is described as discoverer of the earth.

The various combinations of numbers which we observe in the myth have also nothing strange about them. The four-five division plays a great part within the sky-group, whereas the grouping into seven seems to be associated especially with the relationship of sky to earth. The middle brother, Tongiil, is relegated to the background in the myth; it is the relationship of two brothers and two sisters that is primary. We can thus undoubtedly see Tongiil as a further instance of the fifth figure who stands for unity. This four-five grouping is in its turn supplanted by the triad. This is self-evident in a society, such as that of Kei, in which unilateral affinal alliances fulfil such a prominent function. Tongiil is also the central figure in the triad, between the opposed activities of Parpara and Hian. This completely explains the fact that these activities belong to *both* classifications, for this follows from the independent appearance of the triple unity.

It is clear from the course of the companion myth, that which deals with the earth/underworld opposition, that this relationship is regarded as being entirely identical with that between the sexes in the former myth. According to the system of classification in this culture, the earth/underworld opposition pertains to the dualism of social function. The former is subsumed under one classification-group together with the masculine, and the latter under one group with the feminine. We are already familiar with the associations of hunter and agriculture; and the fact that fire is brought into this dualistic system of classification is perhaps a further indication of a relationship with the cosmic dualism. Also, the appearance of the woman as a rather malicious character, and the man as cunning, reminds us of the opposition of sky and earth. As for the malignant character of the woman, however, we should point out that in the unilateral marriage system the wife-giving group is classified as feminine, and that it not only occupies a position of great ascendancy but is even *feared*, and this is one of the important elements in the system.

If the system which is delineated in these myths is compared with what can be observed in the structure of the society, one is struck by the remarkable points of resemblance. In addition to the *fam*-groups divided into seven, there is the village divided in traditional fashion into four or five. The latter grouping is absolutely identical with the mythical five-fold division into three brothers and two sisters. In one case two masculine and two feminine groups are opposed to each other, while in another there are three feminine groups. Most of the time this opposition seems to be reduced to the dualism of the sexes conceived as separate groups. The latter, together with Geurtjen's hesitation on the point, leads to the presumption that the four-five division in question is traditional, and is not necessarily accompanied by an actual grouping into four or five "family groups". It is similarly unclear whether these modes of grouping in fact apply to a single village or whether they affect a whole district. The antagonism of the villages of Ngilngof and Dulah is in effect one between the districts of Tual and Dulah.[4] In discussing the functionaries, also, we have pointed out that what are elsewhere tribal officials are village officials on Kei and Tanimbar. It seems, therefore, that in various ways the village has taken over the rights of the tribe (i.e., the village-complex). The four-five division of the tribe seems to be repeated in each village, but it is clear that this mode of division is conceived entirely within the sphere of the dualism of social function. In the myth the unity of the group of five is represented by a third man, and the unity of Dulah is evidently symbolised by a third feminine group. This is apparently connected with the fact that in the one case it is a sky-group that is in question, and in the other an earth-group. The masculine predominates in the celestial, and the feminine in the terrestrial. In Timor, too, as we have said, the territory of the whole tribe is brought into the dualism of social function. The third brother is identical with the principal ruler,

---

[4] Geurtjens, 1921, pp. 153, 154.

and the third woman is identical with figures such as "little mother Idar" and "little mother Kelmanut", who in turn are undoubtedly aspects of the little old woman in the underworld. She must therefore be the representative of unity in the sphere of social-functional dualism, just as the principal ruler is in the local-cosmic area. Both figures belong to the feminine half of the first-named classification group, but the former belongs to the earth-half and the latter to the sky-half. To this extent they are thus complementary aspects of one and the same thing. We have already stressed the double character of the ruler, and now his connexion with the cultivation of rice becomes if possible even clearer. The little old woman is also thought of on Kei as a sort of dual being: Tewaharu (the woman with two faces) looks with her "seeing" eye into the world of the living, and with her "blind" eye into the realm of the dead.[5] We have already seen that the principal ruler is considered the human counterpart of the supreme being, while the little old woman seems to exist only as a mythical figure. Perhaps the principal ruler (the sacrificer on Tanimbar) unites these functions in his person, in that he is the "mother" of the village or kingdom.

The relations between *fām* descended from one forefather are not very well known. We have not even any idea whether the seven-fold division is found in reality, or whether it is based on a merely traditional conception. The predominance of the older *fām* has to do, as we have seen, with the dualism of social function. The mythical conflicts between the older and the younger brothers are identical with the quarrels of Parpara and Hian. The seven-fold division, however, was evidently brought under the local-cosmic dualism. The relationships among the villages of Raharing, Ohoi Nangan, and Wowr, also, are not particularly clear. These three villages have, it is said, a single tribal house, but Geurtjens further says that the supreme being let the Raharing people down from the sky. If the three villages, or at least one or more *fām* in each of these villages, are descended from an ancestor who came down from the sky, then their inter-relation is that of the seven-fold division under the local-cosmic dualism. The way in which Raharing and Wowr established their superiority, namely as sky-people over earth-dwellers, is entirely consistent with this. Although elements which belong to the four-five grouping thus appear in the seven-fold system, it is quite clear that these classifications co-exist as distinct principles of grouping. The former is connected particularly with the sexual

---

[5] Geurtjens, 1921, p. 396.

division, and the latter is more connected with the cosmic dualism. With regard to the origin of the different patriarchs (forefathers of the *fām*-groups), the opposition between those who came from the sky and those who did not plays a great part. Those who did not come from the sky include those who came out of a sago palm, a shell-fish, or something of the kind. From what we know about the names of youths and girls, it appears that the whole of nature is classified as masculine or feminine, but unfortunately we have no further details. Geurtjens refers several times to a shell-fish as the origin of a patriarch. Among personal names it seems to be classified as feminine. A foreign region is also of importance as the place of origin of a patriarch, so that in addition to the earth/sky opposition and that of masculine and feminine there is also an effective opposition between the indigenous and the alien.

Nothing is actually known about the inter-relations of the villages, with the exception of the case of the Raharing people, which has been discussed above. We would think in the first place of marriage relationships, of course, and pay special attention to gift-exchange and forms of conflict, but we do not know to what extent these latter factors affect the villages of a complex.

In practically all the societies on *Seran* three important social spheres are met with. In the first place there is the *hena* or *amani* of the Manusela, usually referred to in the literature as "negorij" and on one occasion as a district. A full social life can evidently be carried on within the bounds of this group. The *hena* should thus be thought of as a tribe. But the division of the whole Manusela area into four, when seen in the light of what we have learned elsewhere about quadripartite systems, may point in another direction. Such a four-fold division prompts the inference that the present-day Manusela people were perhaps formerly a single tribe. In the Amahei area the lord of the land is known by a title which is obviously cognate to *amani* and which is used as a synonym for *hena*, viz., *hena pu-uno* or *amano pu-uno*. It is known that the various *hena* in the latter area used to be united in one complex. However this may be, the present *amani* and *hena* undoubtedly represent a social unit which it is usual to call a "tribe". This tribe is divided into a number of *soa*. In the west these are called by the indigenous term *luru*, and certainly correspond to the *lohoki* of Manusela. There is considerable wavering about the territorial and genealogical character of these social groups. The *soa*, as a descent group, is exclusively patrilineal. The third social sphere is the *dati*.

The grouping into *dati* is quite independent of that into *soa*, to the effect that it is impossible to see the *dati* as a simple sub-division of the *soa*. This emerges clearly from Tichelman's descriptions, and is stated in as many words by Van Hoevell with reference to Ambon. The *luma inai* of the Wemale and the *nalano* (*nalane*) of the south coast correspond to these *dati*. In the latter area we also encounter the terms *fam soa* and *nama soa*, meaning perhaps the *fam* or the *nama* of the *soa*. On Buru the *nama* (harbour) is the territory of a *màrah*, and the *fãm* is well known to us from Kei. The reports on the word *soa* as it is also employed on Kei were not entirely unequivocal; although it seemed indeed to be used for a village, it was also applied to a descent group. The composite term *uku-e nalane* can be translated as the *nalane* of the *uku*. The formation of the genitive by placing the word that is qualified in front of the qualifier is a typical feature of the languages in this region, and genitives with the reverse word-order must be regarded as Malayisms. The word *uku* is known to be used by the Manusela as a synonym for *ifa(n)*. The *ifan*, however, must be bracketed with the *dati*, whereas we have seen above that the term *uku*, by contrast, is used with the meaning of *soa*. *Uku* (*suku*) is etymologically related to *soa*. The terms *uku* and *ifan* are reported by different writers. We owe the former to Schadee, and the latter to Willer; Willer's information is old, whereas Schadee's is of recent date. In the west, with which the Manusela are connected, a process of evolution can be discerned in which the hegemony of the *soa* type of organisation came about at the expense of the *dati* type, which disappeared. It may thus be supposed that the older *ifan* corresponds in fact to the *dati*, and the more recent *uku* to the *soa*. In this case Schadee's *uku* can be linked up to Willer's *lohoki*. This view of the issue seems to be confirmed by the notorious ethnographic uncertainty about whether the *soa* is a local or a descent group, and by Tauern's reports, but the extremely vague and confused nature of the evidence does not permit a definitive conclusion. If the *soa*, as a descent group, was exclusively patrilineal, this cannot be said of the *dati* and other groups. The *luma inai* is matrilineal, and Tichelman's information on the *nalano* very clearly contradicts the alleged extreme patriliny of these groups. On Ambon there are women who are heads of *dati*. The institution of *tulung dati* for strangers and upon non-payment of bridewealth is significant in this connexion. An institution of the kind seems to be out of the question as far as the *soa* is concerned: among the Alune, for example, the payment of bridewealth is obviated by the exchange of women between two *soa*. The origin of the *soa* is explained in exactly the same way as is that of the village on Kei, namely by a quite accidental conjunction of a number of family groups of different origins. In this respect the *soa* thus corresponds completely to the district in Timor, i.e., a local group which is one of a number composing the tribe, and which is itself divided into several unrelated descent groups. A number of *dati* are sometimes descended from the same forefather. These will necessarily be *dati* of different *soa*, for otherwise this report could have little meaning. We do in fact possess one example of a *dati* which had representatives in various *hena*, which had formerly made up a complex. It follows incontestably from this that the grouping into *soa* is or was crossed by one into *dati*. This leads us to suppose that members of all the *dati* lived in each *soa*. The *soa*, then, is both a genealogical group and a territorial group, whereas by contrast the *dati* is only a descent group. Perhaps the *nòro* (*nuru, soa*) and the *màrah* of Buru should be seen as similar groups, but unfortunately very little is known about that island. From the little that is known, however, it can be made out that the *màrah* is not simply a sub-clan, or at least has not always been a sub-clan.

Among the Manusela we once more find four headmen, or at any rate four categories of headmen. The *latu* occupies a central position between the *makahitia* and the *ifan*-delegates. According to Willer he governs the whole *amani*, and runs his own *lohoki* in particular. On the other side his functions are connected with a special *ifan*, the *ifan latu*. If the *makahitia* and the *ifan*-delegates are thus opposed to each other as the representatives of the two intersecting principles of grouping in the tribe, the *latu* is the exponent of both. Over against the *latu* there stands a second individual dignitary, the *malesi*, diviner and champion. This figure may be seen as the "warrior" again, whom we have been able to place elsewhere in diametrical opposition to the ruler. Strangely enough, we are told nothing about a "lord of the land". If this is not simply a matter of lack of information, we are dealing here with a grouping which is entirely analogous to that of Timor. One is also struck by such a parallelism in the explicit four-fold division of the *amani* and in the local dualism of the *amani* of Wairama. The practice of "divination" which is reported of the *malesi* is not entirely clear to us, for this would be the first time that priestly functions were ascribed to this official. It is most noteworthy that each *ifan* is said to have two delegates on the governing council. This inclines one to think that there may be a connexion with the division into two *lohoki*, such that each *ifan* was divided into two halves, one in each *lohoki*. This would agree with the relationship between *soa* and *dati* which has been outlined above, but the facts are too vague for anything to be said with certainty.

The opposition of two sorts of functionaries in the south is very striking. On the one side stands the regent with his *soa*-heads, and on the other the lord of the land with the *dati*-heads. The former governs the *hena*, and the latter is the authority on tradition, particularly with regard to land. The *latu* is associated with the local grouping, while the lord of the land is concerned with the land as a social factor, i.e., with the garden plots held by the *dati*. On Ambon, according to Van Hoevell, there were originally no *soa*-lands. The office of *kapitan* appears to be linked with the system of *soa*. One of the *kapitan* is the *kapitan radja*. The latter is thus primarily what the war-leader is in Timor, and as such is opposed to the regent. In Timor, so far as we know, the two functionaries were the representatives of the two local halves of the kingdom. The *latu* and the *kapitan radja* may well belong to different *soa*. Although it is overshadowed by the opposition between the functionaries of the *soa* and the *dati*, we thus find here once more an important triad of figures consisting of the regent, the lord of the land, and the *kapitan radja*.

Our information on the governing officials in the west appears to deal primarily with the Alune, for there is no mention of functionaries connected with the *luma inai* system, but only of *soa*-heads. But from the observations of De Vries the opposition between the two principles of grouping plainly emerges. The regent, with his *soa*-heads, the *alamanan*, and the *mauwen* are closely related by him, as "new" officials, to the *soa*-system. By analogy with what is found in the south, we may presume that the office of *latu nusa*, on the contrary, is based on a grouping of the *dati* type. Among the Wemale this is the *luma inai*. The *mauwen* are especially associated with the *kakehan*, i.e., with the religious. These and the *alamanan* remind us of the *mangsombe* and the *mangatanuk* on Tanimbar. Correspondingly, the regent seems to have much in common with the *orang kaja* of the latter islands. The essential similarity of this system to that of Kei and Tanimbar is evident. As in the Timorese situation, however, the functionaries are not village officials but tribal. In contradistinction to all of the other areas that we have examined so far, here we are dealing not so much with individual functionaries as with groups of officials. Only the lord of the land makes an exception to this rule: in Timor this office was filled by a great number of individuals, but in the western part of Seran he is one of the most important authorities in the tribe. There seems to be a close connexion between this office and that of *kapitan radja*. We have already been able to show that this is so in comparing similar phenomena in Timor and the Tanimbar Islands. Boot's reports would then seem to rest on a confusion between lord of the land and war-leader. He also calls him *masaloi*, which may be identical to the *males(s)i* of the Manusela and the south coast. This somewhat vague figure is often ascribed priestly duties, also, which does not do away with the fact that in the west the *latu nusa* is sharply distinguished from the *mauwen*. The opposition between regent and *kapitan radja* within the *soa*-grouping, found on the south coast, probably corresponds to that between regent and *mauwen* in the west.

There is a profound opposition between *soa* and *dati*. The religious character of the former in opposition to the social character of the latter comes out indisputably from the reports of De Vries and Tichelman. The observations of the latter on the *dati* are of particular interest in connexion with this point, and the relationship of the *soa* to the *mauwen* and the *kakehan* is one of the main pillars in De Vries's whole demonstration. After what has already been said, the correspondence between the *soa*-system and the local-cosmic grouping elsewhere, on the one hand, and that between the *dati*-system and the social functional grouping, on the other, is immediately obvious. The opposition between the religious forces of the local community and the social forces of the cultivated land, which we have already repeatedly met, entirely corresponds to the different aspects of the dual *soa-dati* grouping. We do not, of course, mean by this that the *dati*-system is entirely non-religious; the ancestral and totemic cults of the *luma inai*, and the priestly functions of the lord of the land, prove the contrary. But these matters would take us too far from our subject; all we have tried to do is to show that in the relationship between the two groups one is religious (though not exclusively) and the other has a more social character.

The numerical ideas which we have encountered elsewhere seem to play a more restricted part in the internal organisation of the Seran tribes. Outside the tribe, however, they are proportionally more important. The well-known oposition of Patasiwa and Patalima (the nine and the five brothers or lands) composes a form of inter-tribal organisation which covers almost the whole of Seran, and even occurs far outside it, but we cannot go more closely into the matter in this place. Let us merely recall the six *mauwen* and the situation on Kei, where a six-fold division was likewise associated with the local-cosmic order.

A seven-fold division also plays a part in the songs from Nusa Laut, published by Van Hoevell. The exceptional position of the seventh once more makes its appearance here: the seven-fold division is essentially a six-fold division. Although the subject of the myth is the founding of the various *hena* (here to be understood as tribes), it is plain that the fundamental feature is a grouping into six *teun* (*soa*). There is an obvious local dualism within this system. Perhaps the opposition between the two *latu* and the five *pati* should be seen as a parallel to the seven-five grouping with which we have become familiar from Kei and other parts. In addition to the opposition between the *latu* of the upper side and the *latu* of the lower side, who to judge by their titles are associated respectively with a *waringin* and the water, there is that between *pati* Manusama, the representative of the whole group, and *upu latu* Lemese, who is later associated with Boano. Here, therefore, a *latu* and a *pati* are opposed to each other, which agrees entirely with what was said above about the two *latu* and the five *pati*. We have previously pointed out that the opposition between one's own tribe and a strange tribe is largely to be understood by reference to the dualism of social function. This is evidently the case here as well.

The evidence on Buru does not take us much further as far as these numerical divisions are concerned. There one finds tribes which are divided into three, five, or seven *nòro*, such as, for example, the tribe of the "*nòro pitu*" with its seven *nòro*, one of which is said to have been divided into four *màrah*. Four of the seven *nòro*-names appear to be practically identical. In this case we would seem to have a concrete case of an opposition between four and seven groups, with the possibility that the seven-fold division was derived from an original four-fold division, but given the absolute inaccessibility of the necessary evidence there is not much value to be ascribed to this surmise.

---

[6] In connexion with these numerical ideas, and particularly the significance of the supernumerary group symbolising unity, see McGee (1899) and Van Ossenbruggen (1918).

CHAPTER VI

CONCLUSIONS

Over the whole of the area described we find peculiarities of social structure which show that, in spite of the extreme unilateral character of the descent systems, both patrilineal and matrilineal descent are yet taken into account. One of the most striking facts is that in almost every one of the larger regions into which the area may be divided there is a people who are sharply distinguished from their patrilineal neighbours by their matrilineal descent groups: Kodi on Sumba, south Tétun in Timor, the Wemale of western Seran, and perhaps Wolo Wae in Endeh. Attempts to explain the points of difference between the Alune and the Wemale by postulating a later immigration of the former have been decisively refuted by Duyvendak.[1] Nor can much weight be attached to Grijzen's opinion that the south Tétun are likewise later immigrants. In spite of everything, the various cultures in question exhibit too great a homogeneity to make it necessary for us to resort to migration-hypotheses of this kind. Furthermore, the different rules of descent among the south Tétun can, as we shall see, readily be explained by factors inherent to the culture itself. A dual form of organisation, such as we have thought possible to infer from the marriage system, seems, to the extent that the defective evidence permits any definite judgement, not to survive anywhere in an intact state. The solitary exception to this situation is presented perhaps by Kodi, where a matrilineal clan system is linked to patrilocal marriage customs. The dualistic tendencies are particularly clear in the matter of bridewealth. Only if the bridewealth is paid do the children belong to the father, and only then is the marriage patrilocal. Strictly speaking, however, this is not a dualistic rule, for in this case the departure from the usual

---

[1] Duyvendak, 1926. A summary is to be found in De Josselin de Jong (1933, p. 378). Well-known anthropologists have also tried to explain corresponding phenomena in the structure of other societies by reference to autochthonous and immigrant, older and younger, strata; cf. Malinowski (1926, pp. 72-79) on the system of clans and sub-clans in the Trobriand Islands.

reckoning of descent affects only one generation. Nevertheless, the customs of adoption and the surrender of children which occur over practically the entire area constitute a significant infringement of the absolutely unilateral character of the descent system. The precise import of these features is very difficult to determine, because of the extreme insufficiency of the data. The literature quite incorrectly tends to represent bridewealth as closely connected with patriliny, and this tendency is accompanied as a rule by the view that bridewealth is a purchase price. But bridewealth is beyond question part of an exchange of gifts which usually accompanies marriage. We have seen that in many areas where bridewealth is said to be unknown this gift-exchange is nevertheless practised. This exchange similarly occurs among peoples with matrilineal descent. It should be remarked, however, that in Kodi, for example, this gift-exchange can be connected with the patrilocal marriage customs. Among the two peoples with matrilineal rules of descent and matrilocal marriage (south Tétun and Wemale) it is reported that the payment of bridewealth does not occur, though in fact the custom of the surrender of children is in force. Nothing is known about gift-exchange among the south Tétun and the Wemale, but it seems most improbable that the systematic exchange of traditional valuables which plays such a large part in other societies should be unknown in these. It may be pointed out, in this connexion, that the *luma inai*-building is in fact used primarily for the safe-keeping of such objects. Where such an exchange-custom exists, it is inconceivable that it should not take place at the contraction of marriage, the most enduring form of contact between the clans. Inheritance has an important place among such usages. It is known that, with regard to various possessions, both matrilineal and patrilineal inheritance co-exist in certain societies (Savu, Rote, Seran).

On the other hand, the connexion between double organisation and structural forms of the *soa-dati* type is plain. The *soa* is a patrilineal local group; the *dati* is a descent group numerous features of which recall its original matrilineal character. Let us once more draw attention to the relation of certain goods to the *dati*, and the inheritance of them within the *dati*. At the present day it seems that one of the two rules of descent, which were originally on an equal footing in such a system, has become more and more preponderant, with the result that the opposed rule has almost completely disappeared. The incompleteness of the ethnographic material should be kept particularly in mind in this connexion, for it is possible that it misleads us into accepting an extreme unilaterality even in cases where significant traces of a former double-unilateral system are still to be found. We have only to remember the report according to which the various tribes of Timor have a social structure compounded of both patrilineal and matrilineal systems. Whatever the truth of the matter, the *soa* seems to be a survival of a former patrilineal clan, and the *dati* a survival of a former matrilineal clan. The social structure of the Kei Islands is entirely consistent with this hypothesis. The *soa*, the former patrilineal clan, may be seen in the village, and the old matrilineal clan is to be seen in the *fām*, or at any rate in the group of seven *fām*. The four-five division of the village indicates an original division into four matrilineal clans, and the seven-fold division of each *fām*-group points to six patrilineal clans. Each patrilineal clan was thus a class composed of members of all the matrilineal clans, and each matrilineal clan a class including members of all the patrilineal clans. Reference may be made here to the figures presented earlier, in which dual groupings of this kind have been schematically worked out. The significance of the various numerical combinations will be taken up again below. For the present, we have arrived at a position where we can specify in more detail the place of the local-cosmic dualism outlined above, and that of the division by social function, in the social framework. The former pertains to the *soa*-system and is connected with the patrilineal grouping; the latter is connected with the *dati* and is thus based on the matrilineal grouping. The local-cosmic dualism seems primarily to have had a religious significance, and was based on the opposition of sky and earth. In this dual unity the earth was the older, but also the lesser and particularly the stupider, half, whereas by contrast the sky was the younger but cleverer half. In ritual and myth, figures associated with the sky performed sacrifices, particularly of human victims, in connexion with the cultivation of rice. The representatives of the earth were plainly associated with evil, but it was also the earth which brought forth edible plants. In the dualism of social function, the most prominent opposition was that between the sexes. The masculine element was related to head-hunting, the hunting of game, and fishing; the feminine element was associated with agriculture. In this antagonism the feminine half was the older and at the same time the superior, but it also displayed a certain malevolence. The opposition between earth and underworld seems also to have been subsumed under this scheme.

In nearly all of the areas described we have encountered the district, a local unit composed of several unrelated descent groups; a number of such districts made up the larger unit of tribe or kingdom. We have already stressed the essential similarity between district and *soa*. The presumption, therefore, is that the district, like the *soa*, represents a former patrilineal clan. The heterogeneous descent groups will then be fragments of former matrilineal clans. As one of the two principles of grouping, especially the patrilineal one, came to preponderate, the descent groups progressively supplanted the matrilineal clan, while the district — and possibly other local groups — continued the traditions of the patrilineal clan. The local group is primarily a religious unit, and this character is often accentuated by the figure of the ruler. That the descent groups have in many respects retained the character of matrilineal clans is clearly shown by their part in affinal relations. The nature which they display in this context agrees entirely with what has been said above about the dualism of social function. The corresponding groups are classified as masculine and feminine. The feminine group is the older and predominant, and inspires a salutary fear in its masculine partner. Gift-exchange, a special form of conflict, is one of the integrating components of their interrelationship. They also confront each other as representatives of the corresponding functional categories of the system. The masculine group bring what they have taken in their function as hunters and fishermen, and the feminine group give the produce which they have obtained by their labour on the land.

On Sumba the situation is rather different. In the east, the district traditionally contains four patrilineal clans, each with its own territory. The opposition between social and religious is manifested here in that between ruler and *ratu*. The district seems to derive directly from the tribe, and not to correspond to the local unit which has been referred to as a "district" above. The important inter-tribal relations between the two oldest ancestors, Umbu Walu Mandoku and Umbu Walu Sasar, whose cult is a duty of the rulers,[2] and the familiar affinal relationships of the latter, may be taken to show that the district nevertheless occupies the same place in the system as the local unit does elsewhere. In the west, as we have said, dualism is particularly prominent. To this dualism is linked the familiar opposition between the social and the religious, which, as we know, can be traced back to a combined system of patrilineal and matrilineal clans. Otherwise we know very little — as we have already said — about this part of

---

[2] Wielenga, *Mac.*, 1908, p. 142; 1909, p. 335; 1923, p. 307.

Sumba. On Rote, double dualism has again a very important place. One one side there is the opposition of *manè* and *fèto*, and on the other there is the opposition between these two officials and the *daé-langgak*, the religious functionary par excellence. The former opposition is, as we know, grounded in the dualism of social function, and the latter in the local-cosmic dualism. Although in all *nusak* the *leo* are grouped into a *manè*-half and a *fèto*-half, it seems that one of the two "original groups" of the *nusak* of Termanu is the half of the *daé-langgak* and that the other is that of the ruling officials. The uncertainty regarding the local character of the *manè*-half and the *fèto*-half is entirely consistent with the fact that the *manè/fèto* opposition belongs to the dualism of social function, as is borne out by the circumstance that they are represented as father and son. We have already pointed out that it is only in a matrilineal system that this can make any sense.

The peculiar position of regions such as Kodi, south Tétun, and Wemale is no longer so surprising that we might need to call upon a migration-hypothesis in order to explain it. The mingling of patrilineal and matrilineal elements which we encounter in this area is a natural result of a former double-unilateral system. At the present day it seems that nearly everywhere one of the principles of grouping is overwhelmingly predominant. In most cases this is the patrilineal principle, and in only a few instances is it the matrilineal. We should not dare to offer an explanation of this differentiation here, but it is possible that field research can throw some light on the question. Whether these matrilineal "islands" have any significance in the system of higher forms of organisation is a question that we cannot go into now. The preponderance of one of the two modes of reckoning descent seems to have left some effect on the form in which the bridewealth presents itself. We have already pointed out that the bridewealth is not a purchase price, but forms part of an extensive system of gift-exchange, and that the payment of bridewealth may not be so closely connected with a patrilineal rule of descent. It appears, nevertheless, that in societies in which the latter mode of reckoning descent predominates there has been an intensification of the system of gift-exchange such that bridewealth, although still part of a reciprocal system of giving and taking, has in fact acquired something of the character of a "purchase price". In certain areas this is very markedly the case when new relationships are entered into. The surrender of children offers the possibility of more or less avoiding the expense of this gift-giving. If the matrilineal rule of descent predominates, and the patrilocal rule of marital residence disappears, it seems on the contrary that gift-exchange as part of the contraction of marriage is to some extent weakened (though it will never entirely vanish, as we have thought possible to deduce on purely rational grounds), whereas the surrender of children comes to occupy a correspondingly more important position. It can thus be observed that there is some connexion between patrilocal marriage and the payment of bridewealth, whereas the switch over to one of the possible rules of descent is more likely to result in the custom of relinquishing children.

Consistently with the development outlined above, the lord of the land, who in the first place is a functionary of the *dati*-system, i.e., a dignitary from the matrilineal clan system, today appears as head of the patrilineal descent groups. As we have said, the descent groups of the district and the modern patrilineal clans are connected in essence to the earlier matrilineal clans. In addition, however, we have found the lord of the land provided also with the paraphernalia of a principal ruler. This in fact presents further difficulties for our line of thought. It may be that the duplex character which many sources ascribe to the ruler can provide some explanation here, namely that just as the ruler stands for unity in the paternal dualism, so the lord of the land re-presents the dual unity of the maternal dualism.

Two combinations of numbers play an important part, viz., the four-five group and the six-seven group. The significance of the fifth and the seventh group as representatives of unity has been expounded above in some detail. This supernumerary group has a particularly important place in myths, but the hypothetical fifth or seventh unit has also had an independent existence conferred upon it here and there in the reality of the social structure. In general it has seemed possible to relate the four-five division to the social-functional order, and the six-seven division to the local-cosmic (Fialarang, Djenilu, Kei, Nusa Laut, Seran). The five-fold division of the village on Kei, for example, must be genetically connected to the matrilineal clan organisation, and the seven-fold division of each *fām*-group to the former patrilineal clan system. What is actually found corresponds almost entirely with this hypothesis. The five-fold division is based on the opposition of the sexes; the seven-fold division is connected with the cosmic dualism. It might seem to contradict this system that the interrelations of the patriarchs also rest on the sky/earth opposition, while those of the *fām* of one group exhibit features which are con-nected with the dualism of social function. But in the light of the evolution which this system has long undergone, such contradictions are nothing to be surprised at. The patriarchs are *now* the oldest ancestors of the patrilineal clans; the relationship of the *fām* of a single clan has much in common with the relationships among the descent groups in general. The relationship of the *fām* of one group is in essence that between villages (= districts = former patrilineal clans). The relationships among the villages of Raharing, Ohoi Nangan, and Wowr are entirely consistent with this proposition.

The following is a theoretical reconstruction of the Kei type of social structure:

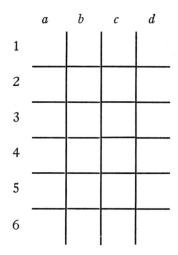

1-6   villages, former patrilineal clans
a-d   *fām*-groups, former matrilineal clans
1*a*-6*d*   former generation-classes

Each village is divided into four (five). This division is based on the opposition of the sexes. The four-fold division reflects the former organisation into matrilineal clans.

Each *fām*-group is divided into seven. This division is connected with the opposition between sky and earth. The six-fold division reflects the former organisation into patrilineal clans.

In the east the double tendencies are manifested in a form which is still strongly reminiscent of the original situation. The double-unilateral system is perpetuated in the *dati-soa* and the *fām*-village groupings. Thus the combinations of numbers on Kei might be taken to indicate an original grouping into four matrilineal clans and six patrilineal clans. We have already observed that it is not absolutely sure what significance may be attributed to this six-seven division, in that we do not know whether it expresses an actual situation or a purely traditional conception. While we think it is possible to recognise such a form of organisation in the district as found in the western part of the area (cf. the *leo* on Rote, with its segments on one side and the *nggolok* on the other; Kodi, with its major and minor *wāla*), it is obvious that the local dual division has the most important place there. The halves of Djenilu and Fialarang which were associated with the sky contained seven groups, and those connected with the earth had four or five. On Rote also both of these combinations of numbers played a part, but there they seemed to have the reverse associations. In the *nusak* of Loleh, ideas about the five/seven opposition such as are found on Kei and in Timor are co-present: the *manè*-half of this *nusak* contains twelve *leo*, which however are supposed to be descended from five brothers, while the *fèto*-half has ten. One writer reports that the *nusak* of Ti contained two phratries, each with eight *leo*; but according to another the masculine phratry contained fourteen *leo* and the feminine phratry twelve. The *nusak* of Oépao, finally, was divided into eight. The oppositions are the same as we encounter in the east, only they are expressed in a more indirect way, connected as they are to the local dualism. In this area a local four-fold division often appears, which may indicate an original division into four patrilineal clans. Our more theoretical consideration of the systems has shown that an original system of four patrilineal clans with unilateral affinal relationships logically entails a correlated system of four matrilineal clans. In this context, therefore, a local division into four is not necessarily particularly important. We have also pointed out that a grouping with four patrilineal clans and four matrilineal clans makes a sixteen-class system very likely. This means that each (marriage-) class will comprise one generation, and that marriage will be confined to the same generation. We are reminded of the social structure of the *nusak* of Ti (Rote), which, according to Van de Wetering at least, is divided into two phratries, each with eight clans, making a total of sixteen. A square number such as this agrees very well with our hypothesis, according to which the *fām*, the *dati*, and the *nggi leo* were originally divided as generation-classes among patrilineal clan, village, *soa*, and district. A very important datum, which also seems to support our hypothesis, is furnished by the adoption-customs in Endeh (Flores). An adopted son is counted as belonging to the generation of his mother. If the woman belongs to matriclan *a* and patriclan 1, and her husband belongs to matriclan *b* and patriclan 2, their son, as member of his mother's matriclan and his father's patriclan, is *a2*. The adoption of *a2* by *a1* changes nothing as far as membership of his matriclan is concerned, but he acquires membership in his mother's patriclan and thus becomes *a1*. The fact that thereafter he belongs to his mother's generation must undoubtedly be connected with a system of marriage-classes, each of which comprises only one generation, as we have described above. If an individual is transferred to another patriclan or matriclan, this must *ipso facto* be accompanied by a change in generation-class.

The six-fold division, which we meet in both the east and the west of the area, might be taken to indicate a system with six matrilineal clans and six patrilineal clans, which would then comprise 36 classes. But a six-fold division readily permits other inferences. Let us recall the situation in Lidak, where there was possibly an original division of six *fukun* between two phratries. In such a case it is conceivable that there was quite probably a division into patrilineal or matrilineal moieties and three matrilineal or patrilineal clans. In a system of this kind odd marriages might take place between members of different generations. The existence of such marriage possibilities, however, is not testified to by any single report. Moreover, the indications of such a mode of grouping are very few. We are thinking particularly of the *kabisu* divided into two, on Sumba, and the *kabisu* with a double totem. It is reported of Tarung, in Lauli, that there are three *kabisu*, one of which is divided into two. We do not know for certain whether this is the only *kabisu* that is divided into two, or whether the others are also split in a similar way. There is a report from Timor that one can take the *kana luan* of one's grandfather if this is threatened with extinction. This report is capable of various interpretations, and is not entirely clear. It inclines one, however, to think of a division into moieties with opposite descent groups, in which case the first and the third generations could indeed belong to the same group. Reference can also be made once more to the already much-discussed connexions among the villages of Raharing, Ohoi Nangan, and Wowr, on Kei. These relationships indubitably have to do with a six-fold division, and yet only three villages are mentioned. Finally, the important part played by dualism as such in the west deserves to be recalled. In Kodi, as we know, six of the 49 *wāla* occupy "a specially prominent place".

If we keep in mind the fact that a six-fold division can very easily give rise to a grouping into seven, it is truly striking, after everything that has been said in this connexion, that the total number of *wāla* is precisely the square of seven. The fact that according to reports the number of *wāla* cannot change, or at any rate that no new ones can be added, does not point to an adventitious proliferation and disappearance of sub-clans, though the number of them might otherwise lead to this inference.[3] Given the defectiveness of the ethnographic material, any kind of definite conclusion is out of the question, and we shall have to confine ourselves to these few remarks.

In view of the tendency towards symmetry which characterises these systems, the combination of four matrilineal clans and six patrilineal clans seems not very likely. While the system on Kei leads to the supposition that such a grouping exists there, the same opposition in Fialarang and Djenilu is related to the local dualism. For the present, therefore, we can only say that the system permits both a six-fold and a four-fold division, and that examples of both are to be found. In addition, the six-seven grouping is today associated with the former paternal principle of grouping, and the four-five system, by contrast, with the maternal. Kodi, however, provides an example of a tribe in which the matrilineal clans are grouped by six. The how and why of these associations are matters which we are not in position to determine here. Yet attention should be drawn to a possible connexion with an arrangement into two matrilineal moieties and three patrilineal clans. The fission or doubling of the two moieties and the three clans could in fact lead to four matrilineal clans and six patrilineal clans,[4] but the motive forces of a potential evolution of this kind are extremely obscure, and we can only point out that the six-fold division is already given in the number of classes. To start from a grouping into four matrilineal clans and four patrilineal clans leads to great difficulty in the explanation of the six-seven division. The preference for threes, which as we have said, constantly makes its appearance with asymmetric connubium, together with the familiar tendency to see

---

[3] Kruyt, 1922a, p. 499.

[4] It is possible, as we have said, that such a doubling took place on Rote. The numbers two (*dua*) and three (*télu*) which occur in the names Dudua Loko and Tételu Liki, the two oldest ancestors of the entire Rote people, may of course indicate a dualistic order within the five-group (Van der Kam, 1934, p. 585). We may recall here, too, the custom in central Timor by which western Fialarang, is divided into six, is called *umah hāt* (the four houses) or *rin besin hāt* (the four iron pillars).

everything in the light of a dually conceived unity, may perhaps provide a way out. However this may be, for the moment no decisive answer can be given to these questions. But it is obvious that tendencies to tripartition have played an important part together with tendencies towards quadripartition, and that over a long period these have led to the formation of an intricate structural scheme which now confronts us. Finally, it should be remarked that a double-unilateral system is often accompanied by a traditional division of the whole society into four great classes. We know how such classifications may serve as the foundation for an all-embracing cosmic order.[5] In the advanced phase of evolution which the system has reached as we now come to learn of it, it is possible that the old tendencies to quadripartition, more or less detached from their basis, still exert a rigorous influence as a logical framework upon all social and cosmic entities, and that this four-fold division is derived only indirectly from a former system of four clans but is grounded directly in a four-class system founded on a double dualism.

We have thus found exclusive cross-cousin marriage as the index of an asymmetric system of connubial relations in which the clans are linked to one another by a closed chain of affinal alliances. As a consequence, individual marital connexions are entirely overshadowed by exclusive cross-cousin marriage. We should also keep in mind, in this connexion, that the classificatory system of kinship terminology has a misleading effect in that it represents relationships as being individual when they are really collective. This asymmetric connubium appears to be based essentially on a double-unilateral system in which both patrilineal and matrilineal clans operate side by side in the organisation of the tribe. We have thought it possible to trace the patrilineal grouping back to a form of organisation of the *soa* type. Although the term *soa* is not in fact indigenous in most regions, and although its loose employment has often led to confusion, the correspondence with organisational units such as the village on Kei and the district in Timor is so convincing as to furnish a satisfactory assurance of an essential similarity. The matrilineal grouping survives in forms of organisation of the *dati* type. The *soa*, etc., make their appearance today primarily as local groups, and the *dati* of which the *soa* is composed, as descent groups, particularly as sub-clans. These descent groups are genetically related to the classes, segments of the former

---

[5] Cf. Durkheim and Mauss, 1903.

matrilineal clan, into which the previous patrilineal clan was divided. The *soa* is conceived more under a religious aspect, in contrast to the *dati*, which has a more explicitly social character. The *soa*-organisation is subsumed under the local-cosmic dualism, in which the opposition between sky and earth takes first place. The *dati*-grouping is related to the social-functional division, which is based in the first instance on the opposition between the sexes and on the functional division into hunters, fishers, and warriors on one side and agriculturalists on the other. The relationship between earth and underworld, and inter-tribal relationships as well, are also brought into this scheme. In the local-cosmic dualism the younger sky represents the better half, and the older earth the stupid and evil half. In the other dualism the older group is pre-eminent, and the fear which it inspires is one of the grounds for its authority. The paternal principle of grouping is per-petuated in a religious form of organisation, and the maternal in a social form. The double system has been best preserved in the east, whereas in the west the opposition of social and religious is more closely linked to the local dualism. The two ancient principles of grouping are also manifested in two combinations of numbers. The six-seven division is associated with the paternal, local-cosmic, and religious principle, and the four-five grouping is associated with the maternal, social-functional principle. In the east this opposition re-appears mainly in the double form, in which the two principles inter-sect; in the west the opposition, like that of the religious and the social, is connected with a territorial dual division. The four-five division points to an original organisation into four matrilineal clans and four patrilineal clans; the six-seven division indicates rather an original grouping into two moieties and three otherwise-defined clans. We have not been able to say much with certainty about the fundamental grounds of this opposition. All we can say is that both the four-fold and the six-fold modes of division must have existed in this area for a long time, and that both may be traced back to a form of organisation which may well be combined with asymmetric con-nubium. We may also state that these numerical oppositions in them-selves accord perfectly with the familiar dualistic scheme. Although we can establish a close connexion in this way between the four-five division and the former matrilineal elements in the social structure, it should be remembered that a local quadripartition is also important everywhere, while Kodi furnishes an example of a matrilateral six-fold division. Generally speaking, a greater extension can be ascribed to the four-fold division that to the six-fold. On this point attention should be drawn to a possible connexion with a division of the whole society into four great marriage classes. Within the group of four the triad occupied a very important position. This preference for the triad is a direct consequence of the unilateral system of affinal relationships. From the point of view of the ego-group, the triad represents a closed and self-sufficient social group which provides for the satisfaction of all its social needs; it is a tribe, as it were, within a tribe. These elements are found everywhere in the figures of the three, four, or five foremost officials. These ruling groups are esentially alike, and differ only in minor respects. The most important figure among these functionaries is the principal ruler, the sacrificer. He occupies a central position in the triad, from which the opposed powers of the two other dignitaries are derived. He is the representative of the unity of the tribe. In the four-group system he belongs simultaneously to the sky-half of the cosmic dualism and to the feminine half of the social dualism. This explains his function as sacrificer, as well as his involvement in the cultivation of rice. He is the human counterpart of the supreme being. His most important characteristic is his inactivity. His mere presence is enough to maintain the entire social fabric. In this respect the similarity between the ruler and a *deus otiosus* is truly striking. As representative of unity, he is the source of the simultaneously opposed and complementary powers which pervade the society and are especially embodied in the regalia. In Timor he has a complete parallel in the figure of the "warrior"; the latter belongs at once to the earth-half of the cosmic dualism and to the masculine half of the social dualism. In some cases this figure seems to coincide with the lord of the land. We recall here the lord of the land on Savu and Rote, the figure of mother-father Leki, who has adopted many features of a principal ruler, in the first place his double character. The presumption is therefore that the principal ruler represents especially the duplex unity of the paternal dualism, while the other figure stands for that of the maternal dualism. The latter person is also connected with figures such as the little old woman in the underworld, who can also be considered a dual being. As a religious figure, the principal ruler, the supreme being, stands next to, and in opposition to, the social figures of the warrior and the little old woman. Together they reflect a unitary conception of the whole cosmos: the principal ruler as a two-fold being also exhibits feminine qualities, and the little old woman retreats more or less into the background. The lord of the land also often meets a similar fate.

On Seran he is clearly a functionary of the *dati*-organisation, and while on Kei and Tanimbar he still forms part of the supreme college of rulers his importance is not rated very highly by various ethnographers. On Sumba he is met with as head of a clan, and in central Timor his office is shared by a large number of persons. In spite of all shifts and displacements, therefore, the group of important functionaries is classified in a double fashion after the model of the bilateral type of structure: a celestial group opposed to a terrestrial, and a masculine opposed to a feminine.

The two intersecting conceptions seem often to be combined in a single dualism, in which the younger but cleverer masculine sky-group is opposed to the older and stupider but more powerful feminine earth-group. In spite of this phenomenon, which may be seen as the result of the preponderance of one of the two principles of grouping, it very often seems possible still to discover older conceptions of a twofold kind. It is self-evident that by no means all of the associations of this system of classification have been brought out by the results of our inquiry. More intensive research in the field will probably be able to throw more light on the matter.

ABBREVIATIONS

B.S.C.B.	*Berichten van den Sint Claver Bond.*
B.T.L.V.N.I.	*Bijdragen tot de Taal-, Land- en Volkenkunde van Neder-landsch-Indië.*
I.A.E.	*Internationales Archiv für Ethnographie.*
J.[R.]A.I.	*Journal of the [Royal] Anthropological Institute of Great Britain and Ireland.*
K.T.	*Koloniaal Tijdschrift.*
Mac.	*De Macedonier.*
M.E.B.	*Mededeelingen van het Bureau voor de Bestuurszaken der Buitengewesten, bewerkt door het Encyclopaedisch Bureau.*
M.N.Z.	*Mededeelingen van wege het Nederlandsch Zendelinggenootschap.*
M.T.Z.	*Mededeelingen: Tijdschrift voor Zendingswetenschap.*
Studiën	*Studiën op godsdienstig, wetenschappelijk en letterkundig gebied.*
T.B.B.	*Tijdschrift voor het Binnenlands Bestuur.*
T.I.T.L.V.	*Tijdschrift voor Indische Taal-, Land- en Volkenkunde.*
T.K.N.A.G.	*Tijdschrift van het Koninklijk Nederlandsch Aardrijkskundig Genootschap.*
T.N.I.	*Tijdschrift voor Nederlandsch-Indië.*
V.B.G.K.W.	*Verhandelingen van het Bataviaasch Genootschap van Kunsten en Wetenschappen.*

BIBLIOGRAPHY

Anon.
1892 "Het landschap Amarassi." *T.B.B.*, vol. 7, pp. 201-227.

Beckering, J. D. H.
1911 "Beschrijving der eilanden Adonara en Lomblèm, behoorende tot de Solorgroep." *T.K.N.A.G.*, vol. 28, pp. 167-202.

Bleeker, P.
1856 *Reis door de Minahassa en den Molukschen Archipel....* (2 vols.) Batavia.

Boot, J.
1893 "Korte schets der noordkust van Ceram." *T.K.N.A.G.*, vol. 10, pp. 650-678, 885-902, 1163-1204.

Brumund, J. F. G.
1845 "Aanteekeningen gehouden op eene reis in het oostelijke gedeelte van den Indischen Archipel." *T.N.I.*, vol. 7, pp. 39-89, 251-299.

Bruynis, J. L.
1919 "Twee landschappen op Timor : Amarassi en Zuid Beloe." *T.K.N.A.G.*, vol. 36, pp. 169-198.

Calon, L. F.
1890 "Woordenlijstje van het dialect van Sikka (Midden-Flores)." [Dutch-Sikka.] *T.I.T.L.V.*, vol. 33, pp. 501-530.
1891 "Woordenlijstje van het dialect van Sikka (Midden-Flores). (Sikka-neesch-Hollandsch.)" *T.I.T.L.V.*, vol. 34, pp. 283-363.
1892a "Eenige opmerkingen over het dialect van Sikka, gevolgd door eenige bemerkingen over de vorige lijstjes, eenige spreekwijzen, enz." *T.I.T.L.V.*, vol. 35, pp. 129-199.
1892b "Woordenlijst van het dialect van Lio (West-Flores)." *T.I.T.L.V.*, vol. 35, pp. 200-208.

Clercq, F. S. A. de
1874 "Allerlei over het eiland Roti." *B.T.L.V.N.I.*, vol. 21, pp. 291-312.

Colenbrander, J. F.
1916 "Iets over de Savoeneesche adat in betrekking tot huwelijk en erfrecht." *T.B.B.*, vol. 50, pp. 44-48.

Couvreur, A. J. L.
1908 "Een dienstreis benoorden Larantoeka (Oost-Flores), 23-28 April, 1907." *T.K.N.A.G.*, vol. 25, pp. 551-566.

D.
1851 "Reis naar het rijk van Amanoebang op Timor, in Oktober 1850." *T.N.I.*, vol. 13, pp. 153-179.

D.B.
1852 "Zeden en gewoonten van de bevolking op Timor." *T.N.I.*, vol. 14, pp. 199-224.

Donselaar, W. M.
1872 "Aanteekeningen over het eiland Savoe." *M.N.Z.*, vol. 16, pp. 281-332.

Drabbe, P.
1923 "Het heidensch huwelijk op Tanimbar." *B.T.L.V.N.I.*, vol. 79, pp. 546-568.
1925 "Dood en begrafenis en spiritisme op Tanimbar." *T.K.N.A.G.*, vol. 42, pp. 31-63.
1927 "Waardigheden of ambten in de Tanimbareesche maatschappij." *B.T.L.V.N.I.*, vol. 83, pp. 181-191.

Durkheim, E., and Mauss, M.
1903 "De quelques formes primitives de classification: contribution à l'étude des représentations collectives." *Année sociologique,* vol. 6 (1901-1902), pp. 1-72. [English edition, translated and edited with an introduction by Rodney Needham: *Primitive Classification.* Chicago: University of Chicago Press, 1963.]

Duyvendak, J. Ph.
1926 *Het Kakean-genootschap van Seran.* Leiden.

Eerde, J. C. van
1920 "Gegevens betreffende de onderafdeeling West-Ceram." *T.K.N.A.G.*, vol. 37, pp. 531-537.

Esser, J.
1877 "Aanteekeningen over Soemba." *T.N.I.*, vol. 6, II, pp. 161-169.

Forbes, H. O.
1884 "On the ethnology of Timor-laut." *J.A.I.*, vol. 13, pp. 8-29.

Francis, E.
1838 "Timor en onderhoorigheden in 1831." *T.N.I.*, vol. 1, I, pp. 353-400; II, pp. 25-80.

Geurtjens, H.
1921 *Uit een vreemde wereld, of het leven en streven der inlanders op de Kei-eilanden.* 's-Hertogenbosch.
1924 *Keieesche legenden* (eerste stuk). *V.B.G.K.W.*, vol. 65.

Gifford, E. W.
1916 "Miwok moieties." *University of California Publications in American Archaeology and Ethnology,* vol. 12, pp. 139-194.

Graafland, N.
1889 "Eenige aanteekeningen op ethnographisch gebied ten aanzien van het eiland Rote." *M.N.Z.*, vol. 33, pp. 351-375.

Gramberg, J. S. G.
1872 "Een maand in de binnenlanden van Timor." *V.B.G.K.W.*, vol. 36.

Grijzen, H. J.
1904 "Mededeelingen omtrent Beloe of Midden-Timor." *V.B.G.K.W.*, vol. 54.

Heijmering, G.
1844   "Zeden en gewoonten op het eiland Timor." *T.N.I.*, vol. 7, III, pp. 121-146, 273-313.

Heijnen, F. C.
1875–76 "Het rijk Larantoeka op het eiland Flores." *Studiën*, vol. 8, no. VI.

Hoevell, G. W. W. C. van
1875   *Ambon en meer bepaaldelijk de Oeliasers, geographisch, ethnographisch en historisch.* Dordrecht.
1882   "Twee zangen in de Ambonsche landtaal." *T.I.T.L.V.*, vol. 27, pp. 69-89.
1890a   "De Kei-eilanden." *T.I.T.L.V.*, vol. 33, pp. 102-159.
1890b   "Tanimbar en Timorlaut-eilanden." *T.I.T.L.V.*, vol. 33, pp. 160-186.

Jackstein, A.
1873   "Eenige notizen over Rotti en de Rottinezen." *T.I.T.L.V.*, vol. 20, pp. 350-356.

Jansen, P. H. A.
1895   "Atapoepoe op het eiland Timor." *B.S.C.B.*, II, pp. 5-11.
1896   "Atapoepoe op het eiland Timor." *B.S.C.B.*, II, pp. 22-26.

Jonker, J. C. G.
1905   "Rottineesche verhalen." *B.T.L.V.N.I.*, vol. 58, pp. 369-464.

Josselin de Jong, J. P. B. de
1928   "The Natchez social system." *Proceedings 23rd International Congress of Americanists*, pp. 553-562.
1929   "De oorsprong van den goddelijken bedrieger." *Mededeelingen der Koninklijke Akademie van Wetenschappen*, Afd. Letterkunde, vol. 68, serie B, no. 1, pp. 1-29.
1933–34 "Religionen der Naturvölker Indonesiens." *Archiv für Religionswissenschaft*, vol. 30, pp. 175-198, 362-382.

Kam, E. G. van der
1934   "Afkomst, volksordening en adatbestuur der Rotineezen." *K.T.*, vol. 23. pp. 585-599.

Kate, H. F. C. ten
1894   "Verslag eener reis in de Timorgroep en Polynesië." *T.K.N.A.G.*, vol. 11, pp. 195-246, 333-390, 541-638, 659-700, 765-823.

Klift, H. van der
1922   "Het monahoe ndao." *M.T.Z.*, vol. 66, pp. 68-77.

Kluppel, J. M.
1873   "De Solor-eilanden." *T.I.T.L.V.*, vol. 20, pp. 378-398.

Kruyt, Alb. C.
1921a   "De Roteneezen." *T.I.T.L.V.*, vol. 60, pp. 266-344.
1921b   "Reis over het eiland Soemba." *T.K.N.A.G.*, vol. 38, pp. 513-553.
1921c   "Verslag van een reis door Timor." *T.K.N.A.G.*, vol. 38, pp. 769-807.
1922a   "De Soembaneezen." *B.T.L.V.N.I.*, vol. 78, pp. 466-608.
1922b   "Een en ander over de To Laki van Mekongga." *T.I.T.L.V.*, vol. 61, pp. 427-470.

1923a "De Timoreezen." *B.T.L.V.N.I.*, vol. 79, pp. 347-490.
1923b "De Toradja's van de Sa'dan-, Masoepoe- en Mamasa-rivieren." *T.I.T.L.V.*, vol. 63, pp. 81-175, 259-401.

Kruyt, A. C. and J.
1921 "Reis naar Kelaka." *T.K.N.A.G.*, vol. 38, pp. 689-704.

Lambooy, P. J.
1927 "Wat de Soembaneesche verhalen ons leren." *Mac.*, vol. 31, pp. 353-358.

Langen, H. G.
1902 *Die Key- oder Kii-Inseln des O.I. Archipelago*. Wien.

Lijnden, D. W. C. van
1851 "Bijdragen tot de kennis van Solor, Allor, Rotti, Savoe en omliggende eilanden." *Natuurkundig Tijdschrift van Nederlandsch-Indië*, vol. 2, pp. 317-336, 388-414.

Locher, G. W.
1932 *The serpent in Kwakiutl religion*. Leiden.

Luttig, H. G.
1933 *The religious system and social organisation of the Herero*. Utrecht.

McGee, W J
1899 "The Beginnings of mathematics." *American Anthropologist*, vol. 1, pp. 646-674.

Malinowski, B.
1926 *Myth in primitive psychology*. London.

Miesen, J. H. W. van der
1902 "Een en ander over Boeroe, inzonderheid wat betreft het district Waisàma, gelegen aan de Z.O. kust." *M.N.Z.*, vol. 46, pp. 427-456.

Müller, S.
1839–44 *Land- en volkenkunde van den Indischen Archipel*. (2 vols.) Leiden.

Nooteboom, C.
1932 *De boomstamkano in Indonesië*. Leiden.

Ossenbruggen, F. D. E. van
1918 "De oorsprong van het Javaansche begrip Montjâ-pat in verband met primitieve classificaties." *Verslagen en Mededeelingen der Koninklijke Akademie van Wetenschappen*, Afdeeling Letterkunde, 5e reeks, 3e deel, pp. 6-45.

Planten, H. O. W.
1892 "De Ewaf of Key-eilanden." *T.K.N.A.G.*, vol. 9, pp. 619-653.

Pos, W.
1901 "Soembaneesche woordenlijst." *B.T.L.V.N.I.*, vol. 53, pp. 184-284.

Rassers, W. H.
1922 *De Pandji-roman*. Leiden.
1925 "Over den zin van het Javaansche drama." *B.T.L.V.N.I.*, vol. 81, pp. 311-381.

1931   "Over den oorsprong van het Javaansche tooneel." *B.T.L.V.N.I.*, vol. 88, pp. 317-450.

Rivers, W. H. R.
1914   *Kinship and social organisation*. London.

Roo van Alderwerelt, J. de
1890   "Eenige mededeelingen over Soemba." *T.I.T.L.V.*, vol. 33, pp. 565-595.

Roos, S.
1872   "Bijdragen tot de kennis van taal, land en volk op het eiland Soemba." *V.B.G.K.W.*, vol. 36.
1877   "Iets over Endeh." *T.I.T.L.V.*, vol. 24, pp. 481-582.

Sachse, F. J. P.
1922   *Seran. M.E.B.*, vol. 29.

Schadee, M. C.
1915   "Heirats- und andere Gebräuche bei den Mansela und Nusawele Alfuren in der Unterabteilung Wahaai der Insel Seram." *I.A.E.*, vol. 22, pp. 129-138.

Schmid, C. van
1842   "Aanteekeningen nopens de zeden, gewoonten en gebruiken, benevens de vooroordeelen en bijgelovigheden der bevolking van de eilanden Saparoea, Haroekoe, Noessa Laut, en van een gedeelte van de zuidkust van Ceram." *T.N.I.*, vol. 5, II, pp. 491-530, 583-622.

Schut, J. A. F.
1918   "Het huwelijk bij de Gèb'emliar op Boeroe." *M.N.Z.*, vol. 62, pp. 16-35, 125-140, 197-210, 296-308.
1921   "Nòro en fèna op Boeroe." *B.T.L V.N.I.*, vol. 77, pp. 615-622.
1923   "Het eten van de eerstelingen van de gierstoogst op Boeroe." *M.N.Z.*, vol. 67, pp. 327-343.

Stresemann, E.
1923   "Religiöse Gebräuche auf Seran." *T.I.T.L.V.*, vol. 62, pp. 305-424.

Suchtelen, B. C. C. M. M. van
1921   *Endeh (Flores). M.E.B.*, vol. 26.

Swieten, Th. van
1897   "Het huwelijk te Larantoeka." *B.S.C.B.*, I, pp. 5-14.

Tauern, O. D.
1918   *Patasiwa und Patalima: vom Molukkeneiland Seran und seinen Bewohnern*. Leipzig.

Teffer, M.
1875   "De Savoe-eilanden." *M.N.Z.*, vol. 19, pp. 205-233.

Tichelman, G. L.
1925   "De onderafdeeling Amahai (Seran)." *T.K.N.A.G.*, vol. 42, pp. 653-724.

Treffers, F.
1914   "Het landschap Laiwoei in Z.O. Celebes en zijne bevolking." *T.K.N.A.G.*, vol. 31, pp. 188-221.

Vries, G. de

1927   *Bij de Berg-Alfoeren op West Seran: zeden, gewoonten en mythologie van een oervolk.* Zutphen.

Wetering, F. H. van de

1922   "De afkomst der Roteneezen van het eiland Rote." *M.N.Z.,* vol. 66, pp. 312-326.

1923*a*   "Het Roteneesche huis." *T.I.T.L.V.,* vol. 62, pp. 452-495.

1923*b*   "De naamgeving op het eiland Rote." *T.I.T.L.V.,* vol. 63, pp. 402-419.

1925   "Het huwelijk op Rote." *T.I.T.L.V.,* vol. 65, pp. 1-36, 589-667.

1926   "De Savoeneezen." *B.T.L.V.N.I.,* vol. 82, pp. 485-575.

Wielenga, D. K.

1908–25 [A large series of small items in the mission periodical *De Macedonier.*]

1913   "Soembaneesche verhalen in het dialect van Kambéra, met vertaling en aanteekeningen." *B.T.L.V.N.I.,* vol. 68, pp. 1-287.

1917   "Vergelijkende woordenlijst der verschillende dialecten op het eiland Soemba en eenige Soembaneesche spreekwijzen." *V.G.B.K.W.,* vol. 61, part 6.

[1926] *Soemba.* 's-Gravenhage.

Willer, T. J.

1858   *Het eiland Boeroe: zijne exploitatie en Halfoersche instellingen.* Amsterdam.

Winthuis, J.

1928   *Das Zweigeschlechterwesen bei den Zentralaustraliern und anderen Völkern.* Leipzig.

INDEX *

Abduction, 53
Abubu, 78
Adat, 56
Administration, 52, 101; and defence, complementary functions of, see: Diarchy
Adonara, 83, 84
Adoption, 19, 76, 80, 154, 160-1
Adultery, 27
Aë, 47
Affinal alliances, 3, 18
Affinal relations, fixed, see: Connubium
Affinal status, relativity of, 100
Africa, 94 n. 2
Agriculture, 30, 60, 65, 125, 138, 141, 144, 155
Ahiolo, 70, 75
Ai biku, 46
Ai halé, 46
Aitōn, 43, 44, 97, 99
Aja, 75
Alamanan, 72, 73, 150
Alas, 47
Alin maun, 14, 15, 89, 101
Alliance groups, number of, 11, 14, 88, 89, 93, 94, 95
Alliance status, relativity of, 89, 102
Alune, 73, 74, 148, 150
Alusi, 31
Amabi, 57, 58
Amahei, 21, 75, 76, 77, 147
Amakono, 51, 52, 113
Amanatun, 16, 46, 54, 55, 56, 57, 59, 60, 103, 118-24, 125, 128
Amani, 67, 68, 69, 70, 147, 149
Amanokwam, 67, 69
Amano pu-uno, 147
Amanuban, 16, 53, 54, 55, 57, 58, 59, 60, 103, 118-24, 125, 128
Amarassi, 16, 57, 59, 127, 128, 129
Ambat ndunir, 32
Ambenu, 50, 52

Amblau, 78
Ambo Roru, 82
Ambon Islands, 77-8, 148, 150
Ambu Modo, 82
Ambu Nggaeh, 82
Ambu Nggobe, 81
Ambush, 55
Amfoan, 50, 52, 53, 54, 66, 115, 116, 118, 135
Amola, 68
Amtiran, 57
Ana ma'ari, 26, 135
Ana matjuwa, 26, 27, 135
Anak makain, 21
Anakala, 18, 28, 135
Anak dati, 76, 77
Analysis, method of, 1-2
Ancestor, ancestors, 11, 16, 22, 25, 35, 36, 37, 38, 39, 42, 44, 45, 50, 52, 58, 61, 62, 66, 67, 73, 74, 78, 79-80, 81, 95, 97, 101, 107, 122, 131, 149, 151, 156, 162 n. 4
Anggrijé, 34
Animals, 75; prohibition on killing certain, 25
Animal-names, 39
Apuwei, 74
Areca nuts, 23
Arm-bands, 34
Arteries, aortic, 33
Aristocracy, aristocrats, 12, 141
Aru marapu, 30
Assembly, 64
Astanara, 43, 44, 98, 100, 101, 102, 104, 105, 106, 111
Astrologer, 68
Asumanu, 42, 43, 44, 97, 99, 101, 103, 104, 107, 115, 129
Ata nain, 49
Ata nggaeh, 81, 82
Ataka beling, 83
Ataka laké, 83
Atok Lekaan, 42

---

* Newly compiled for this edition by the Translator; checked and proof-read by Miss Mariëtte Winkel.

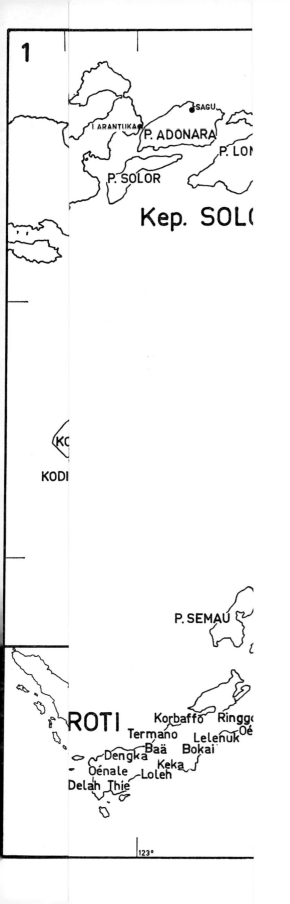

1

SAGU
I. ARANTIIKA
P. ADONARA
P. LON
P. SOLOR
Kep. SOL(

KC
KODI

P. SEMAU

ROTI   Korbaffo   Ringg(
        Termano   Lelenuk Oé
        Baä   Bokai
Dengka Keka
Oénale Loleh
Delah Thie

123°